# Advancing Ethnography in Corporate Environments

# Advancing Ethnography in Corporate Environments

## Challenges and Emerging Opportunities

Brigitte Jordan, Editor

Left
Coast
Press
Inc.

**WALNUT CREEK, CA**

Left Coast Press, Inc.
1630 North Main Street, #400
Walnut Creek, CA 94596
http://www.LCoastPress.com

ISBN 978-1-61132-219-4 hardback

ISBN 978-1-61132-220-0 paperback

ISBN 978-1-61132-221-7 institutional electronic

ISBN 978-1-61132-654-3 consumer electronic

Library of Congress Cataloging-in-Publication Data:

Advancing ethnography in corporate environments: challenges and emerging opportunities / Brigitte Jordan, editor.

  p. cm.

Includes index.

ISBN 978-1-61132-219-4 (hardback : alk. paper) -- ISBN 978-1-61132-220-0 (pbk. : alk. paper) -- ISBN 978-1-61132-221-7 (institutional ebook) --ISBN 978-1-61132-654-3 (consumer ebook)

1. Business anthropology. 2. Corporate culture. I. Jordan, Brigitte.

GN450.8.A49 2013

302.3ʾ5--dc23

                    2012032795

Printed in the United States of America

∞ ™ The paper used in this publication meets the minimum requirements of American National Standard for Information Sciences—Permanence of Paper for Printed Library Materials, ANSI/NISO Z39.48–1992.

Cover design by Piper Wallis

# Contents

## V.

## VI.

Introduction

# Advancing Ethnography in Corporate Settings: Challenges and Emerging Opportunities

*Brigitte Jordan*

## Corporate Ethnography: What Is That?

The idea of a "corporate ethnography" is new to many people. And even people who have heard of the concept remain unclear as to exactly what it means. Corporate ethnography is not easily defined by established disciplinary boundaries. It has strong roots in anthropological methods, theories and conceptual approaches, but is decidedly much more than a graft of academic ethnography onto business contexts.

I am not going to recount here the story of the rise of corporate anthropology and ethnography. That work has been done by others in the introductory chapters of recent books in the field (see the introduction in Cefkin [2009], the papers by Jordan and Suchman in Szymanski and Whalen [2011]) and is repeated at every ritual occasion where the community reflects on where it came from and where it is going (most recently Mack and Squires at the 2011 Ethnographic Praxis in Industry Conference [EPIC]). In addition, several of us provide historical details in this book, most notably Patricia Ensworth.

Judging from attendance at professional conferences and publications in the field, most practitioners of corporate ethnography are not anthropologists, despite the strong association of ethnography with that discipline. Nor, in fact, are corporate ethnographers predominantly academics. Even those who are academics are more likely to be teaching in schools of design or business schools than in traditional anthropology departments. But no matter their background, the common thread among most practitioners seems to be a dual reliance on in-person fieldwork and quantitative data. In general, I would say that a typical practitioner would be a member of anthrodesign (a community listserv)[1] and could be found most reliably at EPIC.[2]

Once skeptical of ethnographic methods, industry—the "corporate" in corporate ethnography—has by now largely accepted them as an important component of corporate research programs. In practice, ethnography in industry typically consists of an eclectic mix of face-to-face and digital, technology-supported methods that

*Advancing Ethnography in Corporate Environments: Challenges and Emerging Opportunities,* edited by Brigitte Jordan, 7–22. ©2013 Left Coast Press Inc. All rights reserved.

might range from conventional participant observation to video-supported shadowing to data analysis in the "cloud." Having grown up in the white spaces between conventional disciplines, corporate ethnography finds its tools and methods in many different arenas of activity, including applied anthropology, product and system design, global marketing, user interface design, and the business sector, and often takes advantage of automatic recording and curating of data.

The contributors to this book see corporate ethnography as an exciting new field that is vitally shaped by and draws heavily on anthropology and its sister disciplines in the social sciences, including sociology, communication studies, and (behavioral) economics, as well as fields solidly based in computer technology, such as Information Technology (IT), Computer Human Interaction (CHI), and Computer Supported Cooperative Work (CSCW). There is an increasingly close liaison between ethnography and design, apparent in the chapters of this book in the prevalence of design recommendations. The chapters by Ellen Isaacs and Ken Riopelle, for example, illustrate how ethnographers are actually involved in the hands-on production of physical products and system specifications.[3]

However, despite these key relationships with a number of academic disciplines, what sets corporate ethnography apart from them is that it "lives" in business. In other words, it derives its ways of knowing and objects of inquiry from industry, and has two fundamental concerns: one, to do research that provides insights into corporate structure and process; and two, to provide real-world solutions to problems that arise in business and industry.

Another major difference is that the output ("results") of corporate ethnography typically consists of "deliverables" for the use of a corporate client or employer, rather than scientific reports and published papers produced for the benefit of academic colleagues. A deliverable may be a design, a workshop, or a PowerPoint presentation to corporate decision-makers, and typically includes concrete recommendations about such things as product design, as Marijke Rijsberman explains, or process enhancement, as discussed by Vidar Hepsø in this volume.

This book wrestles with the key experiences and concerns of practitioners and aspiring players in an exciting emerging market where there are opportunities to address significant problems. It meets a demand in our field for experience-based material that explains methods and approaches, successes and failures, and the breadth as well as limitations in both the theory and the practice of this new field.

## How Did This Book Come To Be?

Over many years I have felt a growing dissatisfaction with the antiquated format of professional meetings that requires hundreds of intelligent people to sit silently for hours, listening to a string of presenters reading in monotone a series of only loosely connected papers. What interaction does exist at these meetings tends to come when a discussant or audience member starts the kind of inherently competitive academic debate that pits one theory, methodology, or data set against another.

What if we could instead develop a panel that would induce an atmosphere of playful cothinking, an offering of multiple perspectives and different ideas nourished by the expertise and experience we would each bring from our different intellectual homes? I wanted something much more informal, less stodgy, something exciting that would generate energy, something closer to conversation than debate. I wanted an opportunity for smart, experienced, dedicated, committed professionals to actually have fun laying out their thinking about topics they thought worth discussing with like-minded colleagues.

I asked Vidar Hepsø, a corporate anthropologist and valued colleague from Norway, to help me organize such a panel for the 2011 meeting of the Society for Applied Anthropology (SfAA). I sent a message to a network of professional friends and colleagues, inviting them to join a nontraditional session that would revolve around issues and dilemmas that we considered to be at the forefront of ethnographic work in industry. A small working group developed a set of crucial topics under the panel title "Challenges and Opportunities in Corporate Ethnography."

Hoping to maintain only a modicum of structure and predictability, our next step was to liberate our panel from the stiff academic presentation format. Thus each theme would be explored in a "dyad": two contributors would take on a common topic, each from a different point of view, but with the goal of sparking creative, generative dialog rather than combative academic debate. There would be no reading of prepared manuscripts and no PowerPoints. After the dyad, the presenters would be open to contributions, questions, and challenges from the audience. We wanted spirited exchanges that would show that it is possible to have different opinions and different perspectives to a problem without deteriorating into competition and one-upmanship.[4]

Although the presenters for this venture had been seduced into joining the panel by the promise that it would be a one-time happening, without papers and with no further obligations, at the postmortem the next morning there was spontaneous agreement among contributors that such a fun and stimulating gathering of curious, smart colleagues should not end with the panel. We discussed a number of formats for developing the dyads further and finally decided on a book. I committed to be the editor of this volume.[5]

I do think it is ironic that an event—designed (and promised) as an ephemeral, elusive, one-time happening that would leave no physical traces—evolved into something as structured as a book, and that the dyad framework I had dreamed up to nudge presentations into dialog rather than debate developed into chapters with structures that actually tamed some of the thoughts and ideas gleefully running wild during the SfAA session.

## Who Are We, the Authors?

Good question! We think of ourselves as part of an emerging new discipline, or maybe just a promising experiment. Most of us are anthropologists but not all.

Most of us have Ph.D.s, but not all. Most of us have taught in academia. Some of us are at the height of our career, acknowledged experts in our domains. And all of us have worked in corporate organizations as employees or outside consultants for years and are passionate about continuing the conversation to which we hope to contribute with this book.

## Dyads and the Dyad Spirit

The dyad format—twin presentations that take on a central topic but from different points of view—allows two lines of thinking to run in parallel, raising questions about different kinds of truths and how to simultaneously follow different approaches to a topic or an issue. It explores potential without premature commitment. Multiple truths, multiple methodologies, multiple theories, multiple outcomes—all are eminently important paths for being successful in this line of work. Later, during writing, the dyads provide structure and a source of support and companionship for the authors.

Even though there is plenty of competition in business, very often the path to a successful outcome is paved with multiple adjustments that pull in the knowledge and experience of multiple contributors. A "with" approach is particularly valuable for engaging in the complex multidisciplinary teams with whom corporate ethnographers typically work. Having to integrate and work jointly with corporate counterparts and negotiating within hierarchical structures where the multiple interests of multiple stakeholders have to be taken into account requires a skillful dance, implicit in many of the chapters but maybe most evident in the chapters by Julia Gluesing and Riopelle as well as Patricia Sunderland and Rita Denny (Dyads 1 and 4) in this volume.

## Our Goals for This Volume

We designed this book to appeal to readers with theoretical interests as well as to those with an applied modus operandi. We want to engage ethnographers who work as corporate employees as well as those in independent consultancies, corporate research labs, and academia. We particularly want to reach teachers and students who will be shaping this space in the future. Especially to them, we thought we could offer not only methodological and conceptual advances but also practical advice. Corporate ethnography is increasingly a source of innovation in theory and method, as well as an important option for the vast majority of anthropology students who do not become academic anthropologists.

This volume, thus, is well-suited not just for corporate ethnographers but also corporate insiders, business leaders, strategists, and managers who want to know more about corporate ethnography and how ethnography can help shape strategy and tactics in their projects. In particular, we have targeted the new breed of corporate insiders who push the cutting edge, the transformative front of business in the twenty-first century, the types that carry titles like media analyst, customer experience designer, data modeler, or social listening expert.

We have tried to provide insights into what it is like to work as an ethnographer in and for large organizations, be they for profit or not, and hands-on lived examples of different kinds of corporate work useful not only for students but also for members of the general public who want to understand the power and conditions of this work. Well aware of the value of theory in our business, and eager to build the new types of theory necessary for the digital era, we nevertheless wrote our chapters hoping to be practical enough to also provide advice for aspiring practitioners and anyone who wants to enter the consulting business. As a consequence, the book offers guidance and background information for people who are engaged in making career decisions.

## Dyads and Chapters

What should you expect from reading this book? I turn now to a brief overview of the themes and contents of the dyads and then of the crosscutting themes that run through the entire volume. Remember that dyads link chapters written by two expert practitioners and their take on a particular hot topic in a "with" rather than "versus" dialog.

### DYAD 1: Conventional Ethnographic Methods
*with* Technology-based Methods

Dyad 1 jumps right into one of today's most hotly debated issues, namely the relationship between conventional ethnographic methods grounded in participant observation and technology-supported methods. This ongoing controversy asks whether new digital methods will make traditional ethnography outdated. In Chapter 1, Julia Gluesing, an anthropologist with global experience in high-tech companies, argues that conventional ethnographic methods are more relevant than ever to understand contemporary work contexts. Ken Riopelle, an engineer and information scientist who frequently partners with Gluesing on projects, argues in Chapter 2 that in the digital age, our five human senses are no longer adequate to make meaning of the digital data deluge and suggests that complementary technology-supported methods need to be used to provide a full (or fuller) picture.

### DYAD 2: Ethnography for Systems Development: Renovating the Legacy
*with* Ethnography and Product Design: Fixing the Future

Dyad 2 extends ethnographic history and methodology into two complex arenas that are particularly important in contemporary corporate organizations, namely the design of systems and products. In Chapter 3, Patricia Ensworth, a business anthropologist with vast experience as a project manager in financial institutions, uses her work in system development to make a comparison between what kinds of ethnographic methods are expected in the ideal case with what the reality is like. Marijke Rijsberman, a design ethnographer with broad project experience, provides the view from a product design perspective by discussing her research on the private and business uses of videoconferencing. Although system development may be more like remodeling a house while product design could be seen as building a new one, the core ethnographic methodologies, based on participant observation and the identification of patterns of behavior and meaning, create many commonalities between the work of the system ethnographer and the product ethnographer.

## DYAD 3: The Value of Rapid Ethnography
### *with* The Limits to Speed in Ethnography

Dyad 3 addresses the role of speed in business from both practical and theoretical points of view. In business, time is a hard taskmaster. For ethnographers the central question is what ethnographic techniques can be adapted for speed without losing the depth and fine granularity of conventional ethnography. In Chapter 5, Ellen Isaacs, a system designer with a keen grip on the value of ethnography for technology and service design, discusses three of her recent projects, ranging from improving urban parking systems to realignment of nursing tasks. She provides detailed insights into rapid ethnography through detailed descriptions of methods and design. Her dyad partner Melissa Cefkin, a corporate anthropologist who has been prominent in keeping "the theory question" alive in our field, raises crucial questions: What are the limits to speed in ethnography? How far can we accommodate the pressure from industry to do our work faster and faster? She suggests a switch from time to temporality that considers such things as the time required to satisfy the logic of a project and the time required for achieving ethnographic understanding.

## DYAD 4: The Cry for More Theory
### *with* The Cry for Practicality

Dyad 4 may be the chapters academic anthropologists will turn to first because it addresses a fundamental issue, one acknowledged openly in academia though more clandestinely in corporate practice: What is the ubiquitous cry for more theory about, even when we are embedded in practical work that needs to get done? Basing their remarks on many years of joint consulting work in marketing and consumer research, Patricia Sunderland, in Chapter 7, introduces the longstanding dualism of theory and practice and its persistence while Rita Denny, in Chapter 8, focuses on the role of theorizing in practitioners' work. Analyzing successes and failures in their consulting projects, they suggest that the corporate funders of their work also have theories, albeit tacit, nonformalized ones, that need to be brought into dialog with the explicit anthropological and academic theories that we bring to the table.

## DYAD 5: Doing Corporate Ethnography as an Insider (Employee) *with* Doing Corporate Ethnography as an Outsider (Employer)

Dyad 5 is concerned with a fundamental structural characteristic of corporate ethnography: the dual nature of engagement (and employment possibilities). Ethnographic work is, roughly speaking, carried out from the outside in by temporary consultants or from the inside out by ethnographers who have been hired by the company for more or less permanent positions as employees. In Chapter 9, Vidar Hepsø, an experienced anthropologist employed for more than 20 years in the Norwegian oil industry, paints a fascinating picture of the issues that arise in the communities of practice charged with provisioning offshore platform installations in the North Sea. He is followed by business anthropologist Francoise Brun-Cottan, who speaks from a career characterized by multiple shifts between insider and outsider status, which is fairly typical in our field. Though their work experiences have been quite different, it is interesting to see that the issues they raise run largely (though not completely) in parallel.

## DYAD 6: The Era of Big Data *with* Pattern Recognition in Human Development

In a large sweep from prehistory to the future of society, Dyad 6 takes on an ambitious set of issues that will shape the future of ethnography. Arguably, the most controversial, implicative, and important topic in the business world today is the question of the impact of Big Data, analytics, and privacy. Chad Maxwell, an applied anthropologist with extensive experience in advertising, marketing, and design research has based Chapter 11 on his work helping companies adjust to (and profit from) the transformations of the digital age. He lays out the impact of digital technology and the massive amount of data it creates. He proposes to chart a new course for ethnographic practitioners in the new era through what he calls "ethnographic analytics." In Chapter 12, as a corporate anthropologist with deep roots in medical anthropology, I attempt to open up "new thinking spaces." I ground my assessment of the issues we face at this time in the evolution of the human species and the changes in humans' ability to make sense of rapid changes in the environment by developing new sensory mechanisms. Taking up an idea advanced earlier in this book by Riopelle and then by Maxwell (that the digital data deluge has outstripped our human sensory capabilities), I conclude the dyad (and the book) by proposing a set of "what's next" issues that complement those proposed by Maxwell.

## Crosscutting Themes

Let me also alert you to some continuing themes threading through the book that, in spite of the variety of topics, provide coherence and mutual relevance. Sometimes these topics are explicitly called out and identified in a chapter; other times they are implicit. For example, methodology issues (and advice) are present in every one of the chapters (though you may have to seek them out). Here I'll highlight a few of the common threads. We'll leave it to you to go looking for more.

### Methods

Explicitly and implicitly, all of us are deeply concerned with methodological issues in our work. Our varied experiences over the last four decades open up a practice-based view on the hybrid arsenal of methods in use by ethnographers doing work in business and industry. Methodology is the very topic of the first dyad, where Gluesing argues forcefully that even (and especially) in global high-tech organizations, research has to be grounded in the intimate copresence and coexperience of participant observation. Riopelle asks if the benefits generated by being there face to face are in danger of being replaced by the affordances of new types of sensors and technologies. Can the new digitally based technologies make conventional methods of data collection and analysis replaceable? He and Gluesing both conclude that ethnography's opportunity lies in a combined use of both types of methodologies. Riopelle even provides very specific examples and step-by-step exercises for readers to try their hand at using algorithms.

Ensworth (in Chapter 3) also makes methods an explicit topic when she reports on her research in system development. She suggests that there are always two aspects to consider: the official "field practices" recommended in books and lectures and the unofficial, rarely talked about methods that emerge with a "reality check" of what happens when a project hits the snags that are guaranteed to appear. Drawing on a wealth of examples from her work, she shows us the clandestine accommodations to reality, the unspoken shortcuts, the tacit agreements that get made to get the work done. This chapter should be particularly valuable to aspiring researchers in the field.

Explicit methodological recommendations are also given in Dyad 6, where Maxwell speculates about what kinds of methods might be appropriate in a world dominated by algorithms and data mining. He argues that the use of analytics, even with its inherent flaws, can be a powerful tool in the ethnographer's methodology toolkit. Jordan agrees, maybe with a bit less enthusiasm, and lays out a detailed set of research recommendations that might lead to a deeper understanding of the transformations we are witnessing and the very significant issues they are generating in society.

Quite apart from these explicit treatments there is a wealth of insights and suggestions in the specific projects reported in the chapters, most of which include more or less explicit methods discussions with valuable ideas and examples.

Chapters such as Isaacs in Dyad 3, or Sunderland and Denny in Dyad 4 are almost instruction manuals for Rapid Ethnography and consumer research, respectively.

## Technology

It will not escape your notice that the first as well as the last dyad of this book focus on the new digital technologies that are generating fundamental changes in how business sees and goes about its work and, even more important, what the implications of these changes are to all of us on a societal level. Ethnography has always been carried out with technology support, from Margaret Mead's notebook and film camera and the 40 pounds of video equipment I used to drag into the field in the 1970s and 1980s, to the ubiquitous tape recorders that still allow us to catch interaction but now with increasing granularity. Combined with a trend to involve former "subjects" as "participants," we have most recently and very productively used portable videorecorders for unobtrusive shadowing, carried out by the ethnographer or study participants themselves. Video diaries, webcam location data, GPS tracking: there are now many kinds of technologies that make possible massive data collection to the point where the actual collection process is no longer an issue. A bit more of an issue is the curating and analysis of such data for which still no easy solutions exist (nor are any offered in this book).[6]

Instrumented data collection is ubiquitous in ethnography now, in corporate work and elsewhere. However, we have entered a new epoch, the era of Big Data, sociodigitization, and analytics, which has generated technologies of a fundamentally different kind that are now available to do Internet-based, multisited, mega data, algorithm-based research. The new gorilla at the corporate ethnography table is "analytics," which consists of attempts to make sense both of data generated on the web (including mobile and social behavior), and of offline data that might come from credit cards, point-of-sale transactions, and call centers, typically captured from customer databases and organizational records.

At this writing, the reaction among academics as well as corporate practitioners is, expectably, divided and still quite volatile. On the one hand there is complete denial ("how long have we had computers?" or "there is nothing new here"); on the other, major segments of the ethnographic community have become very involved, fascinated, energized, engaged, and even committed to big data analytics, both as advocates and as detractors. This situation is reflected in the book. Riopelle and Maxwell, while voicing appropriate cautions, are clearly enthused and emphasize the amazing possibilities opening up both for commercial interests and individuals. They also discuss opportunities in new sensor and archiving technologies that open up opportunities for anthropological data collection and analysis. Jordan, in contrast, is much more concerned about the effects the mining of these unbelievably massive amounts of data, collected and archived automatically, have on our ideas of data collection and analysis. There is a great deal of delight and enthusiastic experimentation with new technologies at this point, and that should be generative of new approaches.[7] The security blanket in these discussions is the continued practical usability and availability of the standard basic ethnographic methods to which everybody is ready to return (or at least pay lip service).

So there is tremendous ambivalence: enthusiastic endorsement of the promise but then also awareness of serious warnings, including the question: what does it mean? (Ladner 2008). We see flights of fancy that try to overcome deeply felt uncertainty with a bravado generated by the suspicion that the positive aspects of the new connectivity will be overwhelmed by exploitation: the reaping of the benefits by the large corporations. This is the period of manifestos, of declarations of a great new world just around the corner on one side and warnings of Armageddon on the other.

However important these issues are, the real essence of this book will be found in the chapters where dyads deal with the mundane successes and failures of ethnographic practice in the real world, a reassuring number of which are not at all or only minimally affected by the promises and threats of analytics.

## Time, Speed, and Temporality in Ethnographic Work

Time is a fundamental symbolic category for understanding the orderliness of corporate life. For us as ethnographers, understanding the organization of time in a new business setting is one of the first requirements for being productive. In business, time is organized according to recurring units such as business quarters or production cycles within which activities occur in an expectedly orderly way. It is up to the ethnographer to figure out what exceptions are allowed and what disturbances create trouble that requires action.

In time-driven organizations, practically all activities are time-sensitive (like the task chains of nurses described by Isaacs in Chapter 5); with the addition of deadlines generated by such things as end-of-quarter or shareholder meetings, they become time-critical. Time-critical activities and projects usually (but not always) involve the bottom line. If such deadlines are missed, heads may roll.

Work is almost always framed in terms of time. ("When is this due?") Given that time is central in business, it is present in some way or other in all the chapters. With compressed timescales, research scope and methods have to be adjusted. In Dyad 3, speed takes center stage with Rapid Ethnography. Isaacs describes three examples of projects carried out under time constrictions and discusses in detail the methodological adjustments she and her team made to provide crucial input to urban parking enforcement, work overload in hospital nursing, and design suggestions for supporting multichannel communication for mobile individuals. Cefkin uses a more theoretical approach and suggests that beyond the preoccupation with time and speed, there is temporality, a higher-level concept that allows us to better understand time from the point of view of what she calls the temporalities of ethnographic understanding, of everyday life, and of project organization.

One of the problems that corporate ethnographers typically encounter is "requirements creep," when, under the twin pressures of speed and organizational complexity, project goals are constantly redefined as various stakeholders provide input even after it is under way. This requires a great deal of flexibility, the ability to step back and reconsider, and adaptability while still holding on to some vision of the desired accomplishment. How to deal with the dangers of requirements creep in ethnographic engagements is visible in many of the larger projects described by Ensworth, Denny, and others.

Even if not explicitly acknowledged, a pervasive orientation to the ways in which time organizes activities in business settings (see Jordan 1990), it is interesting to note that the new communication possibilities provided by the Internet and the global distribution of team members disturb and disrupt many of those established patterns. In the long run, the most critical aspects of time and speed may be the acceleration of production processes that Maxwell and Jordan talk about in Dyad 6.

Many aspects of the organization of time are not explicitly addressed, even though they underlie all corporate work. They affect not only when people do what during a given day or quarter, but also where they can be found and what they are likely to be talking about. With effective distance communication and the ongoing transition to remote work in the global economy, where coordination over different time zones is essential, many of these tacitly organized activities are now disturbed. While there are interesting issues here for future research, our focus for the moment and in this book is on the necessity to do our work within compressed time constraints.

## Theory and Practice

What role does theory play in the ethnography of corporations and other large organizations? This question is most explicitly addressed by Sunderland and Denny in Dyad 4, where they make a powerful argument that the theory we bring from our respective disciplines (in their case anthropology and sociology of marketing) is the most important contribution we bring to the corporate table. They show through a succession of examples and projects ranging from rethinking delicatessen stores to family interaction at breakfast the incessant interplay between the cry for more theory and the cry of practicality, coming to the conclusion that the resolution of the gap lies in understanding and respecting the (usually implicit) theories the client brings to the table. With a delicate, sensitive scalpel they dissect—courageously using their own failures—the sources of miscommunication. They argue that resolving the gap lies in designing and negotiating (early and then again) ongoing conversations that acknowledge both types of theories for a successful solution design.

There is a general view that applied anthropology and ethnography in particular are devoid of theory. But the chapters of this book occupy a space where theory meets practice. Obviously, every time we walk into a problem setting, we bring with us a set of theories of how the world works: explicit ones from our training, implicit ones from our experience. Examples of using both these kinds of theory can be found throughout the book. The more damming accusation, however, is (and always has been) the accusation that applied anthropology (speak ethnography) does not generate theory. It is purportedly purely descriptive and that (pat on the back) is nice, but it does not promote science.

Conversely, one might want to consider that we use exactly the same methods (well, maybe a bit more sophisticated and technology informed) as academic anthropologists, but that in the corporate environment in which we operate, theories, especially named theories, have a bad reputation. So we mostly don't worry about theory at all even though most of our long-term investigations regarding what makes the world of business work are material for theory. The sad fact remains that in the corporate world there is little reward for theory; the reward is for getting things done.

Might we consider the possibility that ethnographic work is potentially as generative of theory as any other kind of empirical work? It requires tracking particular phenomena and their distribution through time and space to arrive at generalizations that eventually could develop into full-fledged named theories. In corporate ethnography, this endeavor is undermined by the conditions of our work, which in most cases precludes a long-term focus. The mental shift that would be required is a move from seeing ethnography as a validating science to seeing it as a discovery science (Whalen and Whalen 2004). With that in mind, one can see, distributed throughout the chapters, a plethora of experiences and insights that could be seen as embryo theories, or theories in waiting. Consider, for example, Isaacs' observations about task allocation in hospital nursing and its relationship to top-down planning of tasks, or Cefkin's theory of temporality that is already anticipating the naming that is necessary for theories to acquire distribution and "a social life" in an appropriate community.

## Identity Conflict and Ethics

To the extent that the capitalist economy is seen as exploitative, working in industry raises ethical questions for many of us, insiders as well as outsiders.[8] The very nature of our work produces issues that range from identity conflicts involving loyalty to company and team to serious ethical worries and concerns, especially about long-term effects. A major issue for all of us is the potential for divided loyalties. To be effective in an organization, you have to be able to speak the language and think the thinking of the company, but that may generate creeping identity conflicts. Such conflicts are evident at various places in the book as part of project descriptions. Both Denny and Sunderland explicitly point to the role of learning to speak the language of the corporation and thereby thinking inside its rules and accepting its unspoken assumptions. That the ethnographer is likely to be in the minority position in crossdisciplinary corporate teams makes it more isolating and more difficult to disagree with company policy and worldview.

Ironically, it is often the very nature of our work that allows us to understand that when we contribute, say, to our funders' operational efficiency (a fairly positive goal), we may also be contributing to people losing their jobs; that when we help them design more effective advertising, we may contribute to the deterioration of people's lives with new products and advertised services. Down the line, we might be part of an effort that contributes to undesirable changes in families, communities and society.

Many of us have struggled with these kinds of questions throughout our working lives. Part of the dynamics of the conflict is a strong identification with ethical principles acquired during our training as humanistic social scientists, while another part is deeply grounded in the ability to see the ways in which changes—no matter how well intentioned—also may have negative consequences. We hope that companies anticipate and deal with those consequences, but to what extent are *we* responsible for them? And what can we do to mitigate negative effects? How can we, for example, help deal with a necessary RIF (Reduction in Force)? What can we do to minimize (or turn positive) the changes to which our work contributes?[9] This is particularly an issue for consulting relationships that are inherently short and narrowly focused and by their very nature do not necessarily raise questions about long-term outcomes. The typical and endemic requirements creep I mentioned earlier, through which project goals are changed on the fly, is a major contributor to situations where at some time during a project you may find yourself producing outcomes you had not envisioned.

In the following chapters, issues of loyalty to the company that employs and funds you are explicitly discussed in Dyad 5 by Hepsø and Brun-Cottan, where Hepsø discusses identity conflicts and Brun-Cottan deals with some pragmatic solutions that her team devised in a case where ethnographic work could have contributed to very negative consequences for a substantial part of society.

Rijsberman, in Chapter 4, gives us a very thoughtful examination of an ethical question. The goals of her research on videoconferencing had not included identifying any misalignments between company goals and consumers' preferences, some of which emerged in her research. Nevertheless, this has led her to ask the broader question: is videoconferencing inherently inimical to the work environment? I think it is these ethical questions, kicked up one level, that stimulate the ethnographic community to investigate higher-level ethical issues.

In academic anthropology, we teach explicitly about the process and the dangers of "going native" when the dual roles of "involved participant" and "objective observer" are no longer in balance. When ethnographic work turns lonely in corporate situations, the conversations that are necessary to keep this balance are often not available. This is one of those situations where having a network of like-minded practitioners in whom to confide can prove invaluable.

## Conclusions

This book occupies the white space between theory and practice. It is an offer to engage in conversation and action to advance corporate ethnography as a new playground and a new market niche for applied social science, anthropology, and ethnography. We are extending this offer to our colleagues in the field, the corporate ethnographers who are already exploring the "corporate jungles" within which we work, as well as to newcomers, including those who are contemplating a career in business ethnography.

We see a rising interest in corporate ethnography in academia with demands from students and professors who are asking for insights, for ways into the world of practicing corporate ethnography, and we hope that our book provides just that. As a matter of fact, we believe that aspiring practitioners will find answers to many of their practical and conceptual questions in the following pages, questions about such things as access, entry, negotiating power structures, pitfalls, and ethics. These can be found here in chapters where experienced practitioners provide insights, project descriptions, models, and even exercises.

But we also want to extend this conversation to practitioners in business who have engaged, or are planning to engage, anthropologists and ethnography. We seek connections to interdisciplinary teams, project stakeholders, managers, and decision-makers: in short, the new breed of practitioners arising within corporations and other large organizations who are ready to explore the white spaces between the social sciences and business.

Throughout this book we have been mindful of the fact that corporate ethnography will be advanced to the extent that we manage to speak to both of these audiences: our conversational partners in business *and* in academia. So we are looking to engage not only with anthropology departments, but also with schools of design and business schools. We want to provide material both for corporate interests and for aspiring practitioners' career choices. This book is equally for scholars, policymakers, and practitioners. And it is to this rich and fertile mix of foundations, experiences, and aspirations that we dedicate our endeavor.

## Acknowledgments

Not all of us who were part of the original SfAA panel were able to carry through with us to the end. However, every one of them made major contributions to our thinking and had an effect on the shape of this volume. Overwhelmed by the realities of their other obligations (remember, this was to be a one-time, ephemeral, fun kind of thing), they have nevertheless remained involved in the fate of "our baby." Not visible in a chapter that bears their name, they are the fairy godmothers who continue to remain connected to us and the volume's career.

I and all of us would particularly like to thank the organizers of the postpanel workshop at the SfAA meetings in March of 2011, especially Peggy Szymanski, who also provided postsession editorial assistance; Mary Walker, whose panel presentation was inspirational; Keren Salomon, whose upcoming publication will draw on our many dialogs; and Roxana Wales, who has fed into our thinking for a long time from NASA and now from Google.

I also very much appreciate the spirit and close attention of Jennifer Collier, our volume editor, and that of Michelle Treviño, our production editor on the Left Coast Press side. On the personal side, I want to thank my family, who with incredible tolerance lived through this year of my nonavailability. (I promise to do better on the next project!) But my deepest thanks go to my partner Robert Irwin, without whose reading, editing, and handholding contributions this volume probably wouldn't exist.

## References

Cefkin, Melissa (ed.)
2009 *Ethnography and the Corporate Encounter: Reflections on Research in and of Corporations.* New York and Oxford: Berghahn Books.

Gray, Jim
2007 "Jim Gray on eScience: A Transformed Scientific Method." [Edited from the last entry on his website at Microsoft Research before he went missing at sea on January 28, 2007.] Available at http://research.microsoft.com/en-us/collaboration/fourthparadigm/4th_paradigm_book _jim_gray_transcript.pdf. Accessed June 1, 2012.

Jordan, Brigitte
1990 Teamwork in an Airlines Operations Room: A Skills Scenario. In *Identifying and Describing the Skills Required by Work. Report of The Secretary's Commission on Achieving Necessary Skills (SCANS)*, pp. A5–A7. Washington, D. C.: U.S. Department of Labor.
2011 Transferring Ethnographic Competence: Personal Reflections on the Past and Future of Work Practice Analysis. In *Making Work Visible: Ethnographically Grounded Case Studies of Work Practice*, edited by Margaret H. Szymanski and Jack Whalen, pp. 344–58. New York: Cambridge University Press.

Ladner, Sam
2008 Watching the Web: An Ontological and Epistemological Critique of Web-Traffic Measurement. In *Handbook of Log File Analysis*, edited by J. Jansen, A. Spink, and I. Taksa, pp. 64–78. Hershey, PA: Idea Group Information Science Reference (IGI Global).

Mack, Alexandra, and Susan Squires
2011 Evolving Ethnographic Practitioners and Their Impact on Ethnographic Praxis. *Proceedings of Ethnographic Praxis in Industry Conference (EPIC)* 2011:18–26.

Slobin, Adrian, and Todd Cherkasky
2010 Ethnography in the Age of Analytics. *Proceedings of Ethnographic Praxis in Industry Conference (EPIC)* 2010:188–98.

Suchman, Lucy
2011 Work Practice and Technology: A Retrospective. In *Making Work Visible: Ethnographically Grounded Case Studies of Work Practice*, edited by Margaret H. Szymanski and Jack Whalen, pp. 21–33. New York: Cambridge University Press.

Szymanski, Margaret H., and Jack Whalen (eds.)
2011 *Making Work Visible: Ethnographically Grounded Case Studies of Work Practice.* New York: Cambridge University Press.

Whalen, Marilyn, and Jack Whalen
2004 Studying Workscapes. In *Discourse and Technology: Multimodal Discourse Analysis*, edited by Philip LeVine and Ron Scollon, pp. 208–229. Washington, D. C.: Georgetown University Press.

## Notes

1   Anthrodesign was started by anthropologist Natalie Hanson in 2002 while she was struggling to reconcile her doctoral studies with full-time employment at the software company SAP, a market leader for supply chain management.

2   EPIC was organized by anthropologists ken anderson from Intel and Tracey Lovejoy from Microsoft in 2005. EPIC publishes peer-reviewed papers presented at the meetings as well as workshops, posters, and artifacts. The *Proceedings*, in their seventh edition at the time of this writing, provide a powerful overview of the development of the field in less than 10 years.

3   Please be aware that I am a deeply entrenched, dyed-in-the-wool anthropologist. You may notice my tendency to let the terms "anthropology" and "anthropological" stand for what in fact by now has a much broader disciplinary basis and influence.

4   Many of us who have come through graduate training and especially the Ph.D. experience (or ordeal) had to fight for years to get the value of our contributions acknowledged and rewarded. Clearly, business values competition and fosters it through performance appraisals and production numbers, not to speak of the dreaded ROI (Return on Investment). It may sound counterintuitive, but in these complex environments a highly competitive spirit may actually be counterproductive to getting something done.

5   As editor, I thought of my work as "herding cats" (though I was always worried that the "cats" might find that offensive). I saw my job as pulling together the variety of viewpoints into a coherent whole, an interesting terrain that has some landmarks and connecting paths. At the same time I tried not to kill the spirit of the original conversation. I wanted us to let live the variety of writing styles from what I call "academese" to "manifesto" style, and thereby preserve the thinking spaces the panel had opened up. I sought to preserve as much as possible the spirit of the original conversation and so you will find very different writing styles, ranging from enthusiastic advocacy to cool assessment to more academic prose.

6   Interestingly, this is not only a problem for the largely qualitative data we rely on in ethnographic research, but also (and maybe to an even greater degree) for the hard sciences. See Gray (2007) for an insightful discussion of the magnitude of this problem.

7   This shift is paralleled only by what the arrival of probability statistics and game theory produced in earlier times. A bit puzzling in this conjecture is the fact that a quick search of the 2010 and 2011 *Proceedings of EPIC* shows a first major paper in 2010 (Slobin and Cherkasky 2010) but comes up with no evidence of major breakthroughs. Yet?

8   There are parallels here with the embedding of anthropologists in military operations in the wars in Iraq and Afghanistan, an issue that has become a point of deep dissension within academic anthropology.

9   Actually, there exists in the community quite a list of possible ways to influence those negative outcomes, most of which include making provisions for including those affected in designing the transition.

Chapter 1

# Being There: The Power of Conventional Ethnographic Methods

*Julia Gluesing*

> The sensitive ethnographer is always open to a slip, to a tear, to an unexpected association.
>
> —*Sherry Turkle*

## Introduction

For anthropologists who study work and organizations and their place in our lives, and for all corporate or business and organizational ethnographers, doing good research still largely depends on doing good conventional ethnography. This usually means spending time with people in their work settings, observing them as they do their work, and talking with them about what that work means to them. Yet the challenge facing corporate ethnographers today is doing ethnography in the global context where work is distributed around the world, across multiple boundaries, in rapidly changing contexts, and where human interaction is mediated by technology. The vexing question is: do conventional ethnographic methods still really work for us in this complex, global business environment where work more often than not takes place over the Internet?

Ethnographers who want to investigate online-mediated work find themselves using technology-based ethnographic methods more and more frequently. They investigate how social networking happens on YouTube (Lange 2007), and they seek to take advantage of the new technologies that can help them tap into the wealth of data about social issues—texts, photos, graphics and other visuals, databases, and algorithms for pattern recognition—that are available online to reveal what groups of people are thinking and doing, how they are organizing and working, and what they value (Hine 2000). Internet search algorithms are helping to uncover both the structure and sentiment of online collaborative innovation networks (Gloor 2004). In addition, there are ethnographers who are advocating new technology-based forms of ethnography when studying computer-mediated communication and community, or cybersociety, and how these virtual communities form in the "electronic frontier" (Boellstorff 2008; Jones 1995; Rheingold 1993). In light of this, many ethnographers as well as their employers are beginning to raise strong arguments for dropping the labor-intensive, time-consuming, and costly conventional ethnographic methods in favor of electronic tools in the investigation of global work that takes place online. The value of conventional ethnography is being questioned.

Although making use of new tools to gain insights into new ways of living and working is indeed convenient, the argument presented in this chapter is that conventional ethnographic methods are more relevant and valuable than ever to understand contemporary work contexts. Global workflows, even those taking place almost solely on the Internet, are still socially negotiated and recontextualized in the local. Being there, practicing participant observation in physical contexts and conducting face-to-face interviews, is critical to uncovering the emergent local, emic meanings and work practices: information that then can flow back into the global technology context. Online work still derives much of its meaning in relationship to local context, organizations, and social groups. A global manager responsible for sustainable materials in manufacturing understands what it means to be sustainable by reference to local plant contexts and work practices and not with reference to any established meaning in the international online work group she manages. For her, work remains a fundamentally socially negotiated activity with reference to local meaning, even when that work is mediated by technology and crosses multiple contexts. For us to do good ethnography that will produce a holistic understanding of modern, mediated work, particularly global work that is distributed across multiple contexts, we must not give up on conventional ethnographic methods.

## So What Are Conventional Ethnographic Methods?

Before discussing why conventional ethnographic methods remain important in the age of abundant, rich, and easily accessible digital information, it is worthwhile to talk about what they are. Ethnography is the trademark methodology of anthropology. As a general method, it is best thought of as a research approach or strategy that seeks to learn about "the social and cultural life of communities, institutions, and other settings" (LeCompte and Schensul 1999:1–2). It is both scientific and investigative. Among cultural anthropologists, the *conventional* primary ethnographic method is *participant observation,* where "the researcher takes part in the daily activities, rituals, interactions, and events of a group of people as one of the means of learning the explicit and tacit aspects of their life routines and their culture" (Dewalt and Dewalt 2002:1). Conventional ethnographic methods are used similarly in any setting. Because this is a book devoted to corporate ethnography, the best way to describe conventional ethnographic methods is with an example that illustrates how they are commonly practiced in corporations.

## A Story of Conventional Ethnography in Action

Early in the 1990s, a multinational corporation in the computer industry, which we will call High Technology Manufacturing (HTM), began to use global teams of about 8 to 12 people to address pressing problems in the product development, sales, and service aspects of its business. This was at a time when global teams, involving distributed work, were a relatively new phenomenon, and not much was known about how they might be alike or different from traditional face-to-face teams. The company chose team members to represent different functional areas such as marketing, engineering, and finance, as well as different offices in Europe, primarily in France and in the United States, and designated English as the common language for the global teams. Participation in the global team was in addition to people's regular work assignments. There were about 30 of these teams at the time, but the company was finding that only about six of them were actually successful in producing the desired results. In spite of the fact that each team had undergone a weeklong orientation program to help them understand their mission and learn about working together as a team, most of the teams were behind schedule in their tasks, and team members were having difficulty getting along. The teams all had process facilitators to help them get their work done, but they still were not making the level of progress their managers expected. The corporation suspected that there might be some fundamental problems in the way the teaming process was structured, but no one, not even the team members themselves, could point to anything specific. The corporation decided that a bilingual (English-French) cultural anthropologist might be able to help, and I was hired to conduct an ethnographic research project that took several months to determine what was contributing to the success or failure of the global teams.

The ethnographic fieldwork began in France when I attended a major conference at which all the HTM global teams were brought together to report on their work. A few new teams had to undergo initial orientation. Teams who were already at work were required to participate in facilitated face-to-face sessions to work on their mission and tasks and engage in some additional training to enhance their teamwork skills. The conference was one of several similar events that I observed. In addition to these observations, I participated in all the team sessions of five global teams, both face-to-face and technology-mediated, gathered all the team documents, and received all the team correspondence over the course of the fieldwork. There were many opportunities to talk with team members informally about their work and to get to know them over lunch, dinner, and other activities. Observing their interactions with one another in many different situations, and listening to them tell stories about their work in general, about their teams, about each other, and about their lives, all counted as "data" and contributed to the research. Formal interviews with managers outside the teams and with all the global team members, not just those in the five teams chosen for specific study, added additional perspectives and context for the study. The research included extended visits on more than one occasion to the work locations in Europe and in the United States where most of the team members had their offices. These visits really provided information about the organizational and sociopolitical contexts that influenced how the team members saw their work and about their habitual work behaviors outside their work with their team. To support all this fieldwork, I created a "portable office" that included plenty of notebooks in a variety of sizes for fieldnotes, a laptop computer, a portable printer, multiple telephone and computer connectors for a variety of plugs and outlets, a stapler, paper clips and scotch tape, a tape recorder and blank tapes, a camera, and plenty of pens and pencils.

Ethnography yielded a typology of the characteristics of successful and unsuccessful global teams and uncovered many misunderstandings within the teams and among the teams and managers that were previously poorly understood. One of the major problems turned out to be the many different definitions for commonly used English terms, such as "market research." Team members used the term assuming that they all had the same understanding of what market research meant. However, as it turned out, what marketing meant in terms of specific behaviors was different in different contexts. At HTM in France, market research commonly meant that one sought out the opinions of technology experts and top managers inside and outside the company. In the United States, market research was very different; it was conducted by talking almost exclusively with customers and potential customers, even those who were customers of competitors. These different meanings meant that one team was unable to compare market research data gathered in France with that gathered in the United States. As a result of this insight and many others that emerged from the ethnographic research, HTM adjusted its training and facilitation to include more emphasis on language and on understanding and clarification across contexts and cultures. Managers also decided to rotate the quarterly face-to-face global team meetings across locations to give all members the opportunity to learn about each other's work contexts and standard work practices. I inductively developed a model for representing how team members develop shared understanding about their goals, and how they can create a composite team culture over time (Gluesing 1998). The model became the basis for structuring, facilitating, and evaluating the HTM global teams. It depicted successful teaming that begins with a market-driven business objective that triggers the teaming process, and concludes with the achievement of the business objective and with individual and team learning. The teaming process itself involves learning about and opening up to differences, negotiating a working process that accommodates different contexts and work practices, and strengthening teaming over time by building connections both inside and outside the team, and balancing power in evolving business conditions.

## What Can We Learn about Conventional Ethnography from the HTM Global Teams Example?

In the fieldwork at HTM, we can identify the characteristics of conventional ethnography, primarily participant observation. They usually include the following seven elements and practices:

1. Using all five senses, the ethnographer serves as the primary tool of data collection, living or staying in a context for an extended period of time;
2. Participating in a wide range of activities that are both routine (standard job and team activities) and extraordinary (global team conference), along with the people who are the full participants in that context (global team members);
3. Learning and using more than one language to communicate with people in their own native language or dialect (French and English);
4. Informally observing during leisure activities is an important part of data collection (often called "deep hanging out"), in addition to formal observation of work;
5. Using everyday, informal conversation as a form of interviewing;
6. Recording observations and thoughts, usually chronologically, in fieldnotes in a variety of settings; and
7. Learning from and building on the perspectives of the people in the research setting (in the case of global teams, in multiple research settings) inductively, using both explicit and tacit information in analysis and writing, to develop local theories for testing and then adapting these theories for general use.

These conventional ethnographic methods have been adapted over the years as life and work have changed, and especially as communication technologies have advanced and proliferated (Bernard 1998). New tools beyond those that were described in the "portable office" used at HTM range from digital recorders and handheld computing devices of all kinds—and now smart phones—for taking notes and capturing what is happening in any given situation the ethnographer might be investigating. Another boon to the toolkit has been the numerous qualitative software analysis packages that aid in data coding, assist in the discovery of themes and patterns in the data, and help build and test theories.

In fact, technology and society continuously coevolve (Gluesing 2008). Technology has long been part subject and part method in conventional ethnography since its conceptual and methodological beginnings (Batteau 2009). Today, in researching the virtual work of global teams, the communication technologies that are the focus of ethnographic study can also become a means of data collection and ethnographic practice. As virtual technologies and virtual work become an ever-present part of our daily work lives, we will continue to witness the adjustment of conventional ethnographic methods to the requirements of research in both online and physical settings (Jordan 2009).

However, what will always constitute the foundation of conventional ethnographic methods is the on-the-ground, face-to-face participation in the life of a group in a physical setting to "see" work from the group members' points of view within the larger context of their daily lives. In doing conventional ethnography, we make the assumption that we must discover and situate what people actually do by observing their activities and learning both about explicit culture that people can articulate and the tacit aspects of culture that largely remain outside of people's awareness or consciousness. Only then we can interpret what that behavior means to the people we are studying, and continue to the larger realm of uncovering patterns, which is a strength of the anthropological approach to ethnography as Jordan posits in "Pattern Recognition in Human Evolution and Why It Matters for Ethnography, Anthropology and Society," the last chapter of this volume. Conventional ethnographers work from the inside out and from the outside in to do research and build theory, framing human behavior and belief within the larger sociopolitical and historical context, and in anthropology, using the concept of culture as a lens through which results are interpreted. Conventional ethnography takes time (Cefkin and Isaacs, this volume) and involves deep exploration of a phenomenon using multiple tools and methods; but, first and foremost, it consists of in situ participant observation.

## The Challenges to Conventional Ethnographic Methods: Can Conventional Ethnography Still Work for Us?

With all the technology advances for gathering data, as well as all the ways work is done in online virtual spaces, it is reasonable to ask what value conventional methods can still bring to ethnographic work, especially given the labor, time, and cost involved (the HTM study in our example of ethnographic methods took about a year to complete). Business clients and practitioners raise three primary challenges to the value of conventional ethnography: (1) convergence in the way we work globally, (2) sophisticated virtual technologies that enable rich communication, and (3) the abundance of digital data and data-mining tools.

These challenges to conventional ethnography are all understandable given the way technology and the Internet have become the foundation on which we accomplish global work, especially in the information economy. Yet, if we more closely examine each of them, we can demonstrate how conventional on-the-ground ethnographic methods are not only still valid, but also indispensible in helping us describe, understand, and explain the world of work, even online.

### CHALLENGE 1: Convergence Is Eliminating the Need for Conventional Ethnography

Global work has come a long way since the early 1990s and the days of the HTM global teams. We are likely on a daily basis to interact with people at a distance just as often as we work with those sitting next to us. With the exponential increase in the globalization of business in the past 10 years, with English as the de facto language of global business, and with the standardization of global business practices, there is convergence in the way work is done and fewer communication barriers. Business practitioners argue that this convergence is eliminating the need for conventional ethnography to illuminate differences and communication misunderstandings, or to help facilitate the integration of practices across boundaries. However, another story about a more contemporary global team illustrates clearly that convergence is not happening as one might expect.

Not long ago, a French-American team trying to work online across multiple work sites found itself in trouble. Their task was to develop objectives for a process to deliver consumer food products, but discussion bogged down with no resolution, and agreement on even simple concepts became more and more difficult. Language didn't appear to be an issue, since everyone used English online. As part of a research project to investigate global teams in several different companies, ethnographers had been following the team's online interactions and gathering work documents to try to understand how the team process was proceeding (Baba et al. 2004). They had perceived the team conflict in their online observations, but had not been able to uncover the root causes of the difficulties.

One day, the American and French members of the team met in Paris in a rare face-to-face meeting to again discuss how to merge their two approaches. They hoped to work out a substantive agreement with concrete goals and activities. The ethnographers were invited to attend the meeting as well. The discussions centered on how to merge the American process, called "Product Family Management," with the process the French called "Nourriture Excellente." At last the team negotiated a term that brought together elements from both the French and American perspectives: "Produits Exemplaires" ("produits" is the French word for products, as in "Product Family Management," and "exemplaires" is close to "excellente", as in "Nourriture Excellente"), and agreed to conduct three projects under this new title. One project was called "Changing Attitudes," and its objective was to improve customer support and understanding about Produits Exemplaires. The team selected two coleaders, one French and the other American, a first in their trans-Atlantic association.

The other two projects under Produits Exemplaires were focused on the food product family, and there would be two components, each on opposite ends of a continuum: one called "Ready to Eat" and the other called "Gourmet Cuisine" (symbolically reflecting the distance between American and French dining customs). There was laughing and joking all around when these projects were presented to the whole team at the face-to-face meeting. One French team member said: "A second passion of Elizabeth is cooking!" To which she replied "Eating, forget cooking, it isn't necessary." This brought on more laughter and joking about different approaches to food and eating among the French and Americans. Eventually, the team members themselves, on their own, created a metaphor for food, how it is grown or raised, prepared, and served. This metaphor became an important boundary object that facilitated understanding of each other's perspectives on their shared work, their project roles, on the individual tasks they were trying to accomplish, and how these tasks contributed to the whole project.

The metaphor and the language of food helped the team begin to think of themselves in a very complementary way in the work that they were doing. In other words, the team members rediscovered their interdependence in achieving their objectives through metaphor. Without "being there" using conventional ethnographic methods, engaging in participant observation in the team meeting and informally over dinners with the team, the ethnographers would not have learned serendipitously about the importance of metaphor in bridging the differences that are a regular part of global work. The ethnographers used this insight to create a template for facilitators that would make the creation of unifying metaphors one of the tools for them to use in building and maintaining global team integration.

However, though the convergence of language and practices facilitated the ease with which the American and French teams could interact, this same convergence actually precipitated the inevitable problems that arise when people of different backgrounds and cultures attempt to work together. It required conventional "being there" ethnography to recognize and document the significant breakthrough that occurred at the meeting and to expand the concept into a company-wide template for action. Even though global work is much more commonplace than it was in the days of HTM, there are still very real, if subtle, differences that are important to performance and success in global teams that require the power of conventional ethnographic methods to uncover and understand. As Sherry Turkle reminds us, "The sensitive ethnographer is always open to a slip, to a tear, to an unexpected association" (2011:xiii).

### CHALLENGE 2: We Can Learn All We Need to Know about Context Using Virtual Technologies

The second challenge to conventional ethnography that business practitioners often make is that there is essentially no longer any need to travel to different locations to observe or interview because sophisticated virtual technologies are just as good as "being there." They question whether context really matters any more with the proliferation of easy-to-use and inexpensive high-quality videoconferencing technologies. They posit that ethnography can be conducted online because we can see and hear people interact as though we were face to face. The argument is that virtual ethnography can tell us all we need to know about interactions in the virtual context. However, the continued relevance of geography and context to global work, and the critical role of face-to-face communication for solving complex problems, becomes clear if we examine more closely how videoconferencing can mask the complexities of global work (Gluesing et al. 2003).

In this case, a team involved members in Europe, the United States, and Asia. The team met face to face periodically; however, most of their work was conducted online. At one face-to-face meeting in Paris, the team seemed to have developed a plan for bringing projects together that had been developed separately in different locations. Two subgroups, one in Paris and one in Asia, then tried to implement the next steps that had been agreed upon. A follow-up videoconference connecting

Paris, Asia, and the United States, however, revealed that the French customer in Paris had rejected the linkage plan, and that the French team members were no longer going to pursue the previously agreed to arrangement to link the two competing projects. This unexpected turn of events angered the team members in China, who demanded to know why they had not been involved in the discussions with the customer. Aggressive conflict broke out as each side blamed the other for the problem, bringing into the fight charges against individual personalities (e.g., "You can't speak French," "I outrank you"). The so-called "videoconference from hell" drew to a close as an American in China left the videoconference room in tears, determined to leave the company. (Some months later she was reassigned to the Paris office after the crisis was satisfactorily resolved.) People remaining in the videoconference after the American left suddenly realized that something had gone terribly wrong, something that could damage their company and their own careers.

In this case, the virtual technologies masked the influence of the changing business conditions specific to the project implementation in different locations. Team members did not realize that they were proceeding in different directions because context was taken for granted or ignored in their online interactions. All of the anxieties and tensions that had been buried below the surface in the online interactions over the past several months emerged as a result of the videoconference crisis. The ethnographers previously had conducted remote interviews, but had not included any questions about context; nor did team members mention anything related to context. It wasn't until the ethnographers engaged in onsite participant observation that they were able to realize how the immediate physical circumstances, such as the weather, time of day, location, and size and type of videoconferencing facilities, affected the nature of the virtual interactions. They also grasped how strongly the local business conditions, especially the conditions on the day of the videoconference, affected the tone of the virtual meeting and team members' participation. Ethnographers, using conventional methods in the weeks following the "videoconference from hell," were able to uncover the importance of making context explicit in global teaming projects.

The ethnographers used their insights to create new protocols for virtual meetings. At the start of each virtual meeting, team members were asked to spend a few minutes talking about what was happening in their locations, sometimes even including the weather and reminders about the time of day. Local context still has an influence on how team members perform in virtual interactions. The new protocol helped team members make tacit knowledge about their own context explicit for remote team members, eliminating some misunderstandings due to previously unarticulated differences in context. It also helped them recognize the anxieties and pressures that were facing their colleagues in their different locations. Again, this story demonstrates that context does indeed still matter in spite of our rich virtual technologies.

More similar conventional ethnographic work with different teams in multiple locations helped the ethnographers discover important common patterns in global teaming work processes as well. They learned that virtual technologies were supportive of integration across distance, but they also found that these same technologies could be quite dangerous when emotions, particularly conflict, in the global teams were high and technologies were used as excuses to avoid interaction or even to heighten already existing conflict. Merging accounts from conventional participant observation in multiple contexts can create an emergent picture of global work patterns as well as how these patterns are enacted in local contexts, uncovering both similarities as well as variations in work practices and meanings across contexts. This emergent picture also can be compared with data gathered from online ethnography, where "locations" and contexts are more likely to be blurred (Wasson 2004) or shifting, to yield important insights about how "context" is produced in global work.

## CHALLENGE 3: Data Mining the Digital Trail Makes Conventional Ethnography Unnecessary

Finally, business practitioners postulate that with the proliferation of virtual, Internet-based organizing, work is increasingly digitized and leaves a data trail that can be captured and analyzed. These digital footprints that people leave allow ethnographers to trace people's activities and observe where they have been and where they are likely to go, as well as what they are saying about their journey. We as ethnographers can learn what we need to know about what work means and about how it gets done by tapping into the technology infrastructure where work is ongoing. With all these tools available to us for data mining textual, visual, and quantitative data, we no longer need to do participant observation to understand what is happening in any given situation.

Another example helps to illustrate how conventional ethnography remains relevant in this age of digital data mining. In this recent case, a project team in a large automotive company relied heavily on their information technology (IT) infrastructure to do their work. The team was working on a new global product being developed both separately and simultaneously in the United States and in Europe. Management decided that the efforts in both locations were similar enough and convergent enough in their approaches to technology that they could merge the U.S. and European teams into a single global project team. The resulting team rapidly grew quite large, and the managers of the team were having difficulty monitoring and managing the team's interactions on such a global scale.

It just so happened that as the project team's merger was taking place, a group of academic researchers studying global networked organizations was working with a special task force in the same company. The task force was trying to determine how to help the project team move their product innovation process along more efficiently to get the product to market faster. The academic researchers, using automated network analysis tools, helped the global automotive project team dynamically map their team's network of interactions by tapping into the corporate email network. In one of their analyses, electronic data showed a spike in global team membership and an increase in the density of the network, as shown in Figure 1.1 (Gluesing et al. in press).

The two major troughs in the "betweenness centrality" line (top line in Figure 1.1) showed that the amount of direct connection among people in the team increased at periods of high activity, usually corresponding to a change the team was undergoing. The network mapping was very useful in that it could visualize the alteration in the network of relationships as it evolved. But, it could not reveal how team members made sense of this change and how it might affect relationships and the meaning of the work for the team members on both sides of the Atlantic. Therefore, the ethnographers who were part of the academic research team set out to understand the perspectives of a cross-section of people about the global innovation product and project, and what the merging of the two teams meant to the team members. The conventional ethnography supplemented and elaborated on the IT-based communication network analysis by providing people's perspectives on their communication relationships related to the project.

**Two 'troughs' in the Network Centrality Plot correspond to periods of high activity.**

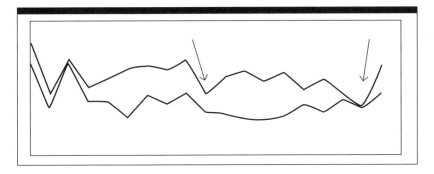

FIGURE 1.1. Centrality plot. Top line depicts the "group betweenness centrality" indicating the degree of direct connections among team members over time in a global product innovation team. Arrows point to two major troughs indicating intense activity and a corresponding increase in direct connections. The second line is the "group degree centrality" indicating the average percentage of members' connections. The third line, which is just visible at the lower left corner, represents the "group density" of the network, which is a ratio of the actual number of connections between members divided by the total number of possible connections. In this case, the density is so small it is barely visible because the actual number of connections between people is small relative to the large size of the group and potential number of connections.

Some of the first thoughts that team members mentioned when the ethnographers interviewed them about the innovation project concerned the emerging partnership with Europe to globalize the product. Team members talked about "roadblocks from overseas . . . a little bit of friction with North America and Europe being connected. People in the United States said "so now what they [Europe] already have on the road we [United States] are now trying to force fit into the product that was here. So what's now defining what the project is, is what Europe already has." There was some resentment at the loss of control among U.S. team members. In Germany, the team members said "positive demonstration of the preliminary concept is also helping" with the merger. However, in the United States again, people said "the original team members are thought to have a lot to do with the momentum behind the project. Their vision, hard work, and persistence have kept the project moving forward in a positive direction." The U.S. team members wanted to ensure that the hard work they had already accomplished was not forgotten.

The ethnographers talked both formally and informally with people in the team to tease out the implications of the merger. The network data indicated that the Europeans had joined the team, and the interviews confirmed that conclusion and expanded on it by revealing that in practice Europe was taking over the project lead, which was later formally announced by the organization's management. The digital data indicated there might be a problem with team integration that could benefit from conventional ethnographic methods to make sense of what was happening from the team members' points of view. The ethnographers were able to help the managers anticipate the consequences of the merger and develop action plans to smooth the transition.

In this same research project, the ethnographers also "shadowed" team members to learn about their daily communication practices and to validate "on the ground" the results of digital network analysis. Shadowing involved following team members as they went about their daily activities, observing and noting items such as the topic of conversation, the type of communication exchange (face-to-face, phone, meeting, audio or videoconference, etc.), the duration of communication events, and the general communication climate or tone (e.g., positive to negative on a scale of 1 to 10), as well as the dynamics or emotionality of the interaction. In shadowing team members, the ethnographers observed that almost everyone was constantly on the move from meeting to meeting and location to location, spending little time at their desks. People were sending and receiving email on their phones and using their phones for other important business functions as well. This pattern would not have been evident in analysis of the automated data. It was very important for the ethnographers to learn how email exchange was actually taking place—via smart phone more than via computer, as it turned out—so that team reporting could be designed for managers that would work on smart phones and not just on the desktop. The phone was central to the global innovation project manager's work, not just as a phone but also as a communication instrument to assist in pacing the work and integrating team relationships. Ethnographers discovered that the smart phone was serving as an important tool to speed along the innovation.

This story about a "mixed-methods" research approach (White and Johansen 2005) contradicts the notion that the wide availability of digital data and the power of online data mining are sufficient to reveal all there is to know about contemporary work practices and their meaning. Conventional ethnographic methods not only provide necessary descriptive data about work practices, but they can also reveal contextually sensitive information about work relations that technology-mediated ethnography has yet to match. Data mining tools are important enablers for the discovery of work patterns and new ways of working as never before (Riopelle, this volume; Maxwell, this volume). And technological methods such as network analysis can help us by pointing to the anomalies and trends, or to particular incidents or locations that might be worth exploring more deeply through "being there" and engaging in conventional ethnographic methods. But ethnography is still essential to reveal the meaning of work to the people doing it. Technology can complement but not substitute for conventional ethnographic methods.

## Conclusion

This chapter has presented the argument that conventional ethnographic methods continue to be relevant and to create value in a work world enabled by powerful technology-based ways of working and doing research about work. The stories of conventional ethnography in practice strongly counter three key challenges to conventional methods in the digital age. Doing conventional ethnography alongside online ethnography is the wave of the future because it can help us understand how work is similarly or differently produced in online and physical spaces (Churchill et al. 2004). This hybrid ethnography is becoming more commonplace in corporate settings (Jordan 2009). Still, as corporate ethnographers, it is important for us not to lose sight of our charge to investigate the ongoing changes in workplace relationships, in work practices, and in the value and place of work in our daily lives. While it is essential that we engage in technology-mediated ethnography that can extend our reach and access to virtual workspaces as well as physical spaces, and our analytical power (as you will learn from Riopelle in this volume), the practice of conventional ethnographic methods continues to have a central place in contemporary corporate ethnography, especially in the global context.

## Acknowledgments

I would like to say a big thank you to the anonymous editor who helped me immensely to craft the right writing style and set the right tone for this chapter on conventional ethnography.

# References

Baba, Marietta, Julia Gluesing, Hilary Ratner, and Kimberly Wagner
2004 The Contexts of Knowing: Natural History of a Globally Distributed Team. *Journal of Organizational Behavior* 25:547–587.

Batteau, Allen
2009 *Culture and Technology*. Long Grove, IL: Waveland Press.

Bernard, H. Russell (ed.)
1998 *Handbook of Methods in Cultural Anthropology*. Walnut Creek, CA: AltaMira Press.

Boellstorff, Tom
2008 *Coming of Age in Second Life: An Anthropologist Explores the Virtually Human*. Princeton, NJ: Princeton University Press.

Churchill, Elizabeth, Andreas Girgensohn, Les Nelson, and Alison Lee
2004 Blending Digital and Physical Spaces for Ubiquitous Community Participation. *Commun ACM* 47(2):38–44.

Dewalt, Kathleen M., and Billie R. Dewalt
2002 *Participant Observation*. Walnut Creek, CA: AltaMira Press.

Gloor, Peter
2004 *Swarm Creativity: Competitive Advantage Through Collaborative Innovation Networks*. Oxford, United Kingdom: Oxford University Press.

Gluesing, Julia
1998 Building Connections and Balancing Power in Global Teams: Toward a Reconceptualization of Culture as Composite. Special Volume on Anthropology of Business Organizations, edited by T. Hamada. *Anthropology of Work Review* 18(2):18–30.

2008 Identity in a Virtual World: The Co-evolution of Technology, Work, and Lifecycle. In *Mobile Work, Mobile Lives: Cultural Accounts of Lived Experiences*, edited by Tracy Meerwarth, with Julia Gluesing and Brigitte Jordan. NAPA Bulletin No. 30. Hoboken, NJ: Blackwell/Wiley.

Gluesing Julia, Tara Alcordo, Marrieta Baba, David Britt, Kimberly Wagner, Willie McKether, Leslie Monplaisir, Hilary Ratner, and Ken Riopelle
2003 The Development of Global Virtual Teams. In *Virtual Teams that Work: Creating Conditions for Virtual Team Effectiveness*, edited by Cristina B. Gibson and Susan G. Cohen, pp. 353–380. San Francisco: Jossey-Bass.

Gluesing, Julia, Kenneth Riopelle and James Danowski
In Press Mixing Ethnography and Information Technology Data Mining to Visualize Innovation Networks in Global Networked Organizations. In *Mixed Methods in Studying Social Networks*, edited by Silvia Dominguez and Betina Hollstein. Cambridge, United Kingdom: Cambridge University Press.

Hine, Christine
2000 *Virtual Ethnography*. London: Sage Press.

Jones, Stephen G.
1995 Understanding Community in the Information Age. In *Cybersociety: Computer-mediated Communication and Community*, edited by Stephen G. Jones, pp. 10–35. Thousand Oaks, CA: Sage Press.

Jordan, Brigitte
2009 Blurring Boundaries: The "Real" and the "Virtual" in Hybrid Spaces. Introduction to Special Section on Knowledge Flow in Online and Offline Spaces. *Human Organization* 68(2):181–193.

Lange, Patricia G.
2007 Publicly Private and Privately Public: Social Networking on YouTube. *Journal of Computer-mediated Communication* 13(1):361–380.

LeCompte, Margaret, and Jean Schensul
1999 *Designing and Conducting Ethnographic Research.* Walnut Creek, CA: AltaMira Press.

Rheingold, Howard
1993 *The Virtual Community: Homesteading on the Electronic Frontier.* Reading, MA: Addison-Wesley.

Turkle, Sherry
2011 *Alone Together.* New York: Basic Books.

Wasson, Christina
2004 Multitasking in Virtual Meetings. *Human Resource Planning* 27(4):47–60.

White, Douglas R., and Ulla C. Johansen
2005 *Network Analysis and Ethnographic Problems: Process Models of a Turkish Nomad Clan.* Lanham, MD: Rowman & Littlefield.

Chapter 2

# Being There:
# The Power of Technology-based Methods

*Ken Riopelle*

> The test of all knowledge is experiment.
> Experiment is the sole judge of scientific "truth."
> —*Richard Feynman*

> Information is the difference which makes a difference.
> —*Gregory Bateson*

## Introduction

Conventional ethnographic methods that emphasize the ethnographer's five human senses are not sufficient to make sense of the modern work world. Virtual work, whereby people work from home, "on the road," or otherwise outside of traditional, centralized offices using information technology (IT), is essentially invisible and beyond the capacity of an ethnographer to comprehend using conventional ethnographic tools alone. Virtual work is no longer confined to a traditional, geographically bounded "field site" with accompanying in situ participant observation. Ethnography today is becoming a hybrid methodology, in which both conventional ethnographic methods and IT-based methods are used as ethnographers alternate between investigation of physical and digital spaces.

I argue that conventional ethnography and technology-based methods are not polar opposites on a straight-line continuum but rather are complementary methods. Gluesing in her chapter (this volume) defines conventional ethnographic methods in corporations as spending time with people in their work settings, observing them as they do their work, and talking with them about what that work means to them. I define technology-based ethnographic methods to broadly mean methods that use information technologies to capture, analyze, and share data. The opportunity these methods present is one of exploration and experimentation in "being there" both in the physical and digital spaces as part of an extended ethnographic investigation, thus reframing the traditional meaning of an ethnographic "field site" and "participant observation" to routinely include digital life.

---

*Advancing Ethnography in Corporate Environments: Challenges and Emerging Opportunities,* edited by Brigitte Jordan, 38–55. ©2013 Left Coast Press Inc. All rights reserved.

## Three Reasons Why Conventional Ethnography Needs Digital Methods: Invisible Work, a Data Glut, and Rapid Technology Advances

As digital technologies become an ever-increasing part of daily work in global corporations, ethnographers also need to embrace information technologies to accomplish their own work, for three major reasons: the invisibility of work conducted remotely and online, the sheer amount of digital information in the workplace, and the continual and rapid advances in information technologies.

### Invisible Work

Information technologies severely limit what an ethnographer can directly observe because work is done on screens of various sizes, making it nearly impossible to tell exactly what work people are doing and with whom they are communicating. Even when an ethnographer is standing directly in front of someone or sitting right next to someone observing them do their work, it is difficult for the ethnographer to know precisely what work is taking place on a digital device. Prior to 1995, work was very visible. Face-to-face communication dominated meetings, telephone calls were synchronous and audible, paper-based correspondence occurred through interoffice mail, postal mail, and faxes, and package delivery in office buildings was evident. A field site was generally geographically bounded, and relationships were visible for participant observation. All those forms of work still exist, but they are now—and have been for some time—moving to the background, while a new digital landscape and communication ecosystem permeate today's workspaces. New mobile devices and messaging services include email, instant messages, push notifications, alerts, wikis, blogs, and the like. There also are new social networking and communication platforms such as Facebook, Twitter, YouTube, LinkedIn, Google+, Skype, GoToMeeting, WebEx, and others that enable group work. Using the "cloud"[1] to store, share, and sync information of all types is both more common-place and more complex than ever. It is also more invisible.

In the past five years, virtual communication technologies have moved especially rapidly to the foreground and dominate the workday inside and outside of the traditional office building. The number of people doing work in the information economy who are actually colocated is rapidly dwindling as more workers are dispersed. Even when people are colocated, the visual and auditory cues that ethnographers traditionally have used to observe the world around them are no longer adequate to capture much of the technology-enabled work being done across time and place. In conventional approaches to methods, the ethnographer is the primary research instrument. However, information technologies are making it difficult for ethnographers to continue in this primary role without embracing the new technologies to help them. Although ethnographers may have 20-20 vision and perfect hearing, technology imposes limits on these senses, impeding an ethnographer's ability to fully observe work in action.

## Data Glut

Information technologies also are generating a second challenge to conventional ethnographic methods: an overload of digital data. The data glut occurs at the individual and company level as well as in the public sphere. Data capturing is occurring in private, secure company intranets with the proliferation of email, web pages, instant messages, and an increasing variety of virtual workspaces. A company's IT infrastructure serves not only as the conduit to carry messages, documents, and related data to and from virtual team members, but also functions as a data capturing and archival resource for email, blogs, wikis, tweets, and other digital media. The volume and detail of the data flowing through and being captured by IT infrastructure is beyond any ethnographer's capacity to capture. The new IT ushers in new data sources of unparalleled quantity and specificity, but often of unknown quality, generated by virtual workers around the world. Capacity for data storage is scaling up to match the enormous amount of data that is being produced and shared, including support for the 48 hours of YouTube videos uploaded each minute, 200 million tweets sent per day, and 7.5 billion photos uploaded to Facebook each month (Parr 2011).

IDC, a technology research firm, estimates that data is growing at 50 percent a year, or more than doubling every two years (Lohr 2012). Accessing, harnessing, and making sense of such data are incredible challenges for ethnographers and a constraint to their ability to add value through direct observation. The IT infrastructure brings with it additional obstacles in the protection of employee privacy, in adhering to different country work laws regarding digital data, and in the protection of intellectual property. All these obstacles can be overwhelming to sort out and to comprehend. However, the effort involved in harnessing the massive amount of digital data is worthwhile because the data can be a valuable source of insight and a complement to conventional ethnographic methods for ethnographers who are willing to engage with the digital work stream.

## Rapid Technology Advances

Information technologies are continually and rapidly evolving, challenging the capacity of everyone to keep up with the technology advances. New tools, such as smart phones and tablets, for example, which come with a software ecosystem of hundreds of thousands of applications, are altering the way work is done, but also are providing new tools that ethnographers can use to support their work, *if* they can keep up and creatively incorporate the new tools into their conventional methods toolkit.

## The Digital Diffusion Dashboard Project: A Story about Adding Value to Ethnography Through IT-based Methods

Virtualization, dispersion, data proliferation, and rapid innovation all pose a real challenge to conventional ethnographic methods, but the challenge can be met. The story of a National Science Foundation (NSF)–funded research grant called "Accelerating the Diffusion of Innovations: A Digital Diffusion Dashboard Methodology for Global Networked Organizations" (NSF 2010) provides a very real demonstration of how IT-based methods can complement and extend conventional ethnographic methods.

The NSF is an independent federal agency created by Congress in 1950 "to promote the progress of science; to advance the national health, prosperity, and welfare; to secure the national defense."[2] The NSF solicits requests for applications (RFAs) to fund and fulfill this mission from both a theoretical and practical perspective through specific programs. The NSF does not define for applicants their research questions, theoretical orientation, investigating methods, sampling, or participating industry partners in the case of corporate research. Rather, the NSF provides a broad set of guidelines for academic researchers to propose a research plan, approach, budget, timeline, and personnel to conduct an investigation that will produce both theoretical and practical outcomes. A panel of experts competitively reviews NSF grant applications and makes recommendations for funding based on merit. All funded grants also are subject to review by a university's Institutional Review Board (IRB). An IRB provides institutional oversight for the conduct of human subject research and must review and approve all data-gathering methods and instruments before research begins. The NSF usually takes about six months to reach a funding decision, and if a grant proposal is funded, it may take another three to six months before the research is actually started.

This approach is in sharp contrast to a company's typical request for proposal (RFP), which often specifies the research questions, methods, and timing the responding vendor, contractor, or supplier should use in a research study. Rarely, if ever, does a company give priority to the theoretical implications of the research or evaluate its contribution to the broader society as a basis for funding. A company can award a proposal at any time, and it typically takes days or weeks, rather than months, to award a contract. Once this decision is made, work generally begins immediately. An internal company project manager or team, who may or may not have expertise in research methods, commonly reviews and approves a contractor's instruments and methods. Human subject review is not usually a requirement in corporate RFPs. Although some companies may have their own internal review boards, their standards generally are not as strict as those in academe.

Although the NSF's primary mission is basic research, the agency is nevertheless interested in funding research that has practical outcomes. In the case of research in organizations, NSF programs often require that grants be conducted with corporate partners to address important and vexing business issues.

## The Story Begins: A Business Problem

The Digital Diffusion Dashboard (DDD) NSF grant addressed the central business problem of how best to diffuse new ideas, processes, and technologies across a global enterprise given the dynamic, emergent, and elusive character of its communication networks. Executives recognize these needs. A critical factor in organizational competitiveness is the speed at which innovations can be implemented. Although fostering good ideas and producing innovation is central to business success, the speed of execution in today's organizations has become the differentiating factor that provides competitive advantage and is far from assured. Innovations gain their greatest value when they are actually used.

Prior to submitting our NSF grant application, my colleagues and I had been consulting and teaching in the automotive industry for more than a decade. We had observed that despite the increasing ubiquity and sophistication of IT, organizations were not taking advantage of the capabilities inherent in their information infrastructure to manage their global innovation processes and networks. We thought that the IT infrastructure could be used to investigate the diffusion of innovation in global networked organizations. We believed that a company could use its IT infrastructure not only to create, transmit, and store communication messages, but also to learn something about how the innovation of new technology was proceeding across the company's global product development network. These ideas formed the basis for our NSF proposal to develop a new methodology for investigating and leveraging a company's IT infrastructure to accelerate the diffusion of an innovation. We proposed to develop IT-based methods by tapping into the company's infrastructure and to validate our methods using conventional ethnography. The NSF funded the grant for three years beginning in 2005, and the grant received a two-year extension to continue the research until 2010.

## The Story Context: Innovation and
## Diffusion in Automotive Product Development

In our study approach, we defined the term *innovation* as "an idea, practice, or object that is perceived as new by an individual or other unit of adoption" (Rogers 2003:12) and *diffusion* as "the process by which an innovation is communicated through certain channels over time among the members of a social system" (Rogers 2003:11). It is important to clarify what these concepts mean in practice in automotive product development.

An automotive vehicle is one of the most complex technology systems to design and manufacture. The more a single part or a component (made up of several parts) of the system touches another part, the more continual scrutiny and review it must have in product development to ensure the full automotive system will function properly; there are tens of thousands of such parts and components in a single vehicle. Our story example focuses on the study of one automotive innovation with several subcomponent systems. We have given the innovation a pseudonym, Advanced Technology Innovation (ATI), to comply with company confidentiality requirements. The ATI product innovation was not a top-down mandatory component built into a vehicle, like a safety belt or an air bag, for example. Rather, ATI was a bottom-up innovation, which was shaped and reshaped by a team of specialized engineers from different disciplines to determine its system compatibility and its final functional features. An auto product development innovation team must persuade members of the social system targeted for adoption, such as engineers who specialize in the engine, transmission, chassis, and electrical subsystems for a new vehicle program, of the value of adopting their new technology and how it will meet or exceed anticipated user needs as well as satisfy the requirements for engineering cost, timing, weight, performance, safety, and regulatory specifications for inclusion on a vehicle. The adoption or rejection of such innovations can be a long and arduous path, especially when the team is globally distributed, taking anywhere from three to five years from idea to production in a vehicle that is ready for marketplace introduction.

This global automotive product development innovation and diffusion process was the context for our study. Using IT-based methods, we designed and tested a set of indicators, which we assembled into a prototype DDD to help innovation managers visualize, monitor, and manage their global innovations and accelerate innovation in a global networked organization.[3] We created simple, clear, and reusable Dashboard indicators that we thought would help open a new frontier for both scholars and practitioners alike by demonstrating how to leverage a company's data resources, primarily email, to visually manage the diffusion network as it emerges and to monitor the consequences of implementation efforts during the diffusion process. The indicators made visible the ATI Team's network of interactions, the main topics of their conversation, and how they felt about their work over time. ATI managers linked the indicators to their own business performance metrics to get an overall sense of how the innovation diffusion process was proceeding.

Even though we developed the DDD tools in the context of the automobile industry, they have potentially wide applicability and benefit in many other public and private sectors, such as healthcare, retail, government and technology. Tools such as these can also enhance ethnographic investigation in the digital workplace, as will become evident in our story (see also Maxwell, this volume).

## The Primary Characters in the Story: The Study Teams and Stakeholders

There were three teams who collaborated to conduct the NSF DDD study. First, the Global ATI Team and their innovation was the subject of the study. This team was charged with navigating the innovation through the global product development process, obtaining buy-in from the component vehicle engineers, and persuading a target program team to adopt their innovation and include it in the vehicle that would eventually be produced and sold in the marketplace. The Global

ATI Team consisted of 298 people distributed in locations around the world. The ATI Team had its own legal counsel for patents and intellectual property protection, which was important for securing the academic IRB and internal company research approvals. The ATI Team served as the liaison to the corporate Office of General Counsel for global legal and human resource issues.

Second, the NSF and IRB confidentiality requirements for the grant, and the corporate legal requirements, all specified that the data we gathered had to stay within the corporate firewall. Therefore, the company established an Internal Research Team that consisted of five company engineers who managed the internal corporate IT resources, databases, and security for the study. This team also performed the Dashboard testing and indicator validation, and facilitated the ethnographic research. The members served as internal technical experts regarding the product development process and as liaisons to the University Research Team. Four of the five members did not have any direct involvement or responsibility in the Global ATI Team. Only the U.S. manager of the Global ATI Team had an overlapping membership in both the Global ATI Team and the Internal Research Team.

The third team was the University Research Team, which included two other professors and me as the principal investigators on the grant. We were in charge of the study and responsible for the study design, software choice, indicator selection, IRB approvals, and for training the Internal Research Team on how to install and use the software for the study. We had the help of a graduate assistant for the ethnographic portion of the project and of an undergraduate computer programmer.

There were two primary stakeholder groups concerned with the research outcomes. The first group was the company's corporate management, consisting of seven people who reported to the chairman as global vice presidents. They assumed the overall corporate oversight and support for the research and had very practical criteria for evaluating the outcomes. Their motivation for participating as an industry partner for an NSF study was to gain access to leading university research. By providing in-kind resources in the form of managerial and employee time, as well as use of company facilities and equipment, they hoped to receive tools that might give them a competitive advantage. As a part of the NSF proposal, the company's Chief Technology Office submitted a letter of commitment to serve as an industry partner. The second stakeholder group was the NSF Human and Social Dynamics program itself, which funded the study. Their interest was ensuring the study would contribute to the broader societal and public good as well as advance graduate and undergraduate education and training.

## The Story Unfolds: Capturing Digital Data and Building Diffusion Indicators

The automotive company had a complex global server farm and intranet to facilitate employee communication and storage of digital material for its operations. Email was the primary means of communication in the Global ATI Team and was the primary resource to build the Dashboard indicators. Before email could be collected, however, the University Research Team had to comply with IRB and corporate legal and human resource requirements for confidentiality and privacy protection by establishing four procedures:

1. All ATI Team members received an emailed consent form, approved by the IRB, which they returned with their consent or refusal to participate. Team members who elected to participate in the study could opt out at any time.

2. The research teams did not gather all email, only the email that was related to the ATI innovation project. To collect only this subset of email, the ATI Team members participating in the study installed and activated email rules themselves, using common project keywords (emic language). They copied their email, using a "dummy" email address in the "cc" field, to a centralized, secure server email box with restricted access. They could readily see the dummy email address in their email header and delete it if they did not wish to have a particular email sent to the dummy mailbox in the secure server.

3. Two additional filters were placed in the rules. First, if an email was designated as personal, private, or encrypted, it was automatically excluded from data collection. Second, all legal email concerning patents that was labeled as "privileged" was excluded from data collection.

4. No individual email could be read by the University Team. All email content was aggregated as frequency counts for single words or word pairs for analysis. No email message could be reconstructed. Email was also anonymized for any public presentation (e.g., user 1, user 2, user 3, etc.).

The Internal Research Team gathered email correspondence from January 2005 through November 2007 from the Global ATI Team members who formally participated in the project (about 25 percent), resulting in roughly 45,000 emails and their links among more than 2,000 people across the enterprise communicating about the project over time.

Although the data collection process captured a large volume of email that could be used to understand and describe the diffusion of the ATI Team's innovation, there were biases, limitations, and ethical concerns that had to be considered. Only a sample of the ATI Team participated in the study, leaving room for a possible missing-data bias. The email rules also may have missed relevant email that did not contain the keyword terms, and all email attachments were excluded from the analysis, potentially introducing bias and limiting analysis. An ethical concern arose because the participants' email boxes contained email sent, forwarded, or copied from people who did not consent to participate in the study. After some deliberation, the University IRB and the company's human resource staff decided that because all the email was anonymized for analysis and no individual email could be reconstructed, there was no violation of confidentiality or privacy rules. As far as the legal staff was concerned, all employee email belonged to the company. Employees always saw a message to that effect each time they logged onto the corporate intranet.

The Internal Research Team analyzed the 45,000 emails under the guidance of the University Research Team, and together they created the DDD. The Dashboard indicators made the characteristics of the virtual work among 2,000 people globally distributed around the world visible to the human eye in graphical form. Such a task would have been impossible with conventional ethnographic methods. Three Dashboard indicators[4] illustrate just how IT-based methods such as these can enhance and extend ethnographic research: "Who is Talking" (the network), "The Buzz" (the topics), and "The Emotion" (the feelings) indicators. Using these indicators, the research teams depicted the ATI Team members' dispersed networks of relationships, their central topics of conversation, and the rise and fall of their emotion as they interacted over time.

### "Who is Talking"

The "Who is Talking" indicator is a dynamic visualization of the Global ATI Team member interactions over time depicting the network of relations among team members based on their email exchanges. This indicator assessed aspects of the team structure such as who was and was not interacting in the innovation and diffusion process, the changes in team membership, the speed of new member integration, the extent of cross-functional and senior management involvement, supplier support, regional participation, and the impact of management decisions on the network structure. Figure 2.1 is a still-frame snapshot of the Global ATI Team's email network at a single point in time.

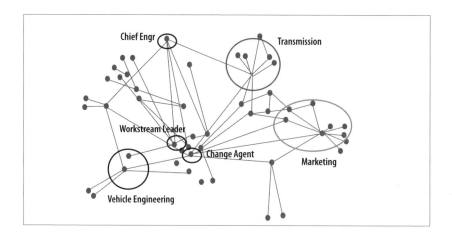

FIGURE 2.1. Visualization of the ATI Team Network. The dots or nodes are people on the team, identified by their roles; the lines represent the email exchanges among them. Nodes that have more email exchanges with one another are positioned closer together.

The dots or nodes are people on the team, and the lines represent their email exchanges. For confidential reasons, key players are identified and labeled by role, such as Change Agent, Workstream Leader, Vehicle Engineer, Chief Engineer, and Transmission (a functional group). Nodes that have more email exchanges with one another are positioned closer together. From this snapshot picture at a point in time, it is easy to see that the Change Agent is quite central in the network and that Marketing and the Chief Engineer have a limited amount of contact with the rest of the key players. It is possible to play a series of these "snapshots" as a movie. The movie enables a visualization of the relationship network as it changes over time.

Ethnographers have been engaged in network analysis (charting kinship and community networks, noting seating arrangements or meeting attendance, and who talks to whom on the shop floor) as a part of fieldwork since anthropology's beginning as a discipline in the nineteenth century. Early anthropologists are often credited with founding the methodology (Bernard 1998; Freeman 2004; Gluesing in press; McKether 2009). Yet even if a team of ethnographers used network analysis as part of their conventional methodology, it would not be possible to achieve the scope and breadth, nor to recreate in near real time a network map such as the one depicted in Figure 2.1, without using the new software tools and the data made available through IT-based methods. IT-based network analysis can help ethnographers studying global networked organizations to prioritize areas that might warrant more in-depth investigation through participant observation or select participants for further interviews to elaborate findings uncovered in the network analysis.

Conventional ethnography is still necessary. In this case, the IT-based network maps do not take into account other means of communication—interpersonal communication, telephone calls, videoconferences, instant messages—and thus do not reflect every type of communication relationship. Ethnographers can elaborate communication patterns visible in the network analysis and provide some "ground truth" about their validity, as we did in this NSF study. The network maps are useful tools, but their limitations should be kept in mind when interpreting the results. Together, IT-based network analysis and conventional ethnographic methods complement one another and can make a powerful analytical combination (see also Jordan, this volume).

## *"The Buzz"*

"The Buzz" indicator helped the research teams studying the Global ATI innovation and diffusion process to quickly grasp what was being talked about in the team. The teams used a software package called WORDij to assess the talk or conversation with analysis routines called Wordlink and Z-Utilities and to develop the indicator. WORDij compares the corpus of text contained in the emails across the network or subnetwork at two different points in time and computes what is new in the conversation, what has remained the same, or what is dropping out of the talk based upon word and word-pair frequency counts with statistical accuracy.

There are five advantages to this method: (1) it is fast; (2) it scales to large amounts of data; (3) it uses the natural language of the participants; (4) it protects the identities of participants because no email can be reconstructed in its original form from the analysis output; and (5) it provides a measure of statistical confidence that the differences uncovered in the analysis are real. For example, in the first three months of one of the engineering projects in an ATI subteam, the group had an innovative idea that was summarized early in the project in word pairs such as "impressed talk," "excited potential," "excited team," "potential exciting," and "benefit opportunity." But later in the project, from months 9 to 12, there was a different set of word pairs that dominated the email exchanges: "too optimistic," "looks optimistic," "not enough," "not support," "cost more," and "more investment." The set of word pairs that was present in the first three months of the project was no longer in the team members' email in these later months. The early optimism in the project subteam had become pessimism stemming from concerns about cost. Eventually, the company disbanded the subteam and cancelled their component of the project. "The Buzz" indicator provided an accurate emotional measure of the team's dilemma.

Ethnographers commonly record conversations, conduct discourse analysis, examine secondary documents, and generally listen to and interpret what is said in the workplace. However, the ability to quickly analyze thousands of emails and assess the differences among them in a few minutes is again beyond the traditional ethnographer's ability. Pairing technological capability with the ethnographer's sense making in context is another powerful combination. The WORDij software works on any text, and ethnographers can use it to compare interview texts, newspaper stories, blogs, tweets, or even their own journal entries to uncover in a very fast, systematic way how "The Buzz" is changing over time and can then concentrate their energies on uncovering the "why" behind the language and the messages. Gregory Bateson once wrote, "Information is *the difference which makes a difference*" (1972:459). WORDij can compute the difference between two sets of text and move ethnographic work ahead with confidence. In the words of James W. Pennebaker in his book *The Secret Life of Pronouns: What our Words Say About Us*: "If you want to get a sense of other people by examining their language, you will actually need to count their words. You can do this by hand—but it is a slow and painful process. Or you can use a computer program" (2012:9).

## *"The Emotion"*

"The Emotion" indicator takes advantage of the Linguistic Inquiry and Word Count (LIWC)[5] software, which is used to calculate an emotional index. It provides a quick picture of how people feel about their work activities, which we labeled the Positivity Index. LIWC reads a text file, one word at a time. As each word is processed, the software searches a dictionary, looking for a match for that word. If a match is found, the appropriate word category scale(s) for that word is/are incremented. As the target text file is being processed, counts for various structural composition elements (e.g., word count and sentence punctuation) are also incremented.

There are 64 standard categories. Two of these categories provide a valence (positive or negative) for the text: positive emotion and negative emotion. Research by Marcial Losada (1999) indicates that a 2.9:1 (positive to negative) ratio is needed for a healthy social system. This is referred to as the "Losada Line." By processing email text over time with the LIWC software, a positivity ratio can be computed and graphed as a measure of a team's emotionality and linked to its performance. If the positivity ratio is above 2.9, individuals and business teams flourish, and if it is below 2.9, they languish (Fredrickson and Losada 2005). High-performance teams have a positive ratio of 5.6:1; mixed teams, 1.8:1; and low-performance teams, 0.4:1. Moreover, there appears to be an upper limit of 11.6:1 where it is possible to have too high a positivity ratio, creating the likelihood that the team will flounder because it does not consider or ignores negative input.

Figure 2.2 is an example of a positivity ratio chart for the Global ATI subteam's performance indicating the key cut points for the Losada Line (2.9), high-performance Teams (5.6), and the upper limit for positivity (11.6).

The positivity ratio for the Global ATI subteam shows that the subteam started out very positive about their innovation component idea, but that their enthusiasm oscillated for eight months from September 2006 to April 2007, and then dove to a very low point from May 2007 to July 2007, with a slight rebound in August 2007. These positivity index charts, in addition to the word analysis, provided a succinct

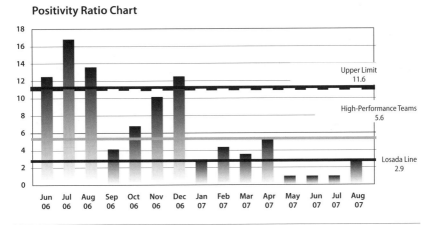

**Positivity Ratio Chart**

FIGURE 2.2. The Positivity Ratio chart for a Global ATI subteam shows the ratio of positive emotion to negative emotion from June 2006 to August 2007. The bottom dark horizontal line is the Losada Line (2.9), which signifies the cut point for a team to flourish, and the top line indicates the upper limit for positivity (11.6). The ratio of high-performance teams (5.6) is indicated by the light-colored horizontal line.

summary of the state of the project team as they drove to product implementation and production. The point is that text analytics can augment and enhance ethnographic methods with speed and accuracy using the natural language of participants in a very systematic manner, which is reusable and repeatable. Indeed, if ethnographers interviewed a sample of team members over time, they would have a sense of the sentiment of the project. But this is very difficult to do if the team is large and distributed. For a global team, "The Emotion" indicator could help affirm or contradict the ethnographer's assessment and provide evidence to sharpen their interview questions or observations. In turn, ethnographers can also enhance the indicator through their fieldwork insights. The LIWC dictionary, which categorizes words, may not capture the unique linguistic vocabulary of a profession or the nuanced talk of a group. It may be necessary to refine the standard LIWC dictionary to supplement or edit the words assigned to a category to more accurately reflect and type the conversation. Each method can help inform the other both to extend the ethnographer's reach and to produce a stronger story.

Taken together, the three DDD indicators, "Who is Talking," "The Buzz," and "The Emotion," make visible the network structure of who is talking with whom and provide a statistical summation of how the conversation is changing along with a picture of team sentiment over time. Given the size and scope of global virtual teams, these measures would be impractical, if not impossible, for ethnographers to construct or replicate using conventional methods. But they can be used effectively to complement these methods for greater leverage and value in corporate ethnography.

## Conclusion

I have asserted and substantiated with examples that conventional ethnographic methods are not sufficient to make sense of the modern work world. Virtual work is increasingly invisible, generating an overwhelming amount of information, moving very quickly, and becoming ever more difficult to grasp as new technology migrates people to a screen culture. To address the modern world with its increasing technology sophistication for data capture, analysis, and sharing, my recommendation for students and faculty as well as for practitioners is "join in and try to keep up." The fundamental skills of observation and pattern recognition remain relevant today (Gluesing, this volume). But ethnographers are required to peer into the screen world and translate these new spaces for understanding. That's where the IT-based methods can really help. Virtual work occurs on private screens with people, databases, and a growing population of software digital assistants that have no geographic bounds, thus reframing the meaning of the traditional "field site" and what it means to do "participant observation." Pen and paper are still important, but the new screen devices and analytics are essential for ethnographic praxis today and in the foreseeable future.

Much time is required to keep up with technology, to learn and relearn what is new across this digital frontier and what its impact will be on both the quality and the quantity of ethnographic production. For faculty members and instructors, rapid advances in technology mean that the tools and techniques they learned in their own undergraduate and graduate training may be obsolete today, and the time required to search for and try out the new technology tools will present a time-consuming challenge, even among practitioners, because of the rapid pace of change.

While we embrace the digital realm and what it can do to augment ethnographic methods, we must also remember that today's digital communication is encapsulated in gadgets and devoid of the surrounding sociopolitical and environmental cues that are essential to understanding context, an important element in any ethnography. The technology is not perfect; it does have cracks in its armor and needs a critical eye to assess its utility. This is where the ethnographer's five senses come into play once again, on the ground, to add this missing dimension. In the final analysis, the ethnographer remains the unifying instrument to integrate the physical and the digital world for an insightful ethnographic story.

Finally, I invite you try out a sample of these tools and evaluate them with your own data to decide for yourself how ethnography can be extended with these new IT-based tools. In the words of Richard Phillips Feynman, "The test of all knowledge is experiment. Experiment is the sole judge of scientific 'truth.'" Feynman (1963:1-1)

## Experiment

Here are three suggested exercises listed in order of software ease of use:

1   Take a sample of any text from email, blogs, meeting minutes, etc., and paste it into the LIWC Try Online website.[6]
    The words in the text will be counted and a percentage calculated for 7 of the 64 LIWC categories, including Self-references ("I," "me," "my"), Social Words, Positive Emotions, Negative Emotions, Overall Cognitive Words, Articles ("a," "an," "the"), and Big Words (more than six letters).
    Calculate a positivity index by dividing the percentage of Positive Emotion by the percentage of Negative Emotion and assess where the result falls on the Losada Line to create your own "The Emotion" indicator. Do you find a relationship between the positivity index and performance?
    This exercise can be done at no cost in just a few minutes . . .
2   Download the WORDij software package for free[7] and try out the Z-Utilities to determine the difference between two sets of text. For example, take your email, a blog, meeting minutes, or any other text for which you have more than one example, and use the Z-Utility to assess what is new in the conversation,

what has remained the same, and what is dropping out of the text over time to create your own "The Buzz" indicator. WORDij runs on a PC, Mac, or Linux computer.

WORDij comes with a complete set of instructions and sample datasets. After downloading the package and reviewing the basic tutorial, you should be able to run the Z-Utilities and see the results in about 1 to 3 hours. Your second run should take only about 5 minutes to complete.

3   For the more ambitious students and practitioners who want to analyze the network structure of email, websites, Facebook, Twitter, and Wikipedia article networks, download and install Condor.[8] Here you are invited to investigate your own email first and create the "Who is Talking" indicator.

This site provides video tutorials about how to use Condor. Condor runs on a PC or Mac.

Depending upon your computer setup, internet speed, and technical skills, Condor may take from 1 to 3 hours to set up and another 1 to 3 hours or longer to import your email, depending upon what email system you are using and the size of your email corpus. After the initial setup is complete, and you are familiar with the software features and options, your second email analysis should only take about 10 minutes to complete. Condor is complex and sophisticated, but it is free for academic use.

## Postscript

The NSF study took place at a tumultuous time in the automotive industry. After the study conclusion, the DDD was not implemented company-wide, despite its endorsement by senior managers, because of corporate downsizing and focus on survival. Approximately 10,000 engineers were let go, representing one-third of the engineering workforce. Nevertheless, a global manager replicated the study at a Tier 1 automotive supplier and implemented the DDD, which she continues to operate today. A second automotive company piloted the DDD, applying the indicators in different team situations and contexts, and the tools were still being used when the grant concluded. The NSF study was twice nominated as an NSF Highlight for the agency's report to Congress and the public. The Dashboard also was a featured centerpiece in a National Institutes of Health (NIH) proposal to evaluate clinical and translational science teams. The grant authors continue to publish about this work and to present at conferences, extending and refining both the methodology and the tools.

## Acknowledgments

I would like to acknowledge the Human and Social Dynamics Program of the NSF (Award no. 0527487) for their study funding. I also would like to thank our colleagues, Peter Gloor at the Massachusetts Institute of Technology (Condor Software), and Andrew Seary (MultiNet/Negopy Software) at Simon Fraser University for letting us use their software for free and for their support with the study.

# References

Bateson, Gregory
1972 *Steps to an Ecology of Mind: Collected Essays in Anthropology, Psychiatry, Evolution, and Epistemology*. Chicago, IL: University of Chicago Press.

Bernard, H. Russell (ed.).
1998 *Handbook of Methods in Cultural Anthropology*. Walnut Creek, CA: AltaMira Press.

Bishop, Amanda, Kenneth Riopelle, Julia Gluesing, James Danowski, and Tara Eaton
2009 Managing Global Compliance through Collaborative Innovation Networks. *COINs 2009 Proceedings: The Social and Behavioral Sciences Procedia* 2(4):6466–6474.

Danowski, James, Julia Gluesing, and Kenneth Riopelle
2008 "Analysis of Email Senders and Receivers and Semantic Message Content Networks in Innovation Management." Paper presented at the International Network for Social Network Analysis (INSNA), St. Petersburg Beach, FL, January 22–27.

2011 The Revolution in Diffusion Caused by New Media. In *The Diffusion of Innovations: A Communication Science Perspective*, edited by Arun Vishwanath and George Barnett, pp. 123–144. New York: Peter Lang.

Eaton, Tara, and Kenneth Riopelle
2007 Accelerating the Diffusion of Innovations: A "Digital Diffusion Dashboard" Methodology for Global Networked Organizations. In *Proceedings of EPIC 2007: The Third Annual Ethnographic Praxis in Industry Conference*, pp. 310–311. Washington, D.C.: American Anthropological Association.

Feynman, Richard Phillips
1963 Atoms in Motion. In *Feynman, The Feynman Lectures on Physics. The New Millennium Edition, Volume 1: Mainly Mechanics, Radiation, and Heat*. Pasadena: California Institute of Technology.

Fredrickson, Barbara L., and Marcial F. Losada
2005 Positive Affect and the Complex Dynamics of Human Flourishing. *American Psychologist* 60(7):678–686.

Freeman, Linton C.
2004 The Development of Social Network Analysis. Vancouver: Empirical Press.

Gluesing, Julia. C.
In press. A Mixed Methods Approach to Understand Global Networked Organizations. In *Anthropology of Organizations Companion*, edited by Ann.T. Jordan and Douglas Caulkins. Boston: Wiley.

Gluesing, Julia, Kenneth Riopelle, and James Danowski
2010 "Gaining Access to Both Email Content and Structure in Corporate Environments: A Novel Partnership Solution." Paper presented at the International Network for Social Network Analysis (INSNA), St. Petersburg Beach, FL, February 10–13.

In press Mixing Ethnography and Information Technology Data Mining to Visualize Innovation Networks in Global Networked Organizations. In *Mixed Methods in Studying Social Networks*, edited by Silvia Dominguez and Betina Hollstein. Cambridge: Cambridge University Press.

Gluesing, Julia, Tara Eaton, Kenneth Riopelle, and James Danowski
2008 "Mixing Ethnography and Information Technology to Assess Organizational Innovation Networks." Paper presented at the International Network for Social Network Analysis (INSNA), St. Petersburg Beach, FL, January 22–27.

Lohr, Steve
2012 The Age of Big Data. *New York Times,* February 11, 2012. Available at http://www.nytimes.com/2012/02/12/sunday-review/big-datas-impact-in-the-world.html?_r=1&emc=eta1._ Accessed June 2, 2012.

Losada, Marcial
1999 The Complex Dynamics of High Performance Teams. *Mathematical and Computer Modeling* 30(9–10):179–192.

McKether, Willie L., Julia C. Gluesing, and Kenneth Riopelle
2009 From Interviews to Social Network Analysis: An Approach for Revealing Social Networks Embedded in Narrative Data. *Field Methods* 21:2:154–180.

National Science Foundation (NSF)
2010 Award Abstract No. 0527487. DHB: Accelerating the Diffusion of Innovations: A Digital Diffusion Dashboard Methodology for Global Networked Organizations. Available at http://www.nsf.gov/awardsearch/showAward.do?AwardNumber=0527487. Accessed June 2, 2012.

Parr, Ben
2011 More Data Was Transmitted over the Internet in 2010 than All Previous Years Combined [video]. Mashable Tech, October 20. Available at http://mashable.com/2011/10/20/kirk-skaugen-web-2/? utm_source=iphoneapp&utm_medium=rss&utm_content=textlink&utm_campaign=iphoneapp. Accessed June 2, 2012.

Pennebaker, James. W.
2012 The Secret Life of Pronouns: What our Words Say About Us. New York: Bloomsbury Press.

Riopelle, Kenneth, and James Danowski
2009 "WORDij." Paper presented at the International Network for Social Network Analysis (INSNA), San Diego, CA, February 12–15.

Riopelle, Kenneth, and Julia Gluesing
2011 "Digital Dashboard Helps Managers Accelerate Innovation." Poster presented at the Second Annual International Science of Team Science Conference, Chicago, IL, April 11–14.

Riopelle Kenneth, Julia Gluesing, and James Danowski
2006 "Acceleration the Diffusion of Innovations: A 'Digital Diffusion Dashboard' Methodology for Glo-bal Networked Organizations." Paper presented at the International Network for Social Network Analysis (INSNA), Vancouver, Canada, April 24–30.

2008 "Organizational Hierarchy Predictors of Symmetric and Asymmetric Dyad and Triad Distributions in a Large Global Organization." Paper presented at the International Network for Social Network Analysis (INSNA), St. Petersburg Beach, FL, January 22–27.

Rogers, Everett M.
2003 Diffusion of Innovations. Fifth edition. New York: Free Press.

# Notes

1   Cloud is short for "cloud computing," defined as "the use of networked facilities for the storage and processing of data rather than a user's local computer, access to data or services typically being via the Internet." From the Oxford English Dictionary, available at http://oed.com/view/Entry34689?redirectedFrom=Cloud+computing (accessed August 08, 2012).

2   See: http://www.nsf.gov/about/ (last accessed on June 2, 2012).

3   For more information about the study methods and results, refer to the numerous presentations and publications that the study has produced (Bishop et al. 2009; Danowski et al. 2008, 2011; Eaton and Riopelle 2007; Gluesing, Eaton, et al. 2008; Gluesing, Riopelle, et al. 2010, in press; Riopelle and Danowski 2009; Riopelle and Gluesing 2011; Riopelle et al. 2006, 2008).

4   There are seven indicators in the DDD: (1) Who is Talking, (2) The Champions, (3) Collaboration, (4) The Buzz, (5) The Emotion, (6) Rate of Adoption, and (7) Value. We chose the three indicators that are most relevant to ethnography to illustrate our story.

5   http://www.liwc.net/ (last accessed on June 2, 2012).

6   http://liwc.net/tryonline.php (last accessed on June 2, 2012). Or download WORDij at https://www.box.com/s/486cdaea032c89a1cab9.

7   http://wordij.net (last accessed on June 2, 2012).

8   https://www.galaxyadvisors.com/science-of-swarms/condor-videos.html (last accessed on June 2, 2012).

Chapter 3

# Ethnography for Systems Development: Renovating the Legacy

*Patricia Ensworth*

> Information underrepresents reality.
>
> *–Jaron Lanier*

## Introduction

The following two chapters focus upon specific implementations of ethnographic practices for development work within corporate environments. While "corporation" is essentially a legal term that can describe both businesses and nonprofit organizations, here we limit the scope of our analysis to for-profit industrial enterprises: groups of people who create products and services and sell them in the marketplace so that the collective entity earns more revenue than it spends on expenses.

Ethnographic praxis in industry has deep roots in several related occupations. The Human Relations movement of the 1930s raised awareness of the impact of social work group dynamics upon productivity, and led to the establishment of the Human Resources function within organizations (Mayo 2003). During the same period, social scientists who used qualitative and quantitative research methods to study consumer behavior for the design of effective advertising founded the American Marketing Society (Burns and Bush 2009). Human Factors Engineering originated during World War II first to ensure the safety of combat aircraft, then the usability of other new technologies, and eventually the ergonomics of Human-Computer Interaction (Wickens et al. 1997). In the 1950s, manufacturing industries embraced Quality Management techniques based upon the principle that understanding the users' perspective is a key success factor for process improvements (Deming 1982). The 1990s introduced Requirements Engineering (Robertson and Robertson 2006) and User Experience Design (Norman 1990), related fields that probe human subjects' cognitive models, sensory responses, and emotional states in relation to prototype artifacts under development.

Anthropologists began taking a serious interest in questions raised by these other disciplines as the mid-twentieth century national independence movements gradually diminished opportunities for fieldwork abroad among preindustrial

*Advancing Ethnography in Corporate Environments: Challenges and Emerging Opportunities,* edited by Brigitte Jordan, 56–75. ©2013 Left Coast Press Inc. All rights reserved.

communities in former U.S. and European Union (EU) colonies. Beginning in the 1980s and continuing until the financial crisis of 2008, American government immigration policies that favored skilled, educated applicants and corporate diversity programs that supported the advancement of formerly marginalized demographic groups fostered a more multicultural workplace habitus. The introduction of email and the Internet as business tools during the 1990s gave rise to international networks of collaboration across time zones and cultural boundaries. After 2000, these same technologies enabled many organizations to outsource work to "near-shore" or "offshore" suppliers located in low-wage areas, achieving higher profits through labor arbitrage and building complex global supply chains. Subsequently enterprises in several countries that once were regarded solely as quasicolonial outsourcing destinations—especially the "BRIC" group including Brazil, Russia, India, and China—have leveraged the investments made by their clients and nurtured sufficient technical infrastructure, human resources, and intellectual capital to challenge the hegemony of U.S. and EU market leaders, particularly in the developing world.

Each of these historical events affecting corporate business activities provided ethnographers with rich scenarios of culture change to observe and analyze. They also enabled some ethnographers to apply their professional skills and insight within corporations for the purposes of facilitating better teamwork, reducing operational risks caused by cross-cultural miscommunication, and enhancing the quality of products and services (Ensworth 2003). As ethnography gained recognition among business managers for its valuable contributions to the bottom line, an important milestone was reached in 2005 when a group of leaders from various innovative companies launched the Ethnographic Praxis in Industry Conference (EPIC). Now an annual gathering with papers published as a scholarly volume, EPIC symbolizes the growing influence of ethnography in the corporate environment.

The two chapters in this section share a number of perspectives. Both authors are full-time practitioners rather than educators or researchers. Both have led teams and managed projects within global corporations whose names appear frequently in the business and technology news. Both are 20-year-plus veterans of development programs in industry, and have participated in the evolutionary changes described earlier in this chapter ever since the era when all phones were landlines and all mail required postage stamps. Both employ ethnographic concepts and methods to get their jobs done.

Nonetheless, the development of systems and products follows different paths, reflects different priorities, and demands different expertise from the ethnographer.

## The Concept of a "System"

The word "system" is derived from the Greek *systema* and signifies an integrated whole comprising multiple parts.[1] The parts are interconnected; the whole possesses a structure and exhibits behaviors.

Systems exist in many domains, both tangible and intangible. Plumbing, electrical wiring, and roads are systems that shape the experiences of people's everyday lives. Science employs systems to classify and explain the physical, natural, and mechanical world. A political system determines how a nation is governed. An economic system establishes the patterns for production, distribution, and consumption of goods and services. A theological system assigns roles and responsibilities to supernatural actors.

Within the four fields of anthropology, systems flourish. For cultural anthropologists, usually the first examples that come to mind are kinship systems, because the realization that in different cultures the parts of a family whole can fit together quite differently—matrilineal versus patrilineal, authority of father versus mother's brother, nuclear unit versus clan loyalty—is such a powerful, memorable insight for the beginning student. In a typical curriculum, one might soon learn about systems of exchange by examining the Trobriand Islanders' Kula ring customs, or systems of meaning by comparing creation myths. Linguists often approach their study of languages through methods of systems analysis. Archaeologists rely upon systems to manage their sites and classify their artifacts. Implicit in the research of physical anthropologists is an assumption that humans are one part among many of a holistic ecosystem.

Corporations' systems are built for well-defined purposes. Every business function owns one: research and development, procurement, manufacturing, quality control, inventory, workflow, operations, sales, marketing, finance, billing, accounting, customer service, internal audit, personnel, time tracking, payroll, document management, facilities management, and training. Each system has inputs, a set of processes, and outputs.

A mere generation ago, most of these corporate systems were manual, paper-based procedures. For the system as a whole to serve its purpose, one of its parts (person A) would type letters and numbers on a piece of paper; then, the paper would be physically moved to another part (person B). Often a social encounter would be enacted, either face to face or by landline telephone, to provide contextual information and solidify the exchange relationship.

The deployment of the personal computer as an office productivity tool in the early 1980s transformed the corporate environment. During the next quarter-century, every system listed here became digitized. Although paper records are sometimes produced as supporting artifacts, today the goal of the system is achieved primarily through the flow of electronic data. Social encounters also take the form of an exchange of digital messages. Thus, the study of any corporate system now inevitably must take into consideration the software that creates, transmits, and stores the information as well as the computer infrastructure that hosts it. Ethnography for systems development in the early twenty-first century draws upon the systems thinking of anthropology, business, and software engineering, a hybrid perspective that cross-fertilizes each discipline's wisdom.

For the purposes of this chapter, we will define a system as a set of relationships, activities, and tools implemented among members of a work process community. In contrast, a product is a single, tangible, manufactured artifact: a car, a cereal, a lotion, a textbook. Though invisible to the end-user, software can also be considered a product if a single master standalone version exists somewhere on a server.

## User Empowerment

As Marijke Rijsberman observes in "Ethnography and Product Design: Fixing the Future" (this volume), the end-users' individual motivations, desires, experiences, and choices have a stronger influence in the development of products than in systems.

Most of the time, the acquisition of a product involves a conscious purchasing decision; a system is often adopted in submission to external forces. Product developers seek to understand the user's needs by exploring fantasies, emotions, self-images, and personal habits (Underhill 2008), while system developers focus more upon tasks, boundaries, rules, and record-keeping. Both product users and system users can be regarded as a translocal ethnoscape (Appadurai 1988): a community dispersed over multiple locations whose members share some bond of affinity. Though their time commitments and skill levels vary, product users form an egalitarian ethnoscape of independent actors with homogeneous roles. The ethnoscape created by system users reflects a hierarchy of authority within which interdependent actors collaborate to perform heterogeneous functions.

The mission of a product developer is to create an object or experience that satisfies an individual, with success measured according to the number of people whose subjective criteria have been met. Although the system developer strives to satisfy end-users and other stakeholders, success is evaluated more objectively based upon the accomplishment of a particular goal through efficient allocation of time and resources (Kerzner 2009). Metaphors of romance and religion convey the attachment of end-users to their favorite products (Luhrmann 2010), yet the highest compliment a happy end-user can pay to a good system is to take it for granted.

During data gathering, unlike the users of a product, the users of a system are rarely offered incentives or rewards for participating in research. Moreover, they must spend more of their time providing information because many systemic processes occur at specific monthly, quarterly, or annual intervals, and multiple cycles should be observed. System development considers forces and constraints about which a large number of users may be ignorant. The answers to the questions, "Why are things the way they are?" and "What alternatives are possible?" may involve legal, financial, and technical specifications that are clearly understood only by subject matter experts in those domains.

Products are born when an individual sees an opportunity, has a vision, and confirms that a sufficient number of other people like the idea to invest in making it a reality. Systems come into being when a group of people trying to get some routine tasks done become exasperated by errors and delays and decide that they want to continue doing mostly the same thing but find a better way, or when something very bad happens and an outside authority tells them they must find a better way. If product development is like building a new house on vacant land, system development is like renovating a dilapidated structure following historic preservation standards while the tenants are still in residence.

Most important, product developers and system developers face in opposite directions with regard to time orientation. As Rijsberman describes, product development looks toward the future and conjures new phenomena through innovation. System development, on the other hand, is usually a process of dragging the heavy baggage of the past inch by inch into the present, with hopefully at least a few options for future evolution.

## The Role of the Ethnographer

In 25 years of work as a business anthropologist for software engineering and information technology (IT), and 10 years as a faculty member leading management training workshops for students from a wide range of industries and organizations, I have never encountered anyone involved in system development whose job title was "ethnographer."

One explanation for this phenomenon might be that corporations—represented by their procurement and human resources managers—assign a high value to credentials based upon professional certifications. There is as yet no Certified Ethnography Professional exam, nor a standard Ethnographic Body of Knowledge. If such a certification were to be created, we could expect to see many more "branded" ethnographers on the job.

The activities that comprise ethnography are performed by staff members or consultants who may be called business analysts, requirements engineers, interaction designers, user experience researchers, taxonomists, or quality assurance managers, to name only the most common choices. Whatever label they wear, their mission is the same: set up camp in the end-users' metaphorical native village, study how the end-users think and behave, provide information and recommendations to the developers, serve as a liaison between the end-users and the developers while the system is being built and deployed, and report results to management.

Under these circumstances, it can be a challenge to identify the specific ethnographic research tasks and explain how they add value to the development process. Unlike methods of inquiry that focus upon users' observable procedures and self-reported behaviors and opinions, ethnography applies the conceptual frameworks from fieldwork in cultural anthropology to understand the functioning of workplace communities. Like a medical anthropologist studying AIDS prevention, a corporate ethnographer might explore the cultural factors affecting whom a worker would trust with confidential data. Like a legal anthropologist studying the balance of power between an indigenous tribe and a global energy company in negotiations over mineral resource extraction on tribal lands, a corporate ethnographer might examine the rights and bargaining positions of union versus nonunion versus contract workers in establishing workplace safety standards. Like a feminist anthropologist studying the transmission of knowledge from an experienced midwife to an apprentice, a corporate ethnographer might document system users' conscious behaviors explained verbally and their unconscious behaviors taught by example. Like an anthropologist organizing a multisite study of an ethnic diaspora, a corporate ethnographer might adapt the research plan for a system deployed entirely within the organizational boundaries and IT firewall of a single enterprise to suit the requirements of a system linking multiple enterprises.

Of course, an ethnographer is not the only type of professional who can perform worthwhile fieldwork. Psychologists, journalists, teachers, sports coaches, market researchers, and people with many other kinds of expertise often learn enough on the job to serve the purpose. However, anthropologists trained in ethnographic research methods start out ahead with a larger toolkit of qualitative and quantitative techniques and higher scientific standards of evidence to test their hypotheses. Moreover, a graduate of a four-field anthropology program brings along habits of thinking that provide unique insights during system development. An understanding of archaeology enables the ethnographer to seek out artifacts from earlier processes, establish their location in space and time, reconstruct the organizational culture that used them, and determine which traditional practices might still be useful to provide continuity with future designs. Physical anthropology prompts the ethnographer to ask questions about the evolution of organizational structures and functions, the material resources a system consumes and produces, and the geographical arrangement of a system's end-users. Linguistics enables the ethnographer to deconstruct and translate technical dialects, to analyze how a system's end-users communicate with each other under various business conditions, and to examine the impact of native language speaking groups on system usage in multicultural organizations. It is a formidable skillset, one that many hiring managers and Human Resources recruiters are at last beginning to appreciate (Fiske et al. 2010).

Fieldwork in cultural anthropology instills several essential principles and practices that the ethnographer carries into the corporate environment:

- RESPECT FOR THE OTHER. The communities we study are different from us in many ways, yet they have valid reasons for their beliefs and customs.
- ACTIVE OBSERVATION AND LISTENING. We strive to absorb information from our sources with our full attention, and without imposing our own ideas or agendas on what we learn.

- PATIENCE. Participant observation—that is, "hanging out" in communities long enough to identify persons of interest, discern patterns, and understand relationships—takes time. It also takes time to digest and analyze our data.
- CONFIDENTIALITY. Under no circumstances will we divulge any information that could endanger our sources. If the outcome of our research has the potential to result in organizational changes affecting our sources, we will disclose that fact at the beginning of the relationship.

For product development, the ethnography practitioners usually support the product management and design functions, and their status as independent impartial observers is widely understood and respected. For system development, this position is more rare because the return on investment is more difficult to quantify. It is uncommon to find a separate, dedicated ethnographic research group inside the organization with its own identity and budget line. Instead, individual practitioners are embedded in development teams and may convene as a loosely organized professional network.

## The Activities of the Ethnographer

When an ethnographer ventures into the field, every engagement is unique. Nonetheless, fieldwork has certain predictable patterns, and anthropology students expect to receive some training before they set forth. Since business anthropology is a relatively new discipline (Suchman 2011), it is far easier to find courses on preparing for an engagement in a remote area of a developing country than in a high-tech office of a Fortune 500 company.

In an attempt to close that gap, and provide a snapshot of current logistics, presented in the next section is an overview of ethnographic methods in system development research. For each of the five steps, there is a section on "Fieldwork Practices" describing an ideal engagement, and a section called "Reality Check" with observations from actual projects.

### Obtaining Access

*Fieldwork Practices*

Every system development ethnography needs a sponsor. The sponsor is the individual, ideally a high-ranking executive, who will pay for the work. With guidance from the ethnographer, the sponsor prepares a goal statement identifying the ethnographer, describing the ethnography's final deliverable (e.g., a report, a set of metrics, a documentary film, a database), and the value of the effort to the system under development. The sponsor sends out the goal statement under his/her own name as a letter of introduction to all senior managers whose staff members' cooperation and involvement will be necessary.

The ethnographer ensures that the sponsor documents the budget for the work, the milestones and deadlines, the intermediate deliverables, the qualitative and quantitative success criteria for the ethnography, the level of security clearance authorized for the ethnographer and his/her associates, the types of decisions the ethnographer may make independently without consulting the sponsor, and the organization's rules for data privacy, intellectual property, audio recording, and video recording.

The sponsor provides the ethnographer with an ID badge, an email account, login credentials to relevant IT systems, a desk and computer and/or secure encrypted access to the organization's virtual private network, and standard productivity tools for word processing documents, presentations, databases, and spreadsheets. Other useful tools for survey generation, data modeling, statistical analysis, qualitative data analysis, and computer screen recording, as well as cameras and other audiovisual equipment, may be available but often must be requested well in advance and included in the budget negotiations.

By the time these preparations are complete, the sponsor and the ethnographer have established a comfortable working relationship. The sponsor understands that he/she will be expected to serve as an escalation point for critical issues, referee conflicts among stakeholders, and chase participants who fail to answer messages or attend meetings. The ethnographer is now ready to walk into the metaphorical village and encounter the natives.

## Reality Check

Sponsors are busy people. They rarely remember all the details, and the ethnographer should maintain the checklist. I have often been obliged to create draft documents for a sponsor to send out.

Licenses for tools are expensive. Unless the ethnographer personally owns the tool, it is necessary to justify the tool's value to the research.

Sometimes the process of obtaining access entails political risks for the sponsor. I worked on one project for a global enterprise software company where the plan envisioned documenting "a day in the life" of several categories of employees. The purpose of the initiative was to reduce operational costs by eliminating redundant data entry and simplifying system workflows. The proposed research design included videotaping users at their desks and recording their keystrokes. A review by the company's legal department revealed that such methods violated union contracts and data privacy laws in several countries that could have potentially benefited from the modifications to the systems. Before the project could be launched, the sponsor needed to meet with the managing directors in each of the relevant countries to negotiate special waivers. It also become important for the sponsor to ensure that high-performing end-users did not exert their influence to arrange for themselves to be excluded from the research and thereby prevent others from learning about their success strategies.

## Establishing Boundaries

### *Fieldwork Practices*

The first challenge faced by an ethnographer conducting research for system development is scope definition. If a unified whole is to be constructed out of multiple parts, what are those parts? The people, processes, activities, information, and infrastructure to be connected must be specified. Typically, the sponsor of the initiative has strong ideas about where the boundaries should be drawn, but the ethnographer's perspectives and methods will discover hidden, reluctant, and ignorant stakeholders.

Ideally, the project manager will have prepared a scope statement documenting the system's boundaries. Otherwise, the ethnographer will immediately make a valuable contribution by completing this task. However, even the most comprehensive project scope document typically focuses upon artifacts and processes. It is often up to the ethnographer to clarify which groups of people fall within the boundaries, and why.

### *Reality Check*

In practice, the decision about the identity of the system is an ever-evolving consensus among those who pay for it, those who build it, those who use it, and those who support it: a "mutually defining relationship," in Rijsberman's words from her chapter in this volume.

Whatever the boundaries of the system look like in the flowchart diagram, the human map is far messier and more contested. Every system has a community of core users and a much larger population of occasional visitors. Behind every process or data interface is an exchange relationship between two or more social groups.

I worked on a publishing workflow system once where some categories of writers were delighted to be invited into the core group because it validated the importance of their content to the enterprise. Other categories of writers begged to be excluded because the system eliminated the multiple rounds of editorial review they were accustomed to: when they clicked "OK," their copy was immediately live on the Internet, a new and anxiety-provoking experience. After the boundaries of the system had been finalized, my team collaborated with the various user groups to identify how their behaviors and communication patterns would change. We devised a phased rollout plan so that each category of users could develop an adequate level of trust in the people managing the system.

## Understanding Stakeholder Motives

### Fieldwork Practices

The next question for the ethnographer involves the purpose of the system. What will all those multiple parts be able to do once they have been connected as a unified whole?

The motive for the system's existence exerts a strong influence on the process of development and the climate for research. While ethnography for product development seeks to make a customer happy enough to buy or to continue using an item, ethnography for system development can be conducted for many different reasons. The best-case scenarios involve more satisfied users, more harmonious relationships, and more efficient procedures. Other motives might include stronger external regulation, improved security, faster performance, cost cutting, elimination of jobs, and outsourcing of less skilled tasks. In any case, it is understood that senior managers wish to implement some significant change.

The role of the ethnographer on a systems development project therefore resembles the role on international aid or ecotourism projects. A powerful sponsor defines the goal and funds the work. The daily lives of different kinds of people will be changed in different ways: some for better, some for worse.

When the system design requires that a group of people perform a single role and comply with a single set of predefined processes, individuals may be obliged to modify their unique behaviors and conform to a new set of standards. The development of the system may create new hierarchies of authority whereby two groups that previously were equal and independent may find themselves in a superior-subordinate relationship, with one empowered to thwart or penalize the other.

Anthropological field methods can help probe beneath the users' surface performances of cooperation and find out what people are really willing to put up with. It sometimes happens that a group on the losing side of a design battle will capitulate for show, and will act as though they are willingly implementing the roles and processes of a system, but in reality they are clandestinely developing "workarounds" to maintain the status quo. Too many workarounds, or workarounds that undermine critical processes, can destroy a system. An ethnographer who has developed a more intimate knowledge of the end-user communities than any other participant in the system development project can identify situations where workarounds are probable and suggest strategies to prevent them.

Ethical issues arise continuously. While identifying stakeholders and documenting their needs, desires, and behaviors, the ethnographer must occasionally decide whether or not to assume the responsibility of speaking up on behalf of voiceless groups and defending the interests of vulnerable populations. Although such advocacy inevitably puts the ethnographer on a collision course with stakeholders who prefer that these end-users remain silent and powerless, experienced project managers support the ethnographer's stance because it improves the probability of the system's long-term success (Ensworth 2011).

## Reality Check

Probing stakeholders' motives and mapping the political landscape they create can involve contentious, emotional encounters that must be handled with tact and diplomacy. One effective technique for keeping the discussion rational is to plot stakeholders' positions on a matrix of attitude and influence. During the design and deployment of the system, additional resources should be allocated to address the issues of user groups in the High Influence/Negative Attitude quadrant (Figure 3.1).

There is truth to the stereotype that systems engineers tend to be introverts. Mostly they prefer building models in solitude to going out and talking to people, especially people who are quite different from them. They also respect authority, at least in principle: they build hardware and software based upon authoritative scientific rules, and by default they rely upon the good judgment of leaders within the organization (at least until proven wrong).

As a result of these professional characteristics, engineers instinctively pay more attention to stakeholders who are like them: well-educated, analytical, and gadget-loving. Over and above the commonsense need to comply with corporate procedures to succeed in their jobs, they privilege the wisdom of management in relation to that of other workplace social groups. Stakeholders who embody alternative perspectives can be excluded from the community formed by the development team because they just don't seem to fit in. This can lead to trouble for the system.

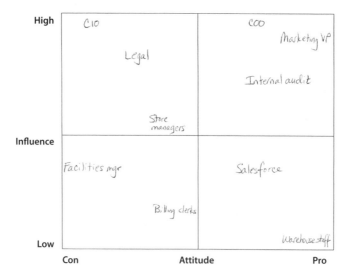

FIGURE 3.1. Stakeholder Analysis Matrix. The most effective technique is to draw the matrix on a whiteboard, write the stakeholders on sticky notes, and then have the development team move the notes around within the matrix until a consensus is reached.

During the Y2K era I was involved in a rescue mission at a global financial services firm where ethnographic research methods discovered the reasons for a new system's failure after other techniques proved ineffective. The company had been in business for more than a hundred years and had developed deep, complex relationships with many long-term institutional customers. Until then, billing had been a manual process dependent upon paper invoices, photocopies, and filing cabinets. With the event of business-to-business secure transactions over the Internet, the time seemed right to go paperless and automate the workflow.

The systems developers interviewed the Chief Financial Officer, the Treasurer, and the Vice Presidents of Accounts Payable, Accounts Receivable, Sales, and Operations. They spent a couple of hours with a billing clerk documenting ideal work processes. They drew flowcharts. They built a prototype and did some usability testing of the screen layouts. They finished the system and deployed it. Everything seemed fine at first.

However, after the first few months, the quality assurance staff noticed an alarming trend. The electronic change log showed that customers were disputing many of the invoices that should have been accurate based upon data input from the salespeople, and billing clerks were retroactively adjusting amounts in the production data. This was unacceptable not only because it created extra work, but also because manipulation of production data by anyone other than system administrators could raise serious issues in an internal audit or regulatory review.

For more than a year, the systems developers tried to figure out the flaws in their logic. New flowcharts were drawn. New versions of the software were released. A Ph.D. in artificial intelligence was hired as a consultant to optimize the data model. Still, the number of exceptions in the change log remained too high.

Eventually, the quality assurance team obtained approval to conduct ethnographic research on the information flow among the human beings connected by the system. A three-week study yielded several interesting insights.

First, the idea that the amount a customer owed could be calculated by a mathematical algorithm using numbers from a standard price list was an illusion. Over the years, this firm had negotiated unique deals, packages, and discounts with nearly every one of its several thousand customers. The bigger the customer, the more convoluted were the terms and conditions.

Second, the details of these unique arrangements existed in so many different formats—contracts, letters, internal memoranda, emails—that it would take a significantly greater effort than anyone anticipated to document and standardize them in a repository accessible via automated queries. Furthermore, they were changing all the time as new products were introduced and salespeople created new incentives.

Finally, the knowledge of all these details resided in the memories of the billing clerks. These 20 women sat together on one floor and formed a cohesive yet isolated social group. For years they had been accustomed to speaking by phone with their counterparts in the customers' Accounts Payable offices and personally resolving any billing questions. Many could trace a customer's billing history back several decades through various acquisitions, divestitures, and mergers.

None of the billing clerks had graduated from college. Most came from close-knit, working-class, religious families. They accepted the fact that they were in dead-end jobs and tried to have fun at the office. They were cynical about authority in general, although proud to work at a highly respected company. They considered the systems engineers a bunch of geeky adolescent boys who did not yet understand the way the world really worked. Once a week they had a potluck lunch in a conference room, played cards, chatted about their families, and exchanged critical information about what the firm's customers were up to. Because the design of the new automated system had eliminated the billing clerks from the workflow of creating invoices, their role was now restricted to fixing mistakes. They were worried about rumors of layoffs in their group.

When the quality assurance group suggested to the system developers that some of the senior billing clerks should be included in the requirements sessions, he reacted as though he had been asked to invite the janitorial staff. When the requirements sessions led to a system modification that gave the billing clerks the ability to review and modify an invoice before it was finalized, the number of customer disputes returned to preautomation levels. When the quality assurance team proposed ethnographic research on the next troubled development project, it took far less than a year to obtain management approval.

## Conducting the Engagement

### Fieldwork Practices

System development ethnography shares many data-gathering methods with product development ethnography: direct observation, participant observation, interviews, surveys, measurements, and focus groups. For analysis, in addition to personas and prototypes there may be flowcharts, process maps, storyboarding, use cases, role-and-responsibility matrices, and walkthroughs. The most notable difference is the type of information the researcher solicits. For product development, what matters most are the informant's feelings and experiences. For system development, it is the informant's personal cognitive map of his/her group and understanding of its values.

Many of the research topics and approaches would be familiar to cultural anthropologists doing fieldwork anywhere. It is important at the outset to understand the identity and common purpose of the group. Origin stories explain who created them and how they came into being. Their history features heroes and villains, migrations, reorganizations, crises averted and overcome. Formal and informal rituals reinforce their group membership, loyalty, and morale. There is a marketplace—physical and/or virtual—where ideas are exchanged and deals are made. New members are initiated through particular customs, and ongoing education is provided in some manner. Kinship structures determine trading partners, organizational allies and enemies, methods of communication, and the group's territorial limits.

To help the system developers design a realistic workflow, the ethnographer asks certain specific questions about both the internal activities the group is collectively responsible for performing and the procedures they follow with external colleagues:

- What are the rules?
- Who makes the rules?
- Who enforces the rules?
- Who referees conflicts?
- What happens to rule-breakers?
- How is virtuous behavior rewarded?
- What is kept secret from outsiders?

Whereas physical systems for plumbing or electricity depend upon the flow of a tangible, measurable substance, human systems depend upon the flow of intangible, unquantifiable communication. Since the cause of a gap or blockage is frequently a breakdown in trust between members of a community, or between multiple communities, the ethnographer explores and documents how trust relationships are established and maintained.

In contrast to other members of the development team who may ask similar questions, the ethnographer's perspective offers three special qualities. First and foremost is emotional intelligence: the anthropological skillset enables an ethnographer to perceive human connections more readily than colleagues trained in management and engineering disciplines. The ethnographer focuses upon social groups, and complements the official data in organization charts about reporting lines and departmental structures by identifying unofficial self-organizing communities of practice. And of course the ethnographer excels at understanding how ethnic, national, religious, and/or tribal cultural values among different user groups can motivate rebellion against the new behaviors imposed by the system developers.

When the ethnographer brings forward his/her findings to the development team, several outcomes are possible. In an environment where human factors in engineering are valued, the data and analysis may be challenged or debated one item at a time, but the ethnographic research as a project deliverable will be appreciated and included among the design specifications. Alternatively, if aggressive deadlines or strict cost controls are creating pressure on the system developers to reduce the scope of the project, the ethnographer will be obliged to repeatedly make a business case explaining the value and relevance of the research. The least rewarding situation occurs when not all of the senior stakeholders on the project agree that ethnographic research is a worthwhile undertaking because they feel the new system is going to come speeding down the organizational tracks like a bullet train and the users damn well better jump on board or they will get run over. Such authoritarian development managers tend to accuse the ethnographer of "going native"—i.e., losing a researcher's objectivity and adopting the end-users' point of view—and it is not meant as a compliment.

## Reality Check

One useful tool to convey information about the structure and roles of trust relationships among user groups is a RACI chart. This spreadsheet designates groups or individuals collaborating in a workflow as Responsible (they do the work), Accountable (they get in trouble if the work isn't done right), Consulted (they contribute expertise), or Informed (they are on the distribution list for reports).

| | Editorial | Sales | Production | Regional Managers | Training | Communications | IT Admin | Web Developer | GUI Developer | Database Developer | CIO |
|---|---|---|---|---|---|---|---|---|---|---|---|
| **Establish Taxonomy** | | | | | | | | | | | |
| Define subject codes | R | | | | | | A | | | C | I |
| Normalize media codes | | | R | | | | A | | | C | I |
| Align regional codes | | | | R | | | A | | | C | I |
| Verify product line data | | | R | | | | A | | | C | I |
| Obtain data model approval | I | | I | I | | | I | I | I | I | R/A |
| **Modify Systems** | | | | | | | | | | | |
| Create data input screens | | | | | | | A | R | C | | I |
| Modify database | | | | | | | A | | C | R | I |
| Modify data feeds | | | | | | | A | | C | R | I |
| Verify business rules from taxonomy | C | C | R | C | | | A | | C | C | I |
| Obtain approval of new functionality | I | I | I | I | | | I | | I | I | R/A |
| **Develop Reports** | | | | | | | | | | | |
| Create sales reports | | A | | | | | | | C | R | I |
| Modify production reports | | | A | | | | | | C | R | I |
| Modify website traffic reports | | | | | | | A | | C | R | I |
| Obtain approval of reports | | I | I | | | | | I | I | I | R/A |
| **Create Training** | | | | | | | | | | | |
| Produce webinar | C | C | C | C | R | C | A | C | | | I |
| Launch web page | | | | | | | A | R | | | I |
| Deliver briefings | C | C | C | C | R | C | A | | | | I |

R = Responsible; A = Accountable; C = Consulted; I = Informed

TABLE 3.1. RACI Matrix for clarifying roles and responsibilities among members of a work process community.

During my ethnographic engagements—either working solo or leading a team—I have interacted with end-user communities, the engineers building the system, the specialist subject matter experts, and various other stakeholders. Sometimes the role has been limited to research, and sometimes through the process of translation and negotiation it has evolved into more active participation in the development work of project management, requirements analysis, and user acceptance testing.

A few examples of projects should provide a sense of the types of issues I have encountered and the ways I have found in which ethnographic methods can facilitate solutions:

- A global investment bank with its headquarters in Europe outsourced some systems development for trading floor operations to a supplier based in India. Although detailed written specifications had been created, traders complained that the new system's user interfaces were too slow and clumsy. Through six months of multiple releases, nothing the vendor designed satisfied the end-users. Accusations of incompetence and bad faith were voiced. The relationship deteriorated to the point where litigation was being threatened by both sides. In a what-have-we-got-to-lose spirit, the bank's senior development manager authorized ethnographic research. Participant observation and videotaping of work processes on the trading floor and at the Indian development center revealed that the primary issue was a mismatch in levels of cognitive chaos. The software engineers occupied peaceful, silent, private cubicles and looked at a single screen. The traders' working conditions were bedlam: people sitting elbow-to-elbow in a bullpen, six to eight screens per trader with multiple data feeds on every one, ringing phones with multiple lines, televisions suspended from the ceiling showing multiple channels of news, and a cacophony of customized alarm sounds triggered by price movements. Of course, both the developers and traders felt their own workplace was normal. On the recommendation of the ethnographers, the vendor built a simulated trading environment as a usability lab for the developers. The software designs they subsequently produced seemed much improved to the users.
- A publisher of technical and professional journals wished to create a system for the centralized electronic storage of customer contact information maintained by its salespeople. The salespeople regarded most of this data as personal property, a private record of the history of their interactions with their clients. The company wanted the system to ensure that the history was not lost when a salesperson left; the salespeople worried that the system would allow their bosses to micromanage and undermine their customer relationships. An ethnographer helped persuade the system developers to take the salespeople's privacy concerns more seriously and establish mutually acceptable boundaries of data to be included and excluded.

- A media company planned to introduce a project management system in its branch offices around the world. In several Arab countries, the data input error rates were extremely high during the beta test of the new system. The branch managers blamed the computer hardware and network, but local technicians could find no problems. An ethnographic study indicated that the users assigned to input the data were the most junior, least educated employees. Among the more experienced staff members, the elegance of their Arabic calligraphy was a matter of pride, and they did not wish to abandon paper-based recordkeeping. The ethnographers negotiated a compromise involving an additional step in the workflow whereby a report was printed so that the more experienced staff could review the data before it was submitted to the headquarters project office.

## Facilitating the Transition

### Fieldwork Practices

It is at the deployment of the new system that the true weight of the baggage comprising old work practices becomes apparent. Until then, no matter how many prototypes have been built and walkthroughs conducted, in the minds of the users the new system has been a theoretical possibility.

When the literal or metaphorical switch is flipped, however, it suddenly becomes very real. No doubt there are some users who have been eagerly awaiting its arrival; many more respond negatively because they are being asked to abandon artifacts, behaviors, and relationships with which they are familiar and upon which they depend.

More than anyone else on the development team, the ethnographer understands what the different groups of users need to help them make the transition to a new system. Educational levels, native languages, work environment, and preferred learning methods all matter. Establishing peer-to-peer communities of practice where social transmission of knowledge can occur is an effective technique advocated by many expert business anthropologists (Jordan with Lambert 2009).

To lay the groundwork for a successful user transition program, and protect resources from the last-minute schedule and budget crunch, the ethnographer creates partnerships with the managers of documentation and training as early as possible in the system development project. The ethnographer's list of end-user complaints and suggestions become the design specifications for the next version of the system in an iterative development process.

### Reality Check

As an ethnographer, the most complex and contested deployment of a new system I have experienced was an IT security initiative that established new rules and workflow for privileged access. Following an act of cyberwarfare by a foreign country that targeted U.S. corporations in industries essential to national security, senior management of the attack's victims understood that they needed to reduce the number of employees who could perform powerful administrator functions on key components of their IT infrastructure. The reason for the lockdown was the fact that the foreign hackers had been able to disguise themselves as administrators, break into the network, steal confidential data, and disrupt operations. Many of the victims were U.S. companies with global organizations and employees located in countries around the world.

Until then, it had been the custom for an IT department to grant privileged access on an informal case-by-case basis. Some administrators were staff members, some were consultants, and some were employees of outsourced suppliers. The principal criterion for approval was that someone who already had privileges trusted the applicant enough to say yes. Suddenly, very urgently, a new system needed to be implemented with rigorous new standards defining trustworthiness. For security reasons, it had to have no workarounds and no exceptions. It also had to come into existence without causing the business to grind to a halt.

The perception of risk is a highly culture-specific variable (Douglas 1966). Because the system was being imposed by a top-down management directive, successful deployment depended upon recognizing the actual grassroots communities of practice, educating community leaders about the new realities of cyberwarfare, and then facilitating peer-to-peer coaching and monitoring for compliance.

## Conclusion

In the aftermath of the 2008 global financial crisis, more corporations are adopting anthropological research methods to better understand the human element of their business (Tett 2011). The era of management faith in mathematical algorithms to explain people's values and behavior has given way to a more nuanced strategy that includes emotional intelligence, social groups, and cultural values. This is potentially good for ethnographers working in the corporate environment.

Although mostly invisible to the general population, system development is an expanding field of endeavor, along with the software and computer infrastructure engineering that powers its workflows. In less than a decade, digital technology has imposed information systems upon nearly every aspect of life in affluent countries: buying groceries, driving a car, sending a package, watching a movie, visiting a doctor, taking a vacation, even finding a mate. In most cases, these systems are owned and operated by corporations. Every public system used by external customers is supported by multiple private systems integrating work process communities within an enterprise's firewall. This is the highly structured environment within which the work of system development is carried out. The special expertise that ethnographers bring to that work is attention to the underlying cultural assumptions, beliefs, and values that are also being reengineered. Ethnography can help ensure that such decisions are more conscious and consensual. A successful system then preserves enough of the legacy of the various users' past for all stakeholders to feel confident about the future.

## Acknowledgments

When I was invited to contribute a chapter to this volume based upon a 15-minute paperless presentation at the 2011 Society for Applied Anthropology meeting, in my enthusiasm for the project I somehow overlooked the fact that I had not written any academic essays in more than 30 years. As the book took shape, I felt rather like a ballroom dancer cast in a classical ballet. Sincere thanks are due to Brigitte Jordan and Marijke Rijsberman for their thoughtful editing and patient coaching.

## References

Appadurai, Arjun
    1988 *The Social Life of Things*. Cambridge, United Kingdom: Cambridge University Press.
Burns, Alvin C., and Ronald F. Bush
    2009 *Marketing Research, 6th Edition*. Englewood Cliffs, N.J.: Prentice Hall.
Deming, W. E.
    1982 *Quality, Productivity and Competitive Position*. Cambridge: MIT Press.
Douglas, Mary
    1966 *Purity and Danger: An Analysis of Concepts of Pollution and Taboo*. London: Routledge and Keegan Paul.
Ensworth, Patricia
    2003 Culture Clash. CIO. October 1, 2003. Available online at http://www.cio.com/article/29821/Patricia_Ensworth_on_Managing_Multicultural_Project_Teams_at_Moody_s. Accessed June 1 2012.
    2011 Web 2.0 and Information Security: Challenges for Corporate Ethnography. *Paper presented* at the American Anthropological Association Annual Meeting, November 18, 2011, Montreal, Canada.
Fiske, Shirley J., Linda A. Bennett, Patricia Ensworth, Terry Redding, and Keri Brondo
    2010 *The Changing Face of Anthropology: Anthropology Masters Reflect on Education, Careers, and Professional Organizations*. AAA/CoPAPIA 2009 Anthropology MA Career Survey. Arlington: American Anthropological Association.
Jordan, Brigitte, with Monique Lambert
    2009 Working in Corporate Jungles: Reflections on Ethnographic Praxis in Industry. In *Ethnography and the Corporate Encounter: Reflections on Research in and of Corporations*, edited by Melissa Cefkin, pp. 94–133. New York: Berghahn Books.
Kernzer, Harold
    2009 *Project Management: A Systems Approach to Planning, Scheduling and Controlling, 10th Edition*. Hoboken, N.J.: Wiley.
Lanier, Jaron
    2010 *You Are Not a Gadget*. New York: Alfred A. Knopf.

Luhrmann, Tanya
2010 What Students Can Teach Us About iPhones.Salon.com, May 30 2010. Available at http://www.salon.com/2010/05/30/iphone_college_students/. Accessed June 1, 2012.

Mayo, Elton
2003 *The Human Problems of an Industrial Civilization.* London: Routledge Classics.

Norman, Donald
1990 *The Design of Everyday Things.* New York: Doubleday Business.

Robertson, Suzanne, and James C. Robertson
2006 *Mastering the Requirements Process, 2nd Edition.* Reading, MA: Addison-Wesley Professional.

Suchman, Lucy
2011 Work Practice and Technology: A Retrospective. In *Making Work Visible: Ethnographically Grounded Case Studies of Work Practice,* edited by Margaret H. Szymanski and Jack Whalen, pp. 21-33. Cambridge, United Kingdom: Cambridge University Press.

Tett, Gillian
2011 Interest Group for the Anthropology of Public Policy (IGAPP) Distinguished Lecture, "Anthropology, Policy, and the Global Financial Crisis," American Anthropological Association Annual Meeting, November 18, 2011, Montreal, Canada.

Underhill, Paco
2008 *Why We Buy: The Science of Shopping.* New York: Simon and Schuster.

Wickens, C. D., J. D. Lee, Y. Liu, and S. Gordon-Becker
1997 *An Introduction to Human Factors Engineering, 2nd Edition.* Englewood Cliffs, N.J.: Prentice Hall.

# Note

1   http://en.wikipedia.org/wiki/System, accessed June 7, 2012.

Chapter 4

# Ethnography and Product Design: Fixing the Future

*Marijke Rijsberman*

> We drive into the future using only our rearview mirror.
> —*Marshall McLuhan*

## Introduction

Although the core ethnographic methodology of participant observation creates many commonalities between systems ethnography and product ethnography, the applied turn imposed by the different corporate contexts drives a significant divergence in ethnographic practice. I will focus in this chapter on two important distinguishing features of product ethnography that set it apart from other ethnographic applications and very specifically from systems ethnography. First, the product ethnographer foregrounds individual motivation and desire to an unusual degree. She will often investigate the substrate of culture in which individual wishes and aspirations flourish only to gain a deeper understanding of the individual and individual decision-making, in sharp contrast to systems ethnography, which privileges the system over the individuals who must work within it. The second distinguishing feature springs from the drive towards product innovation that is fundamental to the global capitalist economy. Product innovation, an essential driver of profit and market dominance, brackets the description and understanding of what "is," here and now, in the ethnographer's analysis, and pushes the work of interpretation forwards into a prediction of possible futures. As Patricia Ensworth shows in "Ethnography for System Development" (Chapter 3), the systems ethnographer concerns herself with creating a system in the present that is in compliance with all established regulations and is free from the defects that have plagued preceding systems in the past. The product ethnographer, on the other hand, may find a convenient jumping-off point in the present moment, starting from the customer experience with existing products, but she primarily concerns herself with future product opportunities, whether those take the form of small improvements or radical changes. These two features impose specific methodological requirements on the product ethnographer and tend to weaken the conventional disciplinary boundaries within which ethnography has traditionally been brought to bear.

*Advancing Ethnography in Corporate Environments: Challenges and Emerging Opportunities,* edited by Brigitte Jordan, 76–91. ©2013 Left Coast Press Inc. All rights reserved.

## Products, Behaviors, and Decisions

First, a word about products, in their splendid but also bewildering variety. In a business context, a product is a thing that is manufactured and offered for sale in the marketplace on the presumption that it satisfies a conscious or unconscious desire among potential buyers.[1] That desire may be preexisting, but it may also be created by the product or the family of products to which it belongs. Translated into ethnographic terms, a product exists in or will be introduced to a culturally specific market, which endows the product with a range of meanings and possibilities. In addition, the product has the potential to shape the behavior of the people who own, use, or otherwise embrace it as part of their personal or professional lives, thus redefining the shared meanings and possibilities associated with the product. People and products are thus seen to exist in a mutually defining relationship.

The product ethnographer's bidirectional perspective is not relevant in the same way to all products on offer. Insulin pumps, office copiers, guided missile systems, and mobile photo sharing services, to name just a few examples, zoom in on pockets of human experience that operate within wildly divergent systems of rules and values as well as cultural substrates. The ways in which different types of products are acquired and used in different contexts vary tremendously, while conditions for innovation diverge significantly from industry to industry. The complexity grows exponentially when we consider products being brought to markets across the continents.

These axes of variation have important implications for the two factors in product ethnography I analyze here, the privileging of the individual and the innovation imperative. To keep the discussion manageable, I will focus primarily on products that the individual has a relatively unconstrained ability to decide to buy or, if not buy, then choose to use or not use, as is often the case in the context of contemporary knowledge work. The examples I rely on to illustrate my argument are intentionally drawn from areas in which buying decisions are largely unconstrained (apparel and media experiences) or in which adoption decisions are within the realm of individual choice even if buying decisions are made by others (productivity tools used in collaborative work environments). Where purchase and adoption choices are severely constrained by a larger system, whether it be regulatory, medical, or military, ethnographic practices will tend to shade over into realities described in Patricia Ensworth's chapter concerning systems ethnography in this volume (Chapter 3).

### Situating the Individual

Good product ethnography[2] is grounded, as is all ethnography, in interaction with individuals or groups of individuals, using the fundamental observational and analytical methodologies of participant observation and interviewing and the many variations of these that have been more or less standardized.[3] A well-designed product ethnography includes the observation of people in the environment in which the product in question is or would be used, in interaction with the product itself or with similar products, and in interaction with other people as well as alone. The objective is to gain an understanding of how participants do things, alone and with others, how they imitate and learn from each other, how they compete with each other, how their behaviors are informed by shared values and beliefs, how they might behave differently in private than in social or professional settings, and how conflicts reveal stresses in or between the cultural systems to which they belong. In short, product ethnography is not significantly different from other applications of ethnography with respect to data gathering.

But a crucial difference does arise in how data are analyzed and put to use. By its very nature, product ethnography is about products and especially about opportunities for future product improvements, much more than it is about the people who might buy them. More important, product ethnography trains a different lens on the individual being studied. Traditional ethnography in the service of anthropological study has an interest in the larger whole—however that larger whole may be defined, as a tribe, a culture (with or without the indefinite article), humankind, society, or the human condition—at least one level of abstraction up from the individual. As a recent ethnography textbook puts it: "Ethnography is a research methodology to explore and examine the cultures and societies that are a fundamental part of the human experience" (Murchison 2010:4). In a similar spirit, Franz Boas wrote that "We cannot treat the individual as an isolated unit" (1962:15), meaning that it is impossible to understand the individual without reference to history or culture. Historically, the individual has also been less interesting to anthropologists than the larger unit, however that unit may be conceptualized exactly.

Product ethnographers, on the other hand, find the larger whole much less compelling than the individual. For good or ill, they are interested in patterns in individual behavior and experience more than in the culture that spawns them. As an example, consider the famous eLab opportunity model of colds, which identified stages in the typical experience of the common cold among individuals in the domestic market. While colds undoubtedly have a rich cultural resonance, the model cuts away all context and brings the physical experience rather than the culture of colds into sharp focus, with its identification of the stages of self-diagnosis, getting a cold (GAC), having a cold (HAC), and getting over a cold (GOAC).[4] When it comes to products, individuals trump culture, as it is individuals who go shopping. This is true especially in the Internet age, when there are mechanisms to address experiences and behaviors in the long tail. Moreover, in societies characterized by rapid change, such as the global capitalist economies in which most products are created and sold, individual behavior is on the leading edge and culture tends to catch up later.

The phenomenon is neatly, if perhaps unintentionally, illustrated by Susan Squires in her essay "Doing the Work: Customer Research in the Product Development and Design Industry" (Squires 2002). Squires argues that "the role of research in the creative process is to discover and draw out design implications of real cultural phenomena" (2002:103). Interestingly, both of her examples show that the way in which behavior breaks loose from the values and beliefs espoused by the individuals being studied is much more telling with reference to the products her studies support. Her first example concerns breakfast in the United States, where the cultural values—very much rooted in the past—held by participants prescribe a healthy breakfast for school-age children. Mothers asserted that they feed their kids a nutritious breakfast. Meanwhile, investigation revealed the children in flagrant rebellion, eating nothing or munching on Dad's junk cereal instead. And it was the children's breakaway behavior that pointed the way to a new product idea, portable yogurt.

The example shows that the product ethnographer operates on the leading edge of cultural redefinition, even potentially playing a role in its acceleration. The ethnographic insights of greatest value are not those that capture where the culture is but where it might go. If we take culture as the fabric of shared meanings continually and dialectically created by a group of people, then the product ethnographer looks not just for the patterns, but for the unraveling at the edges.

Squires' other example concerns office workers who averred that videoconferencing helped them collaborate. Despite their convictions, Squires noted, most turned off the videoconferencing feature in their collaboration tools. Even though the technological ideals of the local Silicon Valley culture were clearly represented in the articulated opinions of participants, their actual behavior stood in stark contrast. Again, it was individual behavior that carried the day, but in this case their behavior exerted a force in the opposite direction, not driving change but rather slowing it down. Squires' participants resisted a projected future to which they subscribed in principle, but which they did not support in practice. Their resistance points the way to the fact that, in the final analysis, it is not the fit of a product to the culture but the fit to actual behavior patterns that will make or break the product experience, and will make it worth buying or worth using.[5] The cultural moment may have been ripe for an embrace of video technology, but individual people quietly declined.

Product ethnography, usually inspecting just a small slice of material culture, may bring to bear an anthropological perspective without giving up the primacy of the individual in the analysis. In this regard, product ethnography shows an affinity to the work of Daniel Miller. In his introduction to *Anthropology and the Individual*, he writes, "We start by appropriating anthropological perspectives that were first developed for the study of society and show how these can be adopted for the study of individuals" (Miller 2009:1). Miller uses the concept of an "aesthetic of order"—a "desire for harmony, order and balance . . . and also dissonance, contradiction and irony" (Miller, 2008:5)—intimately tied to possessions as a lens on the individual experience, where the order is unique to the individual even if the objects in it participate in the broader material culture. While Miller is interested in the full panoply of things in the lives of real people, the product ethnographer will typically focus on a particular product and the way it functions in that order. But what product ethnography shares with Miller's study of individuals is the emphasis on individual choice and agency (sometimes expressed in terms of resistance) as well as creativity, in their relation to things, as they are actively making new culture, assembling new patterns of meaning in a messy dialectical process by which the new is synthesized to the old.

## A Balancing Act

The example of videoconferencing is worth inspecting in greater detail for other reasons as well. It conveniently illustrates how the product ethnographer operates within larger product teams. It also gives us a peek at what the ethnographer will typically do when identifying a poor fit between product and individual needs. And finally, it shows how the product ethnographer navigates the tension between studying individuals up close, entering their perspective as much as possible, in a context that is not, ultimately, motivated by those individuals and their needs but by a product and the needs of the business bringing it to market.

The extent to which videoconferencing in the context of work speaks to individual agency and resistance, in friction with the containing organizational and even regional culture, became apparent when I spent a year and a half observing people who designed, developed, sold, and used a variety of videoconferencing tools, in hopes of persuading the rest of working humanity to fall in love with the technology also.[6] The products in question ranged from video integrated into screen-sharing software, to dedicated videophones, to very high-end room-based videoconferencing systems. The company I was working for had made a strategic investment in videoconferencing after noting the rapid adoption of videoconferencing for personal use taking place in the consumer market. That strategic decision was driven by an implicit (but incorrect) assumption that experiences within the two domains are basically congruent. That is, the company envisioned a future showing the same steep adoption curve for business videoconferencing that personal video tools such as Skype had enjoyed.

The first indication that the two experiences, though superficially identical, are in fact fundamentally different came when many of my coworkers confided to me that, though they regularly used video to communicate with friends and family, they were not nearly as comfortable with video in a work environment. As one coworker commented after an online video meeting, "It's exhausting to be on display for two hours." Another colleague observed how rapidly she had unadopted videoconferencing after moving from one group to another within the same company: "In my [old group], my boss made us use video all the time. We all did it, and I got used to it. But now I never use it anymore. I don't have to, so I don't do it." In fact, for most of my coworkers, "back-sliding" was extremely common and adoption dropped off whenever external pressure to use video decreased. In fact, adoption of videoconferencing in work environments is often mandated by management rather than propelled by demand among the rank and file. In my observation, only a small minority used video in the absence of external pressure of one sort or another. This results in an atypical adoption pattern, by which repeated use results in an increased degree of comfort with the technology, as one would expect, but not necessarily in continued use.

Communications about the burdens of video typically came in the form of confidences because the majority sincerely believed that video support does improve the quality of communication and collaboration, very similar to the convictions reported by Squires. There is a widespread belief in corporate environments that video helps to create collaborative working relationships among people who do not have an opportunity to meet in person.[7] Academic studies suggest, however, that videoconferencing helps people work across distances only under a highly specific confluence of circumstances.[8]

However, as an ethnographer supporting one of the company's videoconferencing products, it was not my responsibility to identify and document a misalignment between cultural values and personal preference. Rather, I had been hired to help the team design the best possible video product, and not in isolation, either. As a product ethnographer, one works closely with others who have their own ideal conceptions of what the product should be, guided by the kind of information they usually work with. Based on their understanding of market demand and competitive analysis, product managers dictate feature sets. Designers translate feature requirements into interfaces, working from design principles and patterns. And engineers usually push back on both feature requirements and design proposals based on their insight into what it takes to make the product.

In such a context, the expectation is that the ethnographer will offer practical recommendations for product improvement that can usefully inform group decision-making. However, the ethnographer will typically broaden the scope of the inquiry before narrowing down on the potential for specific improvements. Product ethnography seeks to answer such questions by looking at the specific situated cultural moment from the individual's vantage point, not ignoring culture but not focusing exclusively on a cultural perspective either. With reference to our current example, the broader question is whether videoconferencing is inherently inimical to work environments, whether it can be used to advantage in specific settings if perhaps not in others, or whether design adjustments might alter the experience sufficiently to remove the discomfort felt by many of the individuals who used the product.

Concrete answers began to delineate themselves after more than a hundred interviews and a year and a half of observation outside of formal studies.[9] Personal video and video at work, it became apparent, may be superficially similar, but they speak to individual needs in a completely different way. The reasons for the radical difference in experience between the two can be found precisely in the collision of the individual with the specific cultural context in which work-related video is situated. Personal video satisfies a fundamental emotional need to nurture rich preexisting attachments to other people. Many are willing to put up with draw-backs inherent in the medium to connect to people they miss. In the "pervy" use cases where video supports sexually charged communication between strangers, there is a similar willingness to overlook limitations in the technology because the emotional gain is high. Video-mediated interactions at work, on the other hand, at best satisfy a need to communicate effectively across distances. That need really adheres to a business proposition rather than arising existentially from within the individual. The medium's drawbacks, meanwhile, weigh heavily on the individual.

The most notable drawback is the heightened awareness of appearances that results from the interposition of technology in the interaction between people. Almost all the tools include a "self-view," which interposes a mirror into the con-versation. Two young women describe the experience as follows:

> L: "I turn off the video feature on Skype because I find the fact that I can see the person but we're not in the same room quite creepy.
> M: "Yes, uhm, …"
> L: "You're staring at each other!"
> M: "Well, it's like, well, you're staring at each other, but really they are staring at themselves. Like a mirror. We're not really looking at each other."

We may be used to mirrors in the bathroom, in which we compose our faces for favorable self-inspection, but it is a different proposition to be confronted with a mirror in a social interaction, in which one can see oneself in action. A height-ened sense of "performativity" results. In Erving Goffman's terminology, video-conferencing creates a heightened awareness of "face," not from the inside out, but observed as if from the perspective of another person.[10] This may be somewhat uncomfortable in personal interactions, but in most work environments the dis-comfort is magnified by the twin realities of not being among familiars and of being exposed to greater risk.

Some people, especially those whose jobs typically have a strong performance aspect (sales people, executives), embrace the medium to good effect and put up with the discomfort willingly. An executive described seeing herself on video as a shock: "Every time it's shocking to see myself. There's a moment of, God, do I really look like that? But you get used to it. You do what you have to do." A sales-person with a remote territory, almost all of whose client contacts took place by video conference, explained to me that he had arranged his cubicle to optimize his video performance, having his desk raised so that he could stand during video conferences and make a more animated, personable, and engaged impression on his customers. But for many others, the experience can be uncomfortable to the point of pain, one to avoid whenever possible. One informant, a male informa-tion technology (IT) director in his 50s with a noticeable skin condition, made the point most eloquently when he attributed a great deal of distress to his direct reports, a degree of distress he seemed to feel vividly himself:

"I tell my people not to worry about it. You don't really look like that. It's just a picture. Try not to think about it too much. It's not real. It's not really what you look like. Anyway, when I go to my boss, he doesn't ask me how did everybody look? He asks me, are we making progress? What people look like doesn't make a difference to solving the problem. It doesn't help you get your work done."

In theory, difficult conversations go more smoothly when participants can see each other, especially when they receive the illusion of eye contact. In practice, interlocutors may find themselves transfixed, and even stricken, by externals, very prominently their own.

Videoconferencing dramatizes the participants' professional self-presentation as a performance, as the acting out of a suitable professional persona. This involves both a psychological drama and a social and cultural phenomenon. The individual's performance plays out against a backdrop of often high-stress (localized) performance cultures, where performance is part of a cycle of evaluation and reward (if all goes well) and punishment (if it doesn't). Not only is one's face at stake, but also one's paycheck. This is a climate in which exposure feels risky and unsafe for many. It's what makes being on display so exhausting. In other words, the needs of the larger unit (the company) for better communication and the needs of the individual for safety and avoidance of stressful situations are not well aligned in the videoconferencing experience.

Whereas one significant drawback concerns the representation of self in the video interaction, another drawback concerns the representation of the group. Even with the increase in bandwidth that the video signal can command today, bandwidth limitations still force a display known as "active speaker switching," by which the current speaker is foregrounded, in many tools. In effect, workers can take center stage by their willingness to be assertive.[11] Meeting participants who do not speak may be represented at a much smaller size or may not be represented at all. In effect, the active speaker switching logic overrules videoconferencing participants' conceptions of how people (should) relate to each other professionally. The disjunction may be less jarring in some corners of the translocal ethnoscape of knowledge work than in others,[12] but it is certainly not ideal for technical constraints to dictate group representation and interaction anywhere in the world.

What to do with such findings in the product design context? The product team needs practical advice, not general statements about how disruptive and distracting the videoconferencing experience is for some users or how poorly it matches local ideas of appropriate group dynamics. Working forwards from what is "broken" in the current experience, the ethnographer recommends not only small adjustments that can be implemented immediately but also creates a vision of a future product that more closely matches face-to-face interaction.

A likely short-term recommendation is to downplay the prominence of the "self-view" in the interface. A little more ambitious would be a recommendation to downplay the talking-heads video altogether, in favor of a display optimized for showing documents, small objects such as packaging, or large ones such as whiteboards. Ethnographic observations about cultural differences in group dynamics naturally lead to recommendations to optimize the video tools for appropriate group representation and to optimize differently in different markets. At the same time, the ethnographer must impress upon strategic planners the reasons and urgency of an investment in developing the technology to the point where the self-view is not necessary. That is, if the technology knows how to display the videoconferencing participant to best advantage under varying conditions, then the person can be relieved of the need to check and adjust the display himself and a more natural interaction can then take place in the video channel, to reduce the discomfort that provides a barrier to adoption in the present.

## Coming to Terms with Innovation

The ethnographer's recommendations for product changes usually attach to different time frames in the product lifecycle at the same time, as in the example illustrated here. There are usually two horizons, one referring to an impending release and another referring to a future incarnation of the product. With regard to the near horizon, research questions are highly practical and quite concrete:

- Does this version of the product match the presumed end-user's needs?
- Are end users able to use the interface and the various features provided?

Often these two questions can be adequately answered in the lab and do not require ethnographic study in the individual's own environment. Exceptions concern cases where informants are unable to clearly articulate their own needs, as in the work-related videoconferencing example here, because of a conflict between conscious value judgments and preferences expressed through actual behavior.

With regard to future releases or completely new products, the research questions are usually more difficult and concern the much-discussed mysteries of successful innovation:

- How can the current product be improved; that is, how should it present itself to invite purchase, and what features does it need to have to inspire delight, word-of-mouth advertising, and product loyalty?
- What new products should be made?

Implicit in both is the question of market success. What will consumers buy in sufficient numbers to generate profit, to leapfrog the competition, and to consolidate the brand to support future success? Many companies still attempt to answer these questions without recourse to ethnography, but there is a growing recognition that direct and deep knowledge of (prospective) customers reduces risk in such business decisions. Many "innovation manuals" now emphasize the need to study end-users, whether by academically trained ethnographers, ethnographers who have learned on the job, or simply members of the design and product teams in possession of an inquiring spirit.[13]

The starting point for a product ethnographer tackling the question of product innovation is necessarily current behavior and existing cultural phenomena. In very simple terms, through observation, interviewing, contextual inquiry, and other techniques to gather data about customers, the ethnographer identifies patterns in behavior and meaning relevant to the product in question, as well as the likely customers' value systems and mental models or ways of thinking about the world. Standard ethnographic data gathering and analysis is directly relevant to this endeavor, but a specific focus arises in the context of product innovation around so-called "pain points": any experiences that fall short of delight. Pain points, whether in outcomes or in the steps that must be taken to get there, are especially important because they represent, at least in principle, opportunities for product improvement and, by extension, innovation.

There are in fact situations in which this story accounts quite well for the way a project or some small aspect thereof develops, but it oversimplifies the challenges significantly. For example, fieldwork for an online clothing retailer revealed that while women are comfortable with elaborate classifications of apparel by type, style, and fabric, men generally felt uncomfortable with fine distinctions, because these distinctions presumed a degree of knowledge that they didn't have and didn't think of as desirable to have. As one male informant said:

G: "Sweaters by yarn? What is that? I can't even imagine what it means. By yarn! You're making me shop the way women shop, and I just want a sweater like I had last year. I liked it a lot, and I'd like to buy it again."

Finding a clear pattern of basic categories and simple oppositions among male participants, the research team made a recommendation to simplify the navigation in the online men's store based on a distinction between weekday clothes (for work) and weekend clothes (for leisure) and the highest-level categories (pants, shirts, sweaters, jackets), while maintaining complexity in the women's store.[14]

Not all findings translate so easily into product adjustments. A more representative case may be found in a mobile product that gives people access, via cell phone, to materials stored on one or more laptop or desktop computers: music, photos, movies, documents, and so forth. The first week in the field revealed that only a few participants maintained coherent collections of things on the computer, while the rest had their "stuff" on a variety of devices, including computers in semi-retirement, a range of mobile devices and cameras, and a host of cloud services. Their principal challenge was to remember where to look for things. Having the option to access media stored on a computer obviously isn't much use if you don't consistently store media on the computer. While this is a valuable insight, which may help explain a low rate of adoption, it is not immediately clear what to recommend in terms of an adjustment in the product.

The difficulty derives from the fact that what we see here is emergent behavior, behavior on the move. Not only breakfast is being reorganized in the lives of contemporary Americans. Media habits and preferences are changing at an even faster pace. For much of the twentieth century, the established behavior was to collect media in one place. The proud owner would organize the physical collection nicely for ease of use as well as display. Any media that went digital would in principle receive the same treatment. The intent and desire was to recreate collections in a similar fashion on the computer (or some backup storage device attached to it) sitting in an "office" area at home. In this media world, value and possession are intimately linked, especially in physical objects. Effort expended on managing the collection is part and parcel of the joy of ownership. It is not hard to find people who are squarely in this way of thinking about their digital collections.

The emergent behaviors, on the other hand, are organized around finding and sharing a slightly different class of things: information, experiences, and digital media, first and foremost. Physical possessions are becoming less meaningful and more burdensome among people on the leading edge of these changes, and value is primarily generated not in possession but in discovery, curation, and broadcasting.[15] One aspect of the new model is "awesome sourcing," as one informant described it: "I get credit for finding it. Like, if I find a great recipe, and I share it with my friends, then when they cook it, I get credit. Well, I should get credit." William Gibson described the phenomenon as "an on-going democratization of connoisseurship, in which curatorial privilege is available at every level of society" (Gibson 2012:134).

The new behaviors have arisen from the new ubiquity of information and the new tools offered to help make sense of it. Pain points cluster around anxiety about the possibility of loss—phones are stolen, SD cards are wiped during factory resets, hard drives die, formats become outmoded, sites go down, and other people delete things one counted as part of one's own stuff—and the difficulty and sheer labor of moving media from devices where they are acquired to devices where they can be edited or to "places" where they can safely be stored. There are some solutions that solve for aspects of these pain points, but there aren't any that solve the entire problem, and certainly none that do so delightfully. The opportunity is clear, but the solution is not.

Clay Christensen's distinction between "sustaining innovation" and "disruptive innovation" provides a framework to understand the difference between the two examples (Christensen 1997). In the case of sustaining innovation (such as an improved online apparel shopping experience), we see an established end-user behavior that is being better supported. In the case of disruptive innovation (such as improved personal media management), the new technologies support new behavior. There is certainly no ethnographic observation technique that lets us peer into the future and determine how such new behaviors will evolve. In this example, there is no methodology for determining how the new curatorial consumption model will develop and what solution/s will meet the evolving needs of curatorial consumers. This is not for want of trying. For example, in an effort to get closer to the leading edge, Maria Bezaitis and ken anderson introduced an ethnographic approach they call "Flux" in a recent paper (see Bezaitis and anderson 2011). Characterizing traditional ethnography as being perpetually behind the curve in rapidly changing cultures, they attempt to develop an observational approach that puts the observer where change is happening. However, adjusting one's observational vantage point to better observe those who are making changes does not equate to gaining an ability to make reliable predictions about where the observed emerging behaviors are headed.

To quote William Gibson again, "While science fiction is sometimes good at predicting things, it's seldom good at predicting what those things might actually do to us" (Gibson 2012:15). Unfortunately, there is nothing in the ethnographer's toolkit today that makes him or her any better at predicting how individuals and whole cultures will change as a consequence of the introduction of new technologies. The law of unintended consequences in fact guarantees that the bets are off in the realm of innovations. Scott Berkun makes a similar point when he writes that "not only is the use of an innovation unpredictable after it has been accepted, but the time and motivation for its acceptance is unpredictable as well" (Berkun 2007:148).

To illustrate, let's take another look at the pain points experienced by emerging "curatorial consumers." Tools are already becoming available that try to let them have their cake and eat it too, engaging in high-value curatorial behaviors while outsourcing low-value collection activities to an automated service, so reconstituting ownership for a networked world. Google+ and other services enable automatic uploads to an online album from any networked device. Facebook's new Timeline view presents posts as a collection. Curation tools like Pinterest seek to conflate broadcasting and collection in the same action. Many other examples can be found with little effort. We have no way of knowing whether any of these approaches will become dominant, or whether behavior will simply change more radically, out from under these innovations. Perhaps people will let go of ownership in a more radical way, finding identity and aesthetic order not so much in possession and memories attached to "my stuff" as in the mirror that the social network holds up to them at any given point in time, emphasis shifting from diachronic to synchronic identity. Or perhaps a development we cannot even imagine today will alter the dynamic in even more radical ways.

The failure of observational methods to reliably disclose the future has significant consequences for the product ethnographer. In the first place, the ethnographer needs to reach beyond observation of current patterns of behavior and meaning and adopt some application of a trial-and-error approach that incorporates design activities into the research process. This may take the form of participant brainstorming and other ideation exercises, behavioral prototyping, or other formal co-creation methodologies.[16] The exact methodology used is probably far less important than the introduction of iterations into the research process. If ethnography is to be a valid driver of product innovation, then observation must be taken beyond the problem space—beyond the identification of points of friction between cultural substrate and individual behavior—and into the validation of possible solutions. Iterative approaches allow for testing of cautious predictions, which can be adjusted appropriately if responses are not in line with expectations. Second, even when the ethnographer uses an iterative approach to ground her predictions, a significant dose of caution and humility remains highly salutary.[17] Only time will tell how human behavior will bend to changing times. The only certainty is that the future will not be like the past.

## References

Berkun, Scott
2007 *The Myths of Innovation*. Beijing: O'Reilly.

Bezaitis, Maria, and Ken Anderson
2012 Flux: Changing Social Values and their Value for Business. In *Ethnographic Praxis in Industry Conference 2011 Proceedings* 1:12–17.

Boas, Franz
1962 *Anthropology and Modern Life*. New York: W. W. Norton & Company.

Botsman, Rachel, and Rae Rogers
2010 *What's Mine Is Yours: The Rise of Collaborative Consumption*. New York: Harper Business.

Christensen, Clayton M.
1997 *The Innovator's Dilemma: When New Technologies Cause Great Firms to Fail*. Boston: Harvard Business School Press.

English-Lueck, J. A.
2002 *Cultures@SiliconValley*. Stanford: Stanford University Press.

Gibson, William
2012 *Distrust that Particular Flavor*. New York: G. P. Putnam's Sons.

Goffman, Ervin
1967 *Interaction Ritual: Essays on Face-to-Face Behavior*. Garden City, N.J.: Doubleday.

Guest, Greg, Kathleen M. MacQueen, and Emily E. Namey
2011 *Applied Thematic Analysis*. Los Angeles: Sage Publications.

Halse, Joachim, Eva Brandt, Brendan Clark, and Thomas Binder (eds.)
2010 *Rehearsing the Future*. Copenhagen: The Danish Design School Press.

Hippel, Eric von
2006 *Democratizing Innovation*. Cambridge: MIT Press.

Kelley, Tom, and Jonathan Littman
2001 *The Art of Innovation: Lessons in Creativity from IDEO, America's Leading Design Firm*. New York: Currency/Doubleday.

McKinney, Phil

2012 *Beyond the Obvious: Killer Questions that Spark Game-changing Innovation*. New York: Hyperion.

Miller, Daniel

2008 *The Comfort of Things*. Cambridge, United Kingdom: Polity.

2009 *Anthropology and the Individual: A Material Culture Perspective*. Oxford, United Kingdom: Berg.

Murchison, Julian M.

2010 *Ethnography Essentials: Designing, Conducting, and Presenting your Research*. San Francisco: Jossey-Bass.

Newell, Sue, Maxine Robertson, Harry Scarbrough, and Jackie Swan

2009 *Managing Knowledge Work and Innovation*, second edition. Basingstoke, United Kingdom: Palgrave Macmillan.

Olson, Gary M., and Judith S. Olson

2000 "Distance Matters." *Human-Computer Interaction,* 15: 139-78.

Radka, Rich, and Abby Margolis

2011 Changing Models of Ownership. In *Ethnographic Praxis in Industry Conference 2011 Proceedings* 1:214–228.

Rane, Abhijeet, and Tavishi Agrawal

2011 The Future of Workplaces. GigaOM Pro, March 16, 2011. Available at http://pro.gigaom.com/2011/03/the-future-of-workplaces/. Accessed March 18, 2012.

Sanders, Elizabeth B.-N., and Bo Westerlund

2011 "Experiencing, Exploring, and Experimenting in and with Co-design Spaces." Paper presented at the Nordic Design Research Conference, Helsinki, May 29–31, 2011. Available at http://www.maketools.com/articles-papers/SandersWesterlundNordes2011.pdf. Accessed August 11, 2012.

Squires, Susan

Doing the Work: Customer Research in the Product Development and Design Industry. In *Creating Breakthrough Ideas: The Collaboration of Anthropologists and Designers in the Product Development Industry*, edited by Susan Squires and Bryan Byrne, pp. 102–124. Westport, CT: Bergin & Garvey.

Watts, Duncan J.

2011 *Everything Is Obvious: Once You Know the Answer*. New York: Crown Business.

# Notes

1 "In marketing, a product is anything that can be offered to a market that might satisfy a want or need." See the Wikipedia entry for "Product (business)," http://en.wikipedia.org/wiki/Product_(business), accessed January 7, 2012.

2 In an online comment titled "Does Corporate Ethnography Suck?" Sam Ladner recently summed up a variety of criticisms of corporate ethnography that brand the discipline as trite and stupefying, if not outright deceptive. (See http://ethnographymatters.net/2012/01/13/does-corporate-ethnography-suck-a-cultural-analysis-of-academic-critiques-of-private-sector-ethnography-part-1-of-2/, accessed May 13, 2012.) Business environments typically exert a great deal of pressure on the ethnographer to cut corners, and there are undoubtedly circumstances in which product ethnography has delivered superficial, incomplete, or deceptive findings. Without wishing to argue the case, I assume here that product ethnography, when done carefully, will lead to valid insights, including insights the commissioning business is reluctant to hear.

3   See Squires (2002:105–6) for a mapping of qualitative research methods to different phases of the product lifecycle.

4   See Guest (2011:243) for a description and an illustration of the model.

5   How exactly a positive product experience translates into a purchase is debatable. The situation is complex for any given product and is undoubtedly not the same for different kinds of products. Suffice it to say here that product ethnography is typically only brought to bear when some kind of linkage is assumed to hold true by all parties commissioning and conducting the ethnography.

6   My research was officially based on field interviews and lab studies. However, the observational opportunities within the company, among coworkers using the tools (or not using them), proved invaluable in helping me formulate the questions to ask in field studies, to gain a real understanding of individual decisions and preferences.

7   Interestingly, decision-makers typically believe this more strongly than end-users, given the numbers provided in GigaOM's study "The Future of Workplaces" (Rane and Agrawal 2011). According to the study, 48 percent of decision-makers agreed with the statement "Video calling allows me to collaborate better," whereas only 23 percent of end-users agreed.

8   See for instance Olson and Olson (2000), who argue that "Groups with high common ground and loosely coupled work, with readiness both for collaboration and collaboration technology [i.e., video conferencing, among other technologies], have a chance at succeeding with remote work."

9   This particular example bears directly on the question of appropriate time horizons addressed in the twin chapters "The Value of Rapid Ethnography" and "The Limits to Speed in Ethnography" by Isaacs and Cefkin in this volume. Although some insights into the videoconferencing experience (especially those related to specific features of the user interface) arose after a few observations, the overall character and contours of what makes work-centric videoconferencing different emerged more slowly.

10  In *Interaction Ritual*, Goffman writes, "The term 'face' may be defined as the positive social value a person effectively claims for himself by the line others assume he has taken during a particular contact. Face is an image of self delineated in terms of approved social attributes" (Goffman 1967:5).

11  In some of the videoconferencing tools, this effect is magnified by designs that are organized around creating the illusion of eye contact. While this works well for videoconferences with two participants, it tends to reinforce the spotlight on the most assertive meeting participants in larger meetings, creating a dialogue between them as opposed to a full group interaction.

12  To give just a few domestic examples, in the context of Silicon Valley, individual performance takes place in a setting in which a notion of equal participation governs many people-to-people interactions, and many local participants complain that they wish to see everyone in the meeting at once and at equal size to capture that they are on equal footing. (See English-Lueck [2002] on the expectation of radical equality in Silicon Valley.) Newel et al. make a similar point with their use of the term "adhocracy" to describe knowledge-intensive work: "An adhocracy genuinely de-emphasizes a hierarchical structure" (2009:36). Elsewhere in the United States, where there is more formality and tolerance of the visible manifestation of rank, participants are more likely to wish to "request" a turn to speak by raising their hand and complain that they are invisible under active speaker switching logic.

13  See, for example, Kelley (2001), Berkun (2007), McKinney (2012), and many others. Others argue that a great deal of innovation takes place within end-user communities—what Eric von Hippel (2006) calls the "emerging system of user-centered innovation"—in the form of creative reuse as well as outright product development. A good product ethnographer will be especially alert to any examples of creative reuse.

14   This is not to argue that the organizational change that is required to execute even technologically simple recommendations such as this one is a slam dunk. "Getting traction" for product recommendations is a much discussed challenge among ethnographers in many organizations.

15   Some aspects of the emerging behaviors and mental model have been described in Botsman (2010), especially with regard to changing ideas about the joys and sorrows of owning and caring for physical possessions. As Rich Radka puts it, "In the last 5 years we've seen massive growth in new business models in which people are willing to trade off the right to own a product…for new kinds of social capital" (Radka and Margolis 2011:214).

16   At a talk, Elizabeth Sanders argued that "[l]iving in the future is about co-creation." For a more formal defense of this idea, see Sanders and Westerlund (2011) or Halse et al. (2010).

17   Duncan Watts is particularly informative in his book *Everything is Obvious* (2011) about the ways in which humans tend to overestimate the reliability of their predictions about the future. Product ethnographers in general would do well to read his chapter "The Dream of Prediction" at regular intervals.

Chapter 5

# The Value of Rapid Ethnography

*Ellen Isaacs*

> "We don't have time for that!"
> —*Fortune 500 company client*

## Introduction

In the business world, time is a precious commodity and a tough master. Public companies are scrutinized on a quarterly basis according to their earnings and output. Time is present either explicitly or as an undercurrent in almost every plan and business decision. For ethnographers working in such an environment, fieldwork schedules that once mirrored annual agricultural cycles now must align with the business quarter.

This environment is a far cry from the early days when Margaret Mead and Bronislaw Malinowski were concerned with temporal cycles in nonwestern societies, focusing on seasonal cycles and cultural rights of passage that mark the phases of life (Malinowski 1922; Mead 1928; van Gennep [1909] 1960). With the rise of industrial society, the field's interest in the experience of time began to take on economic concerns as sociologists and anthropologists studied temporal issues within hospitals, factories, and other institutions (Bulmer 1984). Other anthropologists looked at cultural differences in how people orient to time and how strictly they observe schedules (Hall 1983). These studies, conducted within their own culture of university-based research, were carried out in a timescale that matched the academic year.

Today, ethnographers working in corporate settings have to accept the need for speed and adjust their approach. While surely requiring tradeoffs, rapid ethnography brings the ethnographic perspective into organizations in a way that is culturally palatable and gives ethnographers a seat at the table. In corporate settings, ethnographers are rarely used as historians; more frequently, they are asked to be the company's scouting party, to understand consumers' needs, to make sense of their evolving practices, and to explain why those practices matter to the company's strategy and to the design of its products and services.

In this chapter and the one by Melissa Cefkin that follows, we propose a dialogue about the nature of time: what it causes us to do, how it shapes our work, and

*Advancing Ethnography in Corporate Environments: Challenges and Emerging Opportunities,* edited by Brigitte Jordan, 92–107. ©2013 Left Coast Press Inc. All rights reserved.

the compromises it engenders. I begin by describing how I used rapid ethnography in three projects, each with its own analytic focus, methods, and lessons learned. Cefkin responds with a thoughtful discussion of what we may be losing in our ethnographic practice and our findings when we conduct research quickly. She provocatively asks, "What are the limits to speed?" Together, these two papers deal with the realities of practicing ethnography in today's fast-paced business world.

## The Value of Rapid Ethnography

Several times I have worked with clients who were refocusing their product concept to reach the right audience after having missed with an earlier attempt. I suggested spending a month or two directly observing people in their target market so we could understand what they're doing and what they need. Their response: "We don't have time for that!" And yet, as long as three years later, those clients were still searching for the right product concept. I believe if they had invested a handful of weeks in rapid ethnography, they would have saved themselves years of misdirected work.

Still, it's understandable that managers would feel uncomfortable taking time to do open-ended ethnographic observations. You don't know what you'll find, and there's no guarantee you'll have that "a-ha!" insight that will transform your thinking. But in the last two years, I've worked on several ethnography projects that generated specific, long-lasting benefits to the team in a short period of time, so I know it can be done. In fact, I've yet to work on a project that didn't have at least two of the following outcomes:

- Steer the project away from an unproductive direction.
- Refocus the project toward solving a clear, demonstrated problem.
- Open management's eyes to problems or patterns that had been hidden to them, sometimes with simple solutions.
- Inspire technology ideas that could solve an observed problem in a new way.

The following three case studies explain how we generated these benefits. They took from five to ten weeks to complete, with participation from one to four ethnographers (some of them part-time). In the first case, a study of parking enforcement, our client came to us with a specific product concept and wanted to use ethnography to inform its design. In the second case, a hospital had the general idea of supporting nurses and wanted us to identify specific problem areas where technology could assist them. In the third case, a client had the broad agenda of identifying new product opportunities in the area of mobile communication and used ethnography to discover gaps in the current set of offerings to generate ideas. These examples show the use of rapid ethnography for this wide range of uses, from informing the design of a specific product to identifying an opportunity for a new product concept.

EXAMPLE 1: Parking Enforcement

Our client for this project provides services to municipal transportation departments, such as the processing of parking ticket and meter payments. They had the idea of generating a system that would guide parking enforcement officers to potential parking violations to improve their efficiency and increase city revenue. Some cities are already experimenting with this approach by installing systems that have sensors embedded in parking spaces so they can detect when the spaces are occupied. If a meter is not paid, a handheld app guides officers to the parking spot for ticketing (e.g., SFPark in San Francisco, LAExpress Park in Los Angeles, and ParkSmart in New York City). But many cities can't afford such sensor-based systems, so our client wanted to (1) see if we could use historical data on parking violations to predict which blocks are likely to have violations at specific times, and (2) understand parking officers' common practices to help guide the design of the system.

While an engineer on the team ran the analytics on historical parking data, I shadowed three parking enforcement officers (PEOs) in two cities. One city was already using the sensor-based system, and I observed one of its parking officers for half of a shift and interviewed her supervisors the rest of the day. I also accompanied two other PEOs for a full shift each in a different city that didn't have sensors. I video-recorded the PEOs as they drove around looking for parking violations and when they got out of the car to issue tickets or check the meters. As we drove around, I chatted with them to learn more about their work and their perspective on it.

The day after each outing, I wrote up detailed notes based on memory to give the rest of the team quick feedback on the visit. Then I watched the videos and took more careful notes about the PEOs' activities. As I did so, I generated a log or loose transcript of their activity, noting the time and a brief description of what they were doing throughout their shifts. The following is an example of my log:

| Time code | Activity |
|---|---|
| 6:45 | Gets out to look at receipt in windshield to check if it says 8:51 or 8:31, couldn't tell from reflection |
| 7:26 | Gets out to check meter, finds violation, writes a ticket (#5). (Takes 1 min 35 sec) |
| 9:20 | I ask about expectations for tickets, he says depends on beat. Marking beats take more time to mark. In meter beats, you're focused on meter violations but if you run across other violations, you'll get them. |

TABLE 5.1 Sample Parking Enforcement Log

I create these logs primarily as a mechanism to help me truly understand the activity, and secondarily as a way to quickly find key events when I go back to create a video podcast (discussed later) of my findings.

As I reviewed the videos, I was struck—as I always am—at how much I had missed during the original observation and how much more became visible to me through the videos. After having spent a full day with the PEOs, I was now able to understand more about the reasoning behind their activities, especially in the morning when I was just getting a sense of their job. For example, one officer occasionally got out of his car to check the meters on foot rather than scanning them as he slowly drove by. I later realized he usually walked when he was monitoring diagonal parking spaces where it was harder to see the meters from his car and the cars are parked more densely than they are in parallel parking zones.

Spending the time with those videos also helped me realize several inefficiencies in the way they were enforcing parking; inefficiencies that are currently necessary but could be removed or reduced with the right technology solution. Since I am trained primarily as a user experience designer and secondarily as an ethnographer, I'm always looking for the obstacles people put up with and the ways they work around the system to accomplish their goals, since those practices tend to spark ideas about how technology can help them. These insights almost always happen when I'm reviewing the video rather than during the original observation period, since at that point I'm completely focused on trying to understand what the participant is doing from their point of view while also making sure I'm capturing the right activity with my camera. It's only later that I can step back and evaluate what I saw; without the video, much of the detail necessary to generate novel insights is lost.

After discussing my analysis with my team, I produced a 12-minute video podcast that summarized what I had learned and pointed out opportunities for

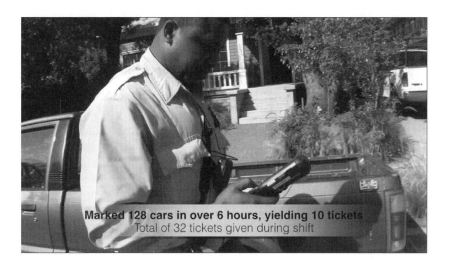

Marked 128 cars in over 6 hours, yielding 10 tickets
Total of 32 tickets given during shift

FIGURE 5.1. Screenshot of video podcast describing findings from observations of parking enforcement.

generating technology improvements (Figure 5.1). I posted the podcast to a secure website and sent a link to our clients, who were able to watch at their convenience. We have found that producing these short video summaries of our findings greatly increases the impact of our work, since the videos show rather than tell what we learned and people find them more engaging than slide sets or documents (Glasnapp and Isaacs 2011). In addition, people seem inclined to forward the link to others in their organization, which helps build a broader base of support for any decisions based on the data.

One of the key findings was that, in the city that already had sensors installed in the parking spaces, the PEO and supervisors were finding the system extremely frustrating and felt that it was *reducing* rather than improving their productivity. I observed the officer as she chased down one "violation" after another only to find that the car had a handicapped placard, or the person had already paid, or there was no car in the parking spot. Her supervisors called these "ghost violations" and complained bitterly about them. The system was handling cars with handicapped placards by having the officers mark them as such, which was supposed to remove the "violation" from the system, but after a while those cars reappeared, so the PEO had to go back to check and mark them again. She wasn't sure why she saw other ghost violations, but she suspected the driver paid after the violation appeared on her screen but the system didn't update quickly enough. Or the meters were miscalibrated. Whatever the reasons, it was clear the system was a hindrance, and in fact she was delighted that we now had video to prove it.

Our client was surprised to hear about these difficulties. Surely the system could be tuned to address these problems, which may have been technical glitches. But it had been in place for about a year and still wasn't running smoothly. It became clear that if a system *with* sensors in the street was creating such frustration and inefficiency, it was less likely that a system based on probabilities from historical data would be successful. The outcome of the analytics on the historical data were consistent with this conclusion: even with seven years of data, most blocks didn't have enough data at enough times to predict violations with reasonable levels of accuracy. So at least in the near term, the study steered the client away from spending a lot of time developing a system that was likely to be ineffective.

Beyond that, the study also suggested several alternative areas for innovation that would solve problems I had observed. One of these concerned enforcement of "marking beats," areas where cars can park for free for a limited amount of time (typically four-hour, two-hour, or one-hour zones). These areas don't have meters, so to enforce them officers have to drive by once to mark the cars (which they sometimes do with chalk but more often by entering license plates into their handheld device), and then return after the right amount of time to identify the cars that were still there. They also have to arrange their time so they can return to the right blocks at the right times. This two-pass effort could be reduced if there were some way for the cars to "know" when they arrived and communicate it to a

PEO's device as the officer drove by. PEOs could then cruise by any street at any time to detect violations.

Our engineering research team held a brainstorming meeting to come up with ideas to enable parking officers to know when cars had arrived. Some were shorter-term with necessary limitations, and others offered greater benefits but required innovations in materials and systems. Both these directions were useful to our client and to our research team. The important point is that the ingenuity of all the smart people in the room could build on my observations to find ways to address a real problem that, if solved, would have a large impact, rather than imagining a possible problem that may not exist or have much impact if resolved.

Of course, these observations by no means gave us a full picture of all that's involved in parking enforcement, and we could make no claims about whether the practices in these two cities were representative of other cities. But they certainly made the client aware of problems with the original project plan, and they identified at least some opportunities for future technology development. Also, the client's company worked with parking offices in many cities, so by sharing the video with others in the company, we were able to verify that our characterization of basic enforcement practices was accurate (in particular about marking beats), while also noting ways that it varied across cities.

This whole project took five weeks from the time I observed the first parking officer to the time I released the video summarizing my findings, including air travel to one of the cities. I was the only one doing the ethnographic work, and I was even splitting my time between this and a secondary project. To be fair, additional time was spent setting up the visits and initially understanding the clients' goals. But since they had good access to the city parking offices, the visits were set up quickly and were constrained only by my schedule.

## EXAMPLE 2: Hospital Nursing

The goal of this project was to develop technology to support nurses in a hospital setting. We partnered with a hospital network and started with the goal of helping nurses *plan and schedule* the many patient care activities that need to be interleaved among many patients. The hospital gave us access to several of its nurses and supervisors so we could get a deeper understanding of how they currently plan their tasks. After conducting a few workshops to understand their jobs, we arranged for three of us to observe three nurses during their shifts on the same day, each of them from a different department. (Two of us were ethnographers and one was a conscientious engineer with ethnographic training.) We video-shadowed the nurses during their whole shifts, occasionally asking clarifying questions when it wasn't disruptive to their work. Since we had already met with them a few times and built up a good rapport, they were relatively comfortable narrating their activities and thought processes for us. Although the two ethnographers recorded continuously, the engineer only captured snippets of video on his phone whenever something of interest was happening. We hated to lose the opportunity to capture that nurse's entire day on video, but we considered it a bonus that the engineer wanted to participate in the shadowing and so settled for the less-than-complete data.

Video recording was tricky because of the hospital's strict privacy requirements, but we managed to get some of the patients' consent; when we could not, we avoided recording the patient and focused only on the nurse. Since we sometimes captured their medical data on computer screens or paper, we postprocessed the video to blur out any such data from patients who hadn't granted permission.

As it turned out, the engineer's abbreviated video recordings had some advantages. Within just a few days of doing the observations, the engineer put together and presented to the team a set of slides that communicated his main observations and showed several short video clips he had recorded. Although his analysis was not deep or thorough, the team appreciated getting a preliminary report shortly after the visit that gave them a sense of what we had learned. After a few weeks, the ethnography team followed up with a more extensive analysis.

During those weeks, the ethnography team went through the continuous footage we had captured of the other two nurses' shifts, again generating detailed transcripts similar to the parking officer logs. A sample is shown here.

| Time code | Activity |
|---|---|
| NURSE'S STATION (Pages Dr. O for Mr. M's potassium) | |
| 1:02:19 | Decides to page Dr. O since she hasn't heard back from her in over a half hour. Has to look up number on computer. |
| 1:02:28 | Calls someone to ask for Dr. O's pager number, writes it on her nurse's brain (a piece of paper summarizing key information for that shift) |
| 1:02:58 | Goes to landline phone to page Dr. O |
| 1:03:11 | Hangs up phone, says, "Now we just wait till they call." |
| **Memory** | **Waiting on Dr. O to return page** |
| HALLWAY (Transition period) | |
| 1:03:21 | Walks over to sink to wash her hands thoroughly |
| 1:04:00 | Puts bandaid on her finger |
| 1:04:09 | She hears someone saying, "Oh, there's the doctor." |
| 1:05:08 | Logs out of computer and gets ready to do med pass |
| 1:05:12 | Tells someone (who?) if Dr. O calls to grab her |
| 1:05:19 | Puts on medical sash |

TABLE 5.2 Sample Hospital Nursing Log

In this log, I grouped the entries into chunks and labeled each one by their location and a short summary of the main activity for that period of time. I added the bold "Memory" note later, after we got interested in how much the nurse was keeping track of in memory. I went back through the logs to note each time a new item got added to her mental list, and when she could remove it (when the task got done).

For this project, we decided to create a series of edited video podcasts, each of which told the story of one patient care "vignette" as it unfolded over time, such as calling a patient issue to a doctor's attention, tracking the progress of medication being prescribed and filled, and then giving it to the patient. We clipped together the bits of video that showed intermittent progress toward completing the task and narrated the story. In addition, we turned our observations about excessive memory load into a "cognitive load timeline" that showed all the tasks handled by one of the nurses on her shift, categorized by type of task, showing how long they took to complete (see Figure 5.2).

What emerged was a clear finding that the nurses were spending a lot of their time simply tracking the status of many ongoing tasks that required coordination among other people, often prodding or unblocking those people so they could carry out the next step in the process. For example, early in her shift, the nurse noted that a patient's potassium level was low. Over the next hour or so, she made several attempts to notify the doctor, first sending a text message, then paging her, and finally corralling her in the hallway. The doctor was about to visit another patient so she said she would soon write a prescription. The nurse kept monitoring the "Pyxis room" (where the pharmacy dropped off medications), but each time she didn't see the potassium-lidocaine mix that should have arrived. Later, when she happened to see a pharmacy tech delivering meds, she asked if it had arrived, but still no luck. At that point, she dug around through multiple screens in the electronic medical record system and discovered that the doctor had prescribed pure potassium, not the mix she had been expecting, and the pharmacy had delivered it a while ago. She had just been looking in the wrong place. The nurse immediately went to give the patient the medicine—three and a half hours after she'd originally noticed the problem.

This was just one episode among many where the nurse had to monitor the task to make sure it got done—all going on in parallel. Keeping track of all these tasks was a heavy cognitive burden, and we saw several times when this nurse didn't complete patient comfort tasks, such as getting an extra blanket or returning a call from a patient's relative. If she couldn't do it immediately, she lost track of the task among the many higher-priority medical activities she was tending to.

We also noticed that the nurses spent a lot of time tracking down phone numbers. At the beginning of each shift, the hospital issued most personnel a mobile phone, to be returned at shift's end so they could be sanitized. Every time the nurses had to reach someone, they had to call the central switchboard, look up

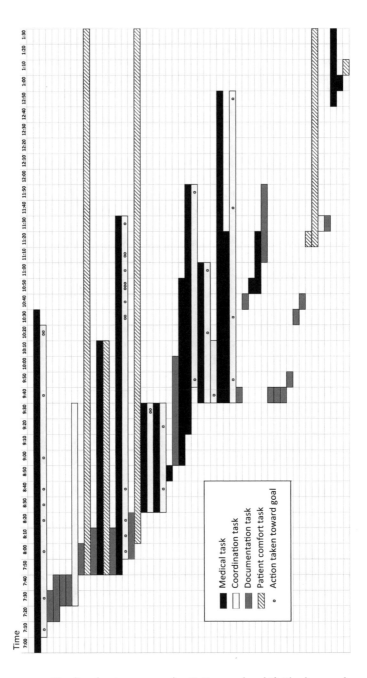

FIGURE 5.2. Timeline showing one nurse's activities over her shift. The diagram shows that the nurse is keeping track of and communicating about many activities across multiple patients all at the same time, leaving little time or mental capacity for patient comfort tasks, such as getting a blanket or returning a call from a patient's relative. As a result, if she couldn't do a patient care task immediately, it often didn't get done.

the number on a piece of paper if it was nearby, or ask someone. Whenever they were asked to get back to someone, the nurses asked for the person's extension and wrote it down on a piece of paper; whenever they made a request of someone else, they provided their number. It was a minor inconvenience, but it caused frequent delays and added up to a meaningful amount of their precious time.

Toward the end of the analysis phase, we met with the nurses and a supervisor and later the management team to show them some of the video vignettes and to discuss our analysis and conclusions. We find it effective to conduct such reviews, since it helps us avoid making unwarranted conclusions based on data that might be unrepresentative of their practices over the long term. The nurse supervisor said that even though she was on the floor with the nurses, she had no idea how much they were keeping track of in their heads. She was also astonished to learn how their phone policy was causing such inefficiencies; she was receptive to the idea of assigning people the same number on every shift. The management team, which wanted nurses to spend more time in the patients' rooms, was deeply impressed by the amount of time the nurses had to spend out of the room to facilitate many of the in-room tasks.

As a result of this analysis, the project shifted its focus toward helping nurses keep track of ongoing *coordination* tasks rather than helping them plan and schedule upcoming tasks, which they were doing with relative ease. This was a profound shift, and yet it was clear to everyone that the data supported it. The team is currently discussing how it can best support coordination among multiple hospital roles and free up nurses to use more of their cognitive capacity for solving patient issues instead of tracking task progress. The ethnographic data is playing an important role in guiding this thinking.

Again, we cannot conclude that our findings generalize to other hospitals or even all types of nursing in that hospital. It's also more than likely that we missed other opportunities for supporting nurse activity. But by showing the videos and our analysis to the nurses and the hospital team, we confirmed that we had accurately captured at least one important part of the story. The most senior nurse on the executive team said to us, "Your knowledge of nursing is light-years ahead of where it was when we started in just a few short months." As a bonus, the nurses were gratified that our analysis made their management aware of how hard they worked to overcome routine obstacles.

This ethnographic work was part of a longer-term project that involves prototype design and development, and our involvement lasted many months. However, the key observation and analysis activities described here were carried out over a two-month period by our three-member team. The initial workshops with the nurses served to establish a relationship with them and gave us a basic understanding of their work, and the one-day shadowing event and the subsequent analysis work revealed the details of the nurses' day and yielded the insights about their cognitive load.

EXAMPLE 3: Mobile Communication

For this project, our client was a consumer electronics company that had the open-ended goal of discovering an opportunity for a product concept involving "mobile telepresence": something that would support people who wished to stay connected to friends and family while moving among many locations throughout the day. There were no guarantees we would uncover new discoveries: indeed, this domain is crowded with technology and has been well researched by both academics and businesses (Grinter and Eldridge 2003; Ito and Okabe 2005; Kirk et al. 2010; Ling and Yttri 2002; Nardi et al. 2000; O'Hara et al. 2006; Okabe 2004). To increase our chances, we attempted a method that as far as we knew had not been tried before. We identified four small groups of people who like to stay in touch and we video-shadowed each group: not just from one person's point of view, but from each member's simultaneously. We arranged for a different researcher to accompany and videorecord each group member over the same period of time so we could see each person's perspective as they connected, engaged, and disconnected over time. There were four of us involved in this project, two full-time and two part-time, and we spent about 10 weeks doing the shadowing and analysis (not including a preliminary phase in which we helped the client choose a domain of study and identified appropriate participants). One member of the client's organization joined us throughout the whole process so he could learn our methodology firsthand.

There were certain logistical issues in video-shadowing in this way, but we were pleasantly surprised at how well it came off. We were able to video record our participants in many public places, including a farmer's market, restaurants and coffee shops, grocery stores, downtown streets, and a department store, as well as in their homes. Only once were we asked to stop recording (in the department store), but we were able to get a manager's approval once we explained our purpose. We got written permission from people who interacted substantially with our participants, and asked for verbal permission from those who spoke with them briefly (such as a waiter or sales clerk).

We wound up with 48 hours of recordings (from 10 people's points of view), so we had to triage. Each researcher scanned through their video to clip episodes of interest for supporting mobile telepresence: cases where participants had problems connecting and sharing, interesting ways they engaged with one another, and so on. We quickly previewed these videos as a team and selected those that seemed most promising for further analysis. For those, we transcribed the conversations, this time in greater detail using a more formal notation. We also clipped the same sequence from the other participants' points of view and synchronized the videos so we could see one video with multiple views in separate windows (see Figure 5.3). The group then met to further analyze those videos and transcripts, discussing patterns across interactions. After we'd shadowed our first group, we held a workshop with the client to give them an early sense of the data, and then we continued with the final three observations.

FIGURE 5.3 These videos, showing three sisters on a three-way phone call, were combined to create one video showing all three points of view at once.

After an intensive two months of work, we identified a phenomenon we dubbed "channel blending," which can be thought of as the opposite of multitasking (Isaacs et al. 2012). We saw small groups of participants, often with several of them in one location and several in one or more remote locations, using multiple devices to carry on one integrated conversation that often included video, music, and/or data (such as their game-playing activities or even their sleep cycles). Rather than splitting their attention among many conversations over different channels (multitasking), people were *blending* the channels together to have one coherent conversation that spanned local and remote spaces.

Yet most of the technologies they used were designed to connect only two people (phone calls, texting, video chat) or large groups of people (Facebook, Twitter, discussion forums), and all of those technologies assumed everyone was in a separate space, alone, using a single device. There seemed to be a clear opportunity for a technology to support small, consistent groups of people (maybe three to six), designed with the assumption that some people may be in the same physical location while some are remote, and that they want to blend together content from multiple devices. We saw a number of variations on this theme, and at the end of the project we had a final workshop where we showed the client many videos and discussed their implications. On the basis of this study, our client initiated an entirely new project to support one of the scenarios included in the broader phenomenon of channel blending.

This project was the biggest of the three discussed here, as it involved intensive work from two of us and substantial work from the part-timers for about 10 weeks. In that time we were able to identify a fundamental need that wasn't being met even with the many technology options available. The finding opened up many possibilities for future product concepts, which could have far-reaching implications for a relatively small upfront investment.

Again, we can't be sure how common channel blending is, but our client was now in a position to have its large consumer research department apply its well-established methods to identify the consumer group(s) that have this need, determine its frequency, and test the product concepts they generated to address this need.

## Conclusion

Time is always a concern for clients who are under pressure to produce products that will succeed in the market. Yet in all these cases, the impact of the ethnographic work had long-lasting effects that more than justified the few months of effort (which was sometimes done in parallel with the rest of the team's activities). In the parking and nursing studies, the clients avoided spending a lot of time and resources developing a solution that was not likely to have success (parking) or great impact (nursing), and were steered in a more productive direction. In the mobile communication study, the client became aware of a gap in the market that offered opportunities for multiple product concepts that could be developed over the next several years.

We were able to produce these results in a short amount of time for several reasons:

- **TEAMWORK.** All the ethnographers who participated in these studies are highly trained and have a lot of experience extracting findings from observational data to inform technology development. Our backgrounds are in sociology, anthropology, and psychology, and we combined our approaches to get the benefit of our diverse training. Beyond that, our clients also contributed to our success. In the parking and nursing studies, the clients were in a position to give us access to key personnel to observe, and those participants were generous in sharing their work experience with us. In the mobile communications study, the client demonstrated its strong commitment to the project by dedicating one of its members to participate full-time in the project and by actively participating in interim workshops that guided our focus of attention. Indeed, all of the clients showed commitment and openness to the process, whatever it might reveal.
- **FOCUS.** Each study focused on a specific type of activity with the goal of identifying opportunities for technology and design constraints. We did not attempt to gain a complete understanding of the underlying cultural norms or the larger significance of our participants' practices. While no doubt fascinating, that type of study would have been impractical to complete in a short timeframe. The benefit of having a narrow goal is that it helps you triage and exclude so you can focus on the data that is most useful for your purposes.
- **RELIANCE ON VIDEO DATA.** We used video as our primary data source, analyzed it in a systematic way, and based our findings directly on evidence captured in the video. This is notable because people sometimes assume that you cannot afford the time to analyze video in a short-term project; instead, they rely on their notes and impressions to form conclusions and use video to illustrate them to the client. By going over the video immediately after recording it, we consistently noticed many rich and subtle activities that were lost on us during our initial observations. There is simply too much to notice at one time. It was through the systematic review of the video that we generated our most compelling insights and built up evidence for our findings, allowing us to tell a convincing story to the client.
- **STRONG, REGULAR COMMUNICATION.** We took conscious steps to communicate frequently—internally with the rest of the team as well as with the client— rather than delivering results at the end. We quickly generated preliminary results soon after doing the observations to give the client confidence that interesting findings were likely, and in some cases to prepare them for findings that challenged the project goals. We then followed those up with more thorough analyses based on video data. In addition to showing our results in

a one-time presentation, in some cases we generated video podcasts that gave the client direct experience with the data and laid out the case for our conclusions. More important, these standalone narrated movies increased the impact of our findings because the client could review them on their own time and share them with others in their organization. Even months later, some of our clients are still showing the videos to their partners and collaborators to get buy-in for the direction suggested by our research.

- LIMITATIONS OF TIME. Still, there's no doubt there are limitations to rapid ethnography. If you spend relatively short periods of time doing intensive observations and analysis, you cannot expect to gain a deep understanding of the many facets of a complex activity, you cannot be sure your findings are representative of a broader market, and you might base conclusions on a distorted picture of the activity you're observing. It's admittedly frustrating to have such rich data and not have the time to delve into it more deeply to gain a richer understanding and uncover a wider range of findings. Still, there are ways to mitigate some of the limitations mentioned. In the nurse study, we validated our findings with the participating nurses as well as their supervisors and upper management. In the parking study, we checked our conclusions with others in the client's organization who had experience with other cities' parking departments. In the mobile communication study, the client planned to use traditional consumer research methods to verify the need for the product concepts they were developing based on the outcome of our study.

By the end of these projects, all the clients felt their "leap of faith" by investing in ethnography had paid off. In fact, the parking study was the client's second engagement with us after they had seen the value from an earlier short-term study. The head of the hospital management team said his team was deeply impressed with the findings, and the consumer company is working to incorporate a version of our ethnographic methods into their own suite of research tools.

Companies that want to be competitive in industries with rapidly evolving products cannot waste time pursuing unproductive strategies. It pays to spend a little time up front to save time later. In fact, it seems to me that such companies don't have time *not* to do these types of observational studies.

# References

Bulmer, Martin
    1984 *The Chicago School of Sociology: Institutionalization, Diversity, and the Rise of Sociological Research.* Chicago: University of Chicago Press.

Glasnapp, James, and Ellen Isaacs
    2011 No More Circling around the Block: Evolving a Rapid Ethnography and Podcasting Method To Guide Innovation in Parking Systems. *Proceedings of Ethnographic Praxis in Industry Conference (EPIC)* 1:190–213.

Grinter, Rebecca, and Margery Eldridge
    2003 Wan2tlk?: Everyday Text Messaging. *Proceedings of Computer Human Interaction*
    441–448.

Hall, Edward T.
    1983 *The Dance of Life: The Other Dimension of Time.* New York: Anchor Books.

Isaacs, Ellen, Margaret M. Szymanski, Yutaka Yamauchi, James Glasnapp, and Kyohei Iwamoto
    2012 Integrating Local and Remote Worlds through Channel Blending. *Proceedings of
    Computer Supported Cooperative Work, ACM* 617–626.

Ito, Mimi, and Daisuke Okabe
    2005 Technosocial Situations: Emergent Structurings of Mobile Email Use. In *Personal,
    Portable, Pedestrian: Mobile Phones in Japanese Life*, edited by M. Ito, M. Matsuda, and D.
    Okabe, pp. 257–273. Cambridge: MIT Press.

Kirk, David, Abigail Sellen, and Xiang Cao
    2010 Home Video Communication: Mediating 'Closeness.' *Proceedings of Computer Supported
    Cooperative Work* 135–144.

Ling, Rich, and Birgitte Yttri
    2002 Hyper-coordination via Mobile Phones in Norway. In *Perpetual Contact: Mobile
    Communication, Private Talk, Public Performance*, edited by J. Katz and M. Aakhus, pp.
    170–192. Cambridge, United Kingdom: Cambridge University Press.

Malinowski, Bronislaw
    1922 *Argonauts of the Western Pacific: An Account of Native Enterprise and Adventure in the
    Archipelagoes of Melanesian New Guinea.* London: Routledge.

Mead, Margaret
    1928 *Coming of Age in Samoa.* New York: William Morrow & Company.

Nardi, Bonnie, Steve Whittaker, and Erin Bradner
    2000 Interaction and Outeraction: Instant Messaging in Action. *Proceedings of Computer
    Supported Cooperative Work* 79–88.

O'Hara, Kenton, Alison Black, and Matthew Lipson
    2006 Everyday Practices with Mobile Video Telephony. *Proceedings of Computer Human
    Interaction* 871–880.

Okabe, Daisuke
    2004 Emergent Social Practices, Situations and Relations through Everyday Camera Phone
    Use. Paper presented at the Mobile Communication and Social Change Conference, October
    18–19, Seoul, Korea. Available at http://www.itofisher.com/mito/archives/okabe_seoul.pdf.
    Accessed August 21, 2012.

van Gennep, Arnold
    (1909) 1960 *The Rites of Passage* [Les Rites de Passage]. London, Routledge.

Chapter 6

# The Limits to Speed in Ethnography

*Melissa Cefkin*

> Attention to the micro-practices slows you down, so let's slow down.
> —*Paul Rabinow et al.*

## Introduction

At the intersection of ethnographic work and business enterprise, researchers are actively experimenting with innovative ways to produce and advance knowledge and are using these experiments to address concrete social phenomena. Examples of this surge are many, including novel forms of data gathering (e.g., "social listening"), participation (e.g., crowdsourcing), and analysis (e.g., integrating text-mined caches of Big Data together with interview and observational data).

Is there something about doing ethnographic work in business contexts that gives rise to this flourishing of experimentation? One could argue that as relentless seekers of process improvements and as purveyors of "the new," businesses are particularly encouraging sites in which to try out new ways of doing things. But just as important, I suspect, are the *constraints* imposed by the business context. Expectations about how work should be performed and the role it should play in shaping business actions abound. Businesses expect it to produce results that inform specific areas of decision-making by generating insight, recommendations, or proposed solutions that are "actionable," often by others. This expectation puts a premium on their specificity, clarity, and portability of results.

Invariably, when it comes to expectations about work, speed matters. Decision-making often moves quickly and may be framed by predetermined cycles (e.g., fiscal quarters). Designs must be developed, tested, and implemented within the terms of a predefined product roadmap (e.g., 18 months) around which the organization may already be staffed and tooled. Policies may need to be clarified and deployed within mandated time frames. Such constraints give rise to an imperative for speed in ethnography.

These constraints have proven to be generative for the ethnographic enterprise. Ethnographers and anthropologists have entered and had a significant impact in corporate environments because of their willingness to work on terms not fully of their own choosing, and there is much to be celebrated in these developments.

*Advancing Ethnography in Corporate Environments: Challenges and Emerging Opportunities,* edited by Brigitte Jordan, 108–121. ©2013 Left Coast Press Inc. All rights reserved.

But it is also important to ask what is at stake in these changing forms of ethnographic work. In this chapter, I reflect on some basic tenets of anthropological ethnographic practice and the distinctive kind of knowledge produced through ethnography as they collide with the limits of speed.

## From Time to Temporality

In their pursuit to perform ethnographic work under tight deadlines, researchers have focused on techniques for rapid data gathering. As Isaac demonstrates (this volume), it is not uncommon for a business ethnographer to count hours and days in the field rather than months and years on any given project. The complete arc of a project, from research definition through solution design and prototyping, may be a matter of weeks, and is probably only rarely more than a few months.

What is going on in these spans of time? From within the practice, one common way of defining what happens is in terms of the phases or steps of the project. From this perspective, then, it is the logic of the project, from definition through data gathering through results, that guides the shape of the work and the allotment of time (a matter I will return to again later). But what if we shift the frame of reference from the logic of the project to the state of the problem or phenomenon itself? A second perspective is the temporal dimension of experience significant to the participants of the settings under investigation. What categories of time are relevant to them? What social and cultural rhythms and cycles mark time differently from one context to the next? A third perspective I call the "time of ethnographic understanding." This is the temporal experience of the ethnographer and, in particular, the time that is required to achieve meaningful social and cultural understanding.

These are questions of *temporality*, of the nature and dimensions of time specific to different people, concepts, and settings. Each of these temporalities illuminates different considerations about the nature of ethnographic work in business contexts and about the kind of knowledge it produces (a set of considerations paralleled by Denny [this volume] in her exploration of the practices and languages of ethnographic theorizing in corporate practice). And each should be considered in thinking about what is at stake in changing forms of research. In light of trends towards greater rapidity, we need to reconcile the ontologically significant temporalities at play in applied business ethnographic work with the demands of these work contexts. My aim is not to argue that corporate ethnographic studies need lengthy and slow to be of value. Not only would that be a foolhardy stance for a practitioner of corporate ethnography such as me to take, it would be a misunderstanding of the constructed nature of research efforts of any kind. It could also be proven patently wrong, as rapid studies have and will continue to produce valuable results (see Isaacs, this volume). However, I do wish to use the lens of time to emphasize the question of what makes ethnographic understanding distinctive in the corporate context, and will suggest that as ethnographers, we in particular must pay attention to the ways in which constructs of time matter.

## The Temporality of Ethnographic Understanding

A key promise of ethnographic work in business is to illuminate ways in which people living in various contexts and conditions (for example, workers in a corporation, people in potential markets, or users of products) understand and interact with the world. Based on this ethnographic analysis, businesses expect to determine how they can best engage to realize the opportunities identified in the analysis, from driving new innovation to improving the design of a product to avoiding missteps in a new strategic direction. In a way, rapid ethnography holds the promise of Cliffs Notes,[1] providing informed but quick access to the important parts of the perspectives meaningful to those choices.

But how do ethnographers know which are the important parts? It may seem relatively easy to render quickly a descriptive account of what is going on, of what is seen and heard. But it can be quite difficult, in fact, given the multiple levels of granularity and various positions worthy of attention. And it can take much longer to understand what is *significant* about what is going on "because what's going on is not obvious and often not quite what is being talked about explicitly" (Rabinow et al. 2008:95). Rabinow, participating in a rich dialogue about doing anthropology of the "here and now," or the contemporary,[2] continues, "[a]lthough at times people do what they are doing and can talk about it quite eloquently. Identifying what is significant can't be done quickly, it seems, or at least there is no rapid means of guaranteeing that one is correct in one's assessment" (Rabinow et al. 2008:95). Gluesing's unpacking of the way language in interaction unfolded over a period of time to create, ultimately, a breakthrough in a team's global practice (this volume) suggests just that. Even when participants speak eloquently about their experiences and the topic at hand, the aim of the ethnographer's analysis is to get at both broader and deeper social and cultural patterns and meanings.

Ethnography is founded on some core underlying perspectives. It is profoundly empirical, aiming to build understanding from what is seen, heard, and experienced rather than seeking to validate or confirm a priori assumptions. Although it emerged from the disciplines most often considered the most "humanistic" of the social sciences (namely anthropology), it also adheres to scientific principles and practices, looking for patterns, finding points of comparison, and testing and reexamining understandings. These practices, in turn, require enough data to identify patterns and recognize variations. As the anthropological lens is focused on lived experience, on the everyday unfolding of people's social and cultural lives, what counts as "enough" data is a body of information that reveals the shifting nuance and experience of the everyday. An understanding of what is significant—culturally, internal to the people and sites under consideration—rests on these principles.

The temporality of ethnographic understanding plays out both at micro and macro levels. Let me illustrate with a couple of examples from my own work.

## Micro Temporality: Seeing Variations in Practice

I was involved in a team ethnographic project to examine and understand how a whole division operated through its headquarters and branch offices. As the services division of Xerox, Xerox Business Services (XBS) provided outsourced document production services—running the copy, print, and sometimes mailroom services inside other organizations. This project was being conducted in the context of a corporate "change initiative" led by the division's human resources and learning and training offices and focused on employee engagement and empowerment.[3] Our team from the Institute for Research on Learning (IRL) was there to provide a systemic assessment of the division (Aronson et al. 1995): to build a picture of life inside the division from the ground up. We organized our research team so that two researchers resided full-time at division headquarters and two others rotated through three different branch offices, staying in each for three to five months. This placement allowed for rich observations of activities and meaning formation from multiple locations at once. Field notes became the currency of information sharing among team members, and were exchanged weekly if not daily between the sites. Conference calls were held frequently, and we assembled at IRL in California

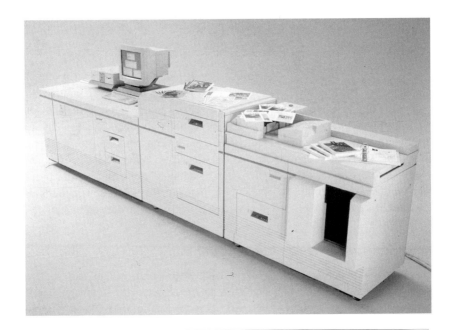

FIGURE 6.1. High-volume production printing machine (courtesy of Xerox Corporation).

periodically for intense face-to-face working sessions. In addition, team members on occasion visited each other's field-site in a kind of research exchange.

At one point, the team stationed at headquarters joined the researchers at a branch office for a week of observations. As a study of work practices throughout the division, one area of focus concerned how operators and staff were adapting to document production using the latest high-volume, high-speed copiers, and the tooling and processes designed to support them. Such copiers (see Figure 6.1) were used for the production and shipment of large-volume, complex orders, such as thousands of user documentation manuals.

After an observation session focused in this area, the visiting team surmised that an opinion they heard expressed by headquarters employees—that the document production process was not being performed to standard and that performance was sloppy—appeared to be accurate. But what the headquarters team missed was that the lead operator in this function had been out the week before, and that a huge special order had arrived unexpectedly, requiring a shift in the schedule and process. What the visiting researchers were observing was the effort to get things back on track. The headquarters team had absorbed an expectation of standard process, whereas the branch office employees understood that the only constant in their world was change. That the work of rebalancing required effort was not so remarkable as to demand being called out by those engaged in the work. It was just the work they were doing, righting the ship, so to speak, which was their job. Because they didn't speak about their effort explicitly, it went unrecognized by the observers from the headquarters team. This case demonstrates that headquarters needed to broaden its perspective of the problem from one of "operator proficiency" to other issues ranging from staffing levels to processes for support exception handling.

This example illustrates a micro-instance of how the temporality of ethnographic sense-making, which begins even as the research is being conducted as well as the timing in which the ethnographer enters and exits the scene, matters. Understanding the situation required contextual understanding and the ability to distinguish signs of what came before from what was happening in the moment. Ethnographers must be sensitive to ways in which the "before and after" that exceeds their horizon may shape actions and meanings. Temporalities of locations take on their own identity. Recognizing the signs that make these temporalities identifiable is part of the process of achieving ethnographic understanding.

## Macro Temporality: Seeing Through Organizational Forms

The temporality of ethnographic understanding also plays out in more macro ways. For example, I have conducted many studies of sales work in different companies and guided by a range of business interests, from informing sales training to the design of tools for global team collaboration. I have pounded the pavement doing door-to-door sales calls with copier reps in rural England and Spain as well as in the heart of New York City, and spent time in planning meetings among highly specialized sales reps focused on high stakes multimillion-dollar contracts between Fortune 500 companies.

Across these many projects I have noted the ubiquity of "sales pipeline meetings" and other practices surrounding the tracking of data on potential sales opportunities (such as contact information, call history records, competitive information, the stage in the sales process). In one project, colleagues and I had the opportunity to study collaboration among globally distributed sales teams. We observed how practices surrounding sales pipeline management, including both the recording of pipeline data and the discussion of it in meetings, played a role in sellers' experiences (Cefkin et al. 2007). We found that efforts to satisfy the process for gathering the pipeline data at times interrupted collegial exchanges between team members. Terse exchanges aimed at tracking down pipeline data in advance of the weekly meeting were common, leading to accusations that some members were more focused on following processes than achieving real results. We also witnessed cases in which the sharing of pipeline information gave rise to new opportunities for collaboration. These observations helped us to understand the role of tools, processes, and corporate directives in shaping communications and perceptions of collegiality across subgroups and locations, and hence the opportunities to positively effect collaboration.

My long-term attention to the meetings held to discuss the sales pipeline, in particular, yielded additional insights (Cefkin 2007). The purpose of these meetings, typically held weekly, is ostensibly for management to review with sales reps the status of potential sales (whether it be new orders, renewals, or upgrades) in the pipeline. In form and practice, such meetings varied by location and over time. For instance, in the 1990s it was not uncommon for potential deals to be recorded manually on index cards or in a spreadsheet and called out one by one and written on a flip chart during the meeting. Over time, information technology (IT) systems have played an increasing role in the capture and transmission of this data. Such variations notwithstanding, my observations have convinced me that the point of these meetings is not purely to share and direct the impact of "information"; it also embodies a particular kind of social and cultural interchange.

I have observed other cases where meetings act as forcing mechanisms, for example, to impose punishment for nonresponsiveness. I came to understand that the sales pipeline meeting not only facilitates a public means of information sharing and exchange—ostensibly enabling both management and team members to identify ways to support each other in advancing opportunities—but also functions to prod sellers to action. Particularly interesting in the case of sales pipeline meetings are their form and rhythm. Conducted in a call-and-response mode between manager and each sales rep, information is reviewed from week to week repeatedly, whether or not any change has occurred. This information, meanwhile, is simultaneously available in the information systems. I posit that the form of the meeting acts to create in sellers a sense of urgency to act. (Bunzel [2002] offers a remarkably similar conclusion in his analysis of weekly status meetings in a coastal hotel where reporting on the numbers conveyed an imperative around the tempo of work expected of different work functions in the hotel.)

My understanding of the varying functions of sales pipeline meetings emerged through long-term engagement with the practice across varying settings. Whereas other sciences—with different subjects of investigation, differently instrumented, and with standards of evidence and proof more clearly tied to measurement—may be able to suddenly render results worthy of attention immediately (due, for instance, to lab readings with visible anomalies), ethnographic understanding does not tend to emerge visibly and all at once. Instead it is interpretive, emergent, and cumulative. What differentiates the knowledge generated from ethnographic research from informed opinion is its basis in systematic data gathering analyzed through tested lenses and held up to examination by others versed in the theories and contexts in question. The temporality of achieving ethnographic understanding is one that unfolds over time.

## The Temporality of Everyday Life

Ethnographic understanding takes time because everyday life is its subject. As Rabinow et al. (2008) suggest, everyday life can't be speeded up: it unfolds in the time it takes to unfold. Indeed, the ethnographic enterprise is founded on this recognition, and the design of ethnographic study, particularly fieldwork, is constructed around it.

Ethnography includes a commitment to account for variations of many points of view within the study context. This is necessary for building a fuller sense of the patterns and values deemed culturally significant and for identifying the varying regimes of value at play, to recognize to whom and under what conditions different factors are important. Sufficiency of coverage is also coupled to considerations of time: the ethnographer's experiences, feelings, and reflections play out only in the ongoing process of doing fieldwork. As Jordan and Lambert aptly remind us, "it means experiencing the boredom as well as the drama of mundane work and everyday life firsthand" (2009:126).

Temporality also factors into the design of field studies, organized with sensitivity towards culturally relevant rhythms and cycles, from growing seasons to election cycles. How does one know what those culturally relevant cycles are? An ethnographer often gains this insight only after spending time amid the action. Consider the earlier example of document production. That example showed that work is necessarily performed in the time in which it takes to do the work. It also hinted at the ways in which the rhythms of that work were shaped through the unit of "the job," through scheduling processes, and through very human elements such as illness and interruptions to schedules. What counted more to the operators than meeting some abstract and inflexible standard of performance measured by codified units of time was getting things back on track. Working from within the temporality of the subjects allows us to know what questions to ask and what factors are key to getting at the important stuff.

Another project illuminates these points more fully. This case is a study of workers who handle relocation and mobility services for large organizations. They secure work permits, visas, movers, living arrangements, schools for children, and so on, as well as confirming policy and allowances for members of organizations moving for short- or long-term assignments to other locations. Many large organizations outsource the work of relocation services to other firms. I engaged in a project in one such organization—a large company providing various outsourced business processes—at a global service delivery center in Manila, Philippines (Figure 6.2). The aims of the project were to inform strategies under discussion (e.g., opportunities for further centralization or decentralization of the teams supporting global clients) as well as to identify areas for improvement (both global process design and local practices).

The research consisted of two five-day field visits to the Manila office for observations and face-to-face interviews, as well as phone interviews and artifact review at a distance. In addition, my research colleague and I engaged the participation of those in the delivery center in designing solutions for such things as improved case management processes and enhanced communications stemming from our analysis and recommendations. We used these participatory design efforts to deepen our ethnographic understanding. While by the standards of corporate ethnography we managed to spend a good chunk of time at the field site and our

Figure 6.2. Service delivery setting (photo by Melissa Cefkin).

total engagement with members of the field site lasted over several months, the specific moments of interaction and immersion were relatively brief.

Although the processes we studied were considered relatively "routine," what we found was that the temporalities of the everyday work were quite complex.[4] The work was "case-based," meaning that each service rep handled a quantity of cases (up to about 120 at once), seeing each relocation through from start to finish. Thus, "the case" itself formed one of the dominant temporalities for service reps. Their actions would revolve around the 90- to 120-day trajectory for each case—initiating the process, securing work permits, scheduling and overseeing the completion of the move, and then finalizing the arrival of the assignee in the new location. Many more tasks, from securing schools for family members to arranging for air-quality testing of residences, also occurred in between.

Because each rep handled multiple cases at once, they were also operating across these trajectories, initiating some cases while being midstream or nearing completion on others. This formed another temporal structure of their work. Further, the reps were also immersed in their own present time, responding to phone calls and instant messages, halting work at their desk to attend a staff meeting, rearranging queues so as to accommodate special requests, stopping for lunch or a coworker's birthday cake, and so on.

The actions and attitudes of the reps were also informed by expectations of the future. Anticipation of such things as whether the relocating assignee would be satisfied in their new assignment or whether any given assignee would be a "repeat customer," someone who would go on assignment again and thus setting up the possibility that current actions would set precedent for future interactions, shaped their expectations. And finally, more periodic cycles of time also informed reps' everyday experience such as impending contract renegotiations with client organizations, company audits, and the monthly tracking of service performance (e.g., number of missed deadlines).

Recognition of these varying temporalities came about from our attention to the everyday practices of the mobility service reps. We had not set out to focus on questions of time or temporality. Had we just focused on case processing—the most explicit and formal of the temporalities and the one around which the work-flow, policies, metrics, and process descriptions were designed—our analysis may have rendered useful targeted process improvement. However, it would have been devoid of broader social and organizational factors shaping the reps' work, which were important to informing the broader strategic questions.

Of course, there is no way to observe empirically what has not yet occurred. Although simulations and forecasts can be powerful tools for anticipating futures, they are not the same as empirically understanding an unfolding situation itself. Efforts to accelerate beyond the temporalities of the everyday means important aspects of the surrounding context—the residues of significant structuring events—may be mistaken as significant when they are not or visa versa. The aim of ethnographic understanding, and its promise in industry contexts, is its attempt to understand what is important from within the realms of practice. It can take time to understand not just what is, but what is important.

## The Temporalities of Organization: Project Time

Ethnographic work in industry most commonly takes the form of a "project." Contrasting with work defined by persistent and repeated activities (such as standard accounting practices), the corporate ethnography project typically has a particular goal such as to design a new product, reformulate a strategy, or provide recommendations for the development of a program. The project is made up of a logical order of steps. First, the researcher must devise effective ways to sufficiently investigate the subject (research design), and second, execute that design (data gathering). The next step is to render a valid and meaningful understanding of the data (analysis), which is then turned into results (deliverables/prototypes). Finally, these are communicated and acted upon. Each step is commonly defined by a specific time frame and set of actions; the ethnographer may specify, for instance, a specific number of field sites to be visited or interviews to be conducted.

How can the project be designed so that researchers can tap into the thoughts, actions, and practices of participants more rapidly? A number of generative advances have been made on these fronts, including those that are productively exploiting information technologies to gain new insight (see, for instance, Maxwell and Riopelle, this volume). This search for efficiency makes sense within the bounds of corporate practice. The organizational imperative to make decisions and take action dominates and transcends the control of almost any given participant in the organizational context, including the researcher. The temporality of the project, in other words, is consistent with corporate practice and should be recognized as a valid temporal construct for ethnographic work. Performing the work and producing results in ways that can be recognized within corporate contexts can be essential to bringing about new understanding and having impact. At the same time, the limits to what is understood by working within these time frames must also be considered, and with it, the potential limits to its value in broadening understanding of the subjects and practices under examination. While it is a valid form for performing corporate work, it also must be recognized that the construct of the project is a construct intended to control time. In this sense, ethnographic work in the corporate sector is subject to the same neoliberal logics of any other market practice.[5]

## The Stakes: Temporalities and the Distinctiveness of Ethnography in Industry

I write this piece in a Janus-faced manner. On any given corporate project, I also commonly spend just hours and days in the field rather than weeks and months, and have become adept at producing results quickly. I will continue to do so and accept these practices as social constructs like any other (including the proverbial one year in the field of traditional ethnographic study). The "success" of ethnographic work in corporate settings, as Blomberg (2009) reminds us, rests on factors other than time and deserves to be recognized in its own terms.

> . . . the ability to deliver value in terms recognizable by the corporations who sponsor the work is not principally gated by these factors of time and money, but instead by the relationships developed within these corporations through which ethnographic insights and sensibilities can have impact. I would submit that a day on the streets in Sao Paulo as viewed through the lens of decades of anthropological and sociological theory and perspective, when connected to the "right" organizational actors, can have significant impact on corporate agendas of technology production or market penetration, even in terms that might warm the hearts of corporate ethnography's most ardent critics. In my view our emphasis should not be on whether corporate ethnographic practices live up to some ideal, but rather on the "appropriate" pairings of opportunities (of access, funding, participants), research problems, and desired outcomes (Blomberg 2009:220).

As Isaac (this volume) effectively demonstrates, rapid ethnographic approaches often provide valuable, business-worthy insight.

Indeed, anthropologists in contemporary settings are often just one kind of expert among many in situations where quickness may be the order of the day, a conundrum explored in the discussion of Rabinow et al. that I use to open this chapter (2008:63). The intrepid business ethnographer, as Solomon (2011) has compellingly argued, has to be willing to move fast to be seen as a valid actor. The question remains (a question echoed in Sunderland's query in this volume about the role of theorizing for ethnographers in industry): when the ethnographer is but one of many experts, what distinguishes her expertise?

In business contexts, "ethnography" is often treated as synonymous with data gathering by way of a field study. It has often been said that the value of ethnography in industry is to "make the invisible visible." Some ethnographic investigations are essentially, and effectively, conducted to "validate corporate hunches and flesh out details" (Jordan and Lambert 2009:125). There is indeed a benefit to the field researcher shining a light on the particular pain points observed in consumers' uses of products, for instance, or the artful practices of workers in managing the complexity of their social and technical surroundings. This should not be undervalued. However, ethnography promises something more than play-by-play reporting to yield near-term insight. Succumbing to the view that the value of ethnography lies in artifacts brought back from the field—a juicy quote here, a telling photo there—puts into question the particular benefits of *ethnographic understanding,* as has been so compellingly argued by Nafus and anderson (2006).

My aim here is *not* to assert that each and every study performed by ethnographers in industry should be lengthy. Ethnographers will necessarily continue to perform particular instances of fieldwork and analysis rapidly and productively. Rather, I assert that reflecting on questions of temporality affords ethnographers an opportunity to refocus on their distinctive contributions vis-à-vis other fields of expertise and to revisit the broader value of ethnography in industry. I agree with Blomberg that *time* per se does not *determine* the ethnographer's ability to see and interpret the phenomenon in question, because indeed ethnographic investigation is not just any old looking and asking. In the words of Ladner: "When researchers add a robust theoretical framework to their corporate ethnography, short time horizons can be mitigated" (Ladner 2012). Because ethnographic work is driven by social and cultural understanding, it demands we pay attention to the temporality of everyday life, to the temporal dimensions of experience significant to the participants of the setting under investigation, and to the temporality of our own interpretive understanding. Ethnography brings socially and culturally informed knowledge to bear in reframing existing understandings so as to make these understandings locally meaningful and available as sites of action. At its best, it also strives to contribute to a refinement or expansion of that social and cultural knowledge, ensuring its ability to affect the worlds affected by business in distinctive ways.

## Acknowledgments

I wish to thank Sam Ladner and Keren Soloman for providing insightful provocations in the shaping of ethnographic projects in industry and Ben Shaw, Susan Stucky, and Paulo Rocha e Oliviera for contributing to my thinking about time and temporality in business practice. Reverberations of Rick Robinson's plea to ethnographers in industry that "we can do better!" can be heard throughout this chapter.

## References

Aronson, Meredith, Libby Bishop, Melissa Cefkin, Brigitte Jordan, Nancy Lawrence, Lindy Sullivan, Connie Preston, and Julia Oesterle
    1995 Reflections on a Journey of Transformation: Learning, Growth, and Change at Xerox Business Services. IRL/XBS Systemic Assessment Project, Final Report. Palo Alto, CA: Institute for Research on Learning.

Blomberg, Jeanette
    2009 Insider Trading: Engaging and Valuing Corporate Ethnography. In *Ethnography and the Corporate Encounter: Reflections on Research in and of Industry*. Melissa Cefkin, ed. Pp. 213–226. New York, Oxford: Berghahn Books.

Bunzel, Dirk
    2002 The Truth of the Organization: Simultaneity, Identity and Discipline in an Australian Hotel. In *Making Time: Time and Management in Modern Organizations*. Richard Whipp, Barbara Adam, and Ida Sabelis, eds. Pp. 168–181. Oxford: Oxford University Press.

Cefkin, Melissa
2007 Numbers May Speak Louder than Words, but is Anybody Listening? Rhythm and Voice in Sales Pipeline Management. *Proceedings of EPIC* 2007:187–199.

Cefkin, Melissa, Ben Shaw, and Susan Stucky
2010 "Quality Time: An Empirical Examination of Experiences of Time in B2B Service Engagements." Paper presented at the Frontiers in Service Conference, Karlstad, Sweden. June 10–13.

Cefkin, Melissa, Jakita Thomas, and Jeanette Blomberg
2007 The Implications of Enterprise-wide Pipeline Management Tools for Organizational Relations and Exchanges. Group '07 Conference Proceedings, Sanibel Island, FL, ACM. Pp. 61–68.

Jordan, Brigitte, and Monique Lambert
2009 Working in Corporate Jungles: Reflections on Ethnographic Praxis in Industry. In *Ethnography and the Corporate Encounter: Reflections on Research in and of Industry*, edited by Melissa Cefkin, pp. 95–136. New York, Oxford: Berghahn Books.

Ladner, Sam
2012 Is Rapid Ethnography Possible? A Cultural Analysis of Academic Critiques of Private-sector Ethnography. Available at http://ethnographymatters.net/2012/01/26/is-rapid-ethnography-possible-a-cultural-analysis-of-academic-critiques-of-private-sector-ethnography-part-2-of-2/. Accessed June 2, 2012.

Nafus, Dawn, and ken anderson
2006 The Real Problem: Rhetorics of Knowing in Corporate Ethnographic Research. *Proceedings of EPIC* 2006:244–58.

Rabinow, Paul, George Marcus, James Faubian, and Tobian Rees
2008 *Designs for an Anthropology of the Contemporary*. Durham & London: Duke University Press.

Solomon, Keren
2011 "Rapid Ethnographic Techniques." Paper presented at the Society for Applied Anthropology Annual Meeting, Seattle, WA, March 29–April 2.

Turner, Chris
2000 *All Hat and No Cattle: Tales of a Corporate Outlaw*. New York. Basic Books.

# Notes

1   Cliffs Notes are summary guides of significant publications and works in many fields designed for student use.

2   Rabinow et al. (2008) provide a rich and provocative exploration of temporalities in performing ethnographic work "of the contemporary." An extended conversation among four anthropologists (Paul Rabinow, George Marcus, James Faubian, and Tobian Rees) explores the challenges of doing anthropological ethnography in sites where anthropologists are but one contingent of many experts. They grapple with the effects of the dynamic, fast-paced worlds of contemporary cultural practice on anthropological work. They suggest that, used to a norm of patient, accumulative achievement, anthropologists experience a kind of "temporal turbulence" in focusing on the here and now (Rabinow et al. 2008:7). Their assertion is that while anthropology requires closeness to what is happening, it also establishes its expertise by bringing a critical distance to the topic, which, when shifted from spatial to temporal frame, suggests a kind of "untimeliness" (Rabinow et al. 2008:58) that encourages reflection. This gives rise to the question (posed by Marcus) of whether this untimeliness needs to be brought into the scene of fieldwork itself. And

if so, how can it be justified in the face of counterpart experts who are operating with expectations of quickness? Marcus suggests that one of the functions of the anthropologist in such settings is in "slowing things down by the tempo of inquiry" (Rabinow et al. 2008:63). Indeed, they put tem-porality at the heart of the contemporary ethnographic endeavor.

3   Chris Turner offers a Texas-inflected retelling of the story of the broader effort in her 2000 book *All Hat and No Cattle: Tales of a Corporate Outlaw.*

4   I reexamined the original data after the completion of the commissioned project together with two research colleagues (Cefkin et al. 2010). It was in this reexamination that we identified the full complexity of the nature of time at play in the service delivery center.

5   I thank Sam Ladner for sharing her thinking around the nature of "fieldwork" time and the ways the construct of "the project" reinforces neoliberal regimes of practice.

Chapter 7

# The Cry for More Theory

*Patricia Sunderland*

> Such a messy oscillation between purified poles demonstrates
> the existence of a monstrosity or hybrid, an impossible object
> that cannot find a voice in the confines of official language.
>
> — *Don Slater*

## Introduction

In this chapter, I focus on the cry for more theory in applied anthropological work. I have used Don Slater's analysis of marketing, referenced in the opening epigram, as analogical muse. The analogy is simple and straightforward: anthropologist-practitioners are also monstrous hybrids.[1] In essence, despite efforts to contextualize applied anthropologists as scholar-practitioners (e.g., Wasson 2006) and well-reasoned arguments that our academic-applied hybridity is a source of strength and an identity to be celebrated (e.g., Blomberg 2005), those of us who ply our trade primarily outside the academy can still find ourselves caught in the suspension between opposed realms of academia and practice. We remain suspect—consider for a moment the ongoing questions regarding ethics in the realm of practice—and we continue to feel the pressure of being squeezed into boxes that do not quite fit. Practicing anthropologists, we would suggest, remain neither here (industry, commerce, policy, government) *nor* there (academia). We are not bound by the purified logics of either realm (i.e., not by the discourses of esteemed theories and practices of intellectualism of the academic realm nor by the discourses of action and pragmatic solution in applied circles). At the same time, as practicing anthropologists we are both here (in industry, commerce, policy, government) *and* there (academia) in subjective experience.

The schism between academic and applied anthropology in the United States and Britain was historically wrought in the context of larger aims and power relations, not least of which was establishing anthropology as a legitimate academic field (Baba 2005, 2009). As Baba (2005) noted, the good news is that social, economic, and political contexts can and do change. In today's world, anthropology's traditional categorizations, including the lines of division between academic and applied anthropology, are dissolving and collapsing. Shifting resources and funding in the academy, an ever-powerful theory of markets to explain behavior, and new technologies, in tandem with global social and economic shifts, are rendering anthropology's traditional field increasingly unrecognizable. Anthropology and anthropologists are charting third spaces (Fischer 2006), studying commerce and financial markets, legal systems, technology, and biotechnology (see Hamilton and Placas 2011), as well as developing tools of translation and mediation that make visible "the differences of interests, access, power, needs, desires, and philosophical perspective" (Fischer 2006:363). Concerns voiced by the academic profession about being involved at all with commercial, social, and political institutions have generally given way to concerns with the terms of engagement (Mullins 2011; Welker et al. 2011). Business anthropology is flourishing and rapidly becoming an internationally organized institution in its own right. The Ethnographic Praxis in Industry Conference (EPIC) was held in Copenhagen in 2008 and Tokyo in 2010; in 2012, the first European EPIC meeting was held in Barcelona. Two international business anthropology journals have been established. *The Journal of Business Anthropology* was created by Brian Moeran and Christina Garsten, located in Denmark and Sweden, respectively. From China, Robert Tian started *The International Journal of Business Anthropology* and organized an International Conference of Business Anthropology at Sun Yat-Sen University in May 2012.

All of these changes make this a particularly important moment to reexamine the theory/practice divide in anthropological milieus, to look again at the cry for more theory versus the cry of practicality. In this chapter I explore some of the dynamics underpinning the persistence of the oppositional dichotomy between theory and practice. In so doing, I ponder what it is about our hybridism that remains monstrous. Why might we still feel—and act—like aberrations? In Chapter 8, Rita Denny contemplates further the experienced tension, examining why theorizing and the work that needs doing are experienced as a zero-sum game, a series of skirmishes that must be won or lost. In the end, for both chapters, the ultimate question is how to further engage ethnography and anthropology as they move beyond the theory/practice divide.

## Hierarchical Cries

If anthropologists in academic settings have traditionally decried the lack of theory in applied work, among anthropologists in industry there is also a persistent plaint for more theory or theorizing (Cefkin 2010; Cohen 2005; Greenwood 2000; Plowman 2005; Robinson 2005). In the anthropological dualism of theory and practice there lurks a hierarchy, with theory in the privileged position. This is true in both academic and applied realms. To praise an academic anthropologist as a "great ethnographer" can be faint praise (i.e., it often carries with it the implicit, unsaid "and not a great theoretician"). Of course it is impossible to separate method from theory. Theoretical issues permeate not only decisions to study whatever it is we study, but also every move we make in the field. Theory has influence over every bit of what we do—and don't—see, hear, and feel. In a nutshell, theory and method are ontologically not separable. At the same time, I have great sympathy for Latour's (1993) perspective that denying hybrid entities is a crucial aspect of upholding modernist oppositions (e.g., theory versus method, academic versus applied, nature versus culture). We are able to think—and often revert to thinking—of theory and method as separate realms, as we do with academic and applied worlds.[2] Institutional arrangements and practices are not to be underestimated either. The need (and time) to publish makes a difference. Most of our academic colleagues must publish. We know that. Some of our applied colleagues are employed in corporations, which also expect, support, and encourage publication efforts. For others there is no such infrastructure, which makes contributing to traditional (i.e., peer reviewed and theoretical discourse–inflected) scholarly conversations a solely personal burden. And it is not easy.

Interestingly, we were recently invited to participate at a prestigious academic workshop. The organizers wanted consumer research practitioners to take part and discussed with us the form that might take. They suggested that perhaps a panel of practitioners in the form of a special session would be ideal and added that while they planned to create an edited book of participants' papers, for the practicing anthropologists there would be no requirement to prepare anything for publication. Without question, the motives were genuine and generous. The organizers wanted practitioners to have a voice in the scholarly meeting and were trying to assure practicing anthropologists' participation by making the constraints less onerous. At the same time, however, does not this once again privilege the academic point of view? Whose voices, whose viewpoints, whose theories will be passed down as part of the permanent record?

## Morality Cries: The Deli Project

In the applied realm, the subjective experience of the hierarchy between theory and practice for anthropologists working in industry is not news. Yet it is interesting to contemplate the ways in which incorporating theory in the work—our own internal cry for more theory—feels like a moral obligation. In the material workings of the theory-practice moral imaginary—in the incorporation of the theory-practice hierarchy into the fabric of our work—we can feel like we are not being anthropologists and we are not doing "good" work unless we explicitly (at least to ourselves) bring in anthropological theory.

For example, in the summer of 2010 we were commissioned to study grocery store delis.[3] Deli areas in U.S. grocery stores have their roots in the German, Jewish, and Italian immigrant delicatessens of the mid-1800s and early 1900s. These were small shops with meats, cheeses, breads, and "made dishes" of ethnic specialization. Transformed by eating and grocery practices of the 1950s, 1960s, and 1970s, deli areas in grocery stores became primarily the staffed counter from which one bought freshly sliced meats and cheese: often bologna, ham, or salami, and rather rubbery varieties of Swiss and American cheese. In the wake of the cultural elaboration in ways of eating and the rise of local, organic and gourmet foods during the 1990s and early 2000s, grocery deli areas once again transformed. At the time of our research, national grocery store chains such as Whole Foods and other upscale, natural food–oriented grocery stores, such as Wegmans in New Jersey or Jimbo's in San Diego, featured imported cheeses displayed as art, open olive or hummus bars, prepared foods to choose from that not only included the ubiquitous rotisserie chickens and veggie wraps, but also vegan spanakopita, "Curry Tofu Mirage," and spicy Thai rice salad.

Our client's company was a corporate leader in the snack food business. Their own array of food offerings had been undergoing change given the changes in the food worlds of consumers. These were food worlds that had been influenced and informed not only by the food offerings of grocery stores, but also by those of green and farmer's markets, restaurants, international travel, and television's celebrity chefs. The corporation was interested in having more of their snack food offerings featured in the deli area of groceries, the area of the store endowed with contemporary cachet. They did not like that many of their older products were relegated to the middle-of-the-store snack and cookie aisle, the "junk food" aisle in consumer and cultural parlance. They certainly did not want their new products landing there. Thus, the corporate goal was to become "thought leaders in deli." To be a "thought leader" held the promise of possessing a more refined understanding of how to package and present their products for grocery store deli areas as well as helping to assure their product placement in the deli due to the relationships with retailers this thought leader status could foster (see Sunderland and Denny 2011).

For us as anthropologists, the project was an interesting one. There was no question; deli areas of grocery stores were fascinating. Among other things, in everyday food provisioning, grocery delis seemed to have become the accepted and esteemed venue for avoiding the pitfalls of junk food not only in grocery store interior aisles but also from traditional fast food locales. Deli shopping was a way to live everyday life without cooking (for many people there was often little time or interest in day-to-day cooking) yet still have freshly prepared foods that were created with fresh ingredients and artisanal flair, the kinds one might expect from higher-end restaurants. Norms of different entrees or sides for each person, perhaps also learned from restaurant eating, could also be obliged. Delis' smorgasbords of gourmet offerings allowed one to choose and create tapas or small-plate treats at home or at work. Sushi and salad bars, taquerias, pizzerias, chef-created stir-fries, hummus, Italian crackers, goat cheese, and fig bars, all side by side. What's not to like?

Moreover, as the project was originally conceived by our client, the research promised a multivantage point understanding. We were to study natural, premium, and traditional grocery stores. "Traditional" grocery stores, a gloss for lower-end stores, meant that we would see delis that had some newer items but also offered lower-end options and had floor plans that were not (yet) altered in line with more contemporary norms. In the original plan, we were slotted to spend considerable time observing in all types of deli areas as well as engaging in discussions with deli managers in addition to the typically requested ethnographic encounters with prerecruited respondents. As it turned out in the end, our client could not secure the necessary permission from the grocery corporate headquarters that would have permitted our research in deli departments and discussions with deli managers nationwide, but we still managed to gain the occasional local permission that allowed us to be in several deli areas for hours on end, notebooks and cameras in hand. We also conducted offsite discussion groups with deli shoppers in San Diego, Atlanta, and southern New Jersey, and from those groups selected 17 people to carry out weeklong video or audio-photo diaries of all their deli shopping and consumption experiences. In the same three cities, we also carried out ethnographic encounters that led us from in-home discussions and tours to shadowed shopping in participants' most and least favorite delis.

We also liked this project from its inception because someone who was excited by ethnography and wanted an anthropological perspective had requested it. She accepted our stated proposal objectives, which focused on the following questions: What does the deli section represent in life and in shopping—practically, emotionally and symbolically? What are the imagined worlds this food section evokes? What are the cultural references framing its meaning? What happens in this section? How do shoppers move through this space? What is their experience? What makes it so? How are deli section foods consumed? In fact, she embraced these objectives. She had worked with us on other studies and she wanted the same kind of, as we imagined it might be called within corporate halls, "anthropological stuff."

Along these lines, the report we produced focused on what we saw as salient cultural ideas and muses surrounding and infusing delis. We discussed food as a form of cultural capital entailing trajectories of travel, discovery, adventure, or health, all of which we detailed with the experiences of our research participants. We talked about how delis fit practically, emotionally, and symbolically within the context of daily life. In a daylong presentation that included numerous illustrative edited video and audio excerpts of the ethnographic material, we then went on to focus more specifically on the dynamics of shopping deli areas versus interior aisles of stores and on the salient contexts for choosing specific delis. Finally, we focused on our client's product categories: how these products were semiotically constructed in delis and in grocery, and how these products were shopped and consumed.

During the lunch break of that daylong presentation, we pulled our client aside because we felt that things were not going well. It seemed to us that our client's own internal client, the person responsible for sales to retailers, the one who would be in front-stage position in that deli thought leadership role, was not persuaded by our analysis. His questions, his comments, his facial expressions, perhaps even his raised eyebrows, concerned us. What looked like side glances and side conversations with his team members also troubled us. Our client was not worried;

she was sure all was well. Unfortunately, by the end of the day, she was proved wrong. We were in big trouble. What were deli "purchase drivers?" What "needs" were consumers fulfilling when they purchased items in the deli? How did they make their decisions (i.e., "What are consumers' decision trees?")? These were the questions he insisted needed answers; these, he maintained, were the questions of interest for both retailers and his corporation, and in our research presentation, we had not answered them.

If in most projects, we can get beyond such a conversational and conceptual impasse by dint of the power of the analysis, as well as the persuasion and influence of our proximal client, in this case we were not so fortunate. The distal client was adamant, and he was not going to budge. We had to address the issues in his terms. In the end, we spent weeks redoing portions of our report, explicitly addressing issues in terms of decision trees and consumer "needs." In other words, we had to accommodate our clients' (theoretical) discourse, not our own. Adhering to the client's own conceptualization of consumption and choice, we increasingly shed our anthropological theory as an explicit source for insight and understanding. The overwhelming feeling for us was loss. Iterative phone calls and iterative re-writes flattened our enthusiasm and identities. The title of "Redo" for the electronic file within the project folder was a sadness-produced and sadness-provoking icon.

We had not wanted to simply frame our analysis and report as "Deli Shopping: Why?" Nor did we want to simply address the issues in the framework and terms of: "What are the purchase drivers? And, which one is most important? Is it an interest in health? Or, is occasion or price the driver?" We saw our goal and our position as anthropologist consultants as providing an anthropological frame that could elucidate the cultural location and logic of grocery deli arenas and in so doing had the capacity to both catalyze and change thinking and action. In the letting go of the anthropological theoretical frame, our feeling was that we had not been successful with our clients and, as a consequence, any "thought leadership" would be constrained by exactly the same models as at the start of the project. Deli thinking, we figured, would remain the same. Anthropological thinking had not had an impact: it had not helped reframe the conceptualization of delis, had not provided a different refracting lens, nor produced superior fidelity in understanding. Anthropological thinking would not have any impact on how our client packaged and presented their products, nor how retailers thought about delis.

As I have illustrated in the retelling of this deli project, the lack of a guiding or framing theory in our work (note the foregrounding of theory in that formulation) meant for us a loss of contribution and, along with that, the capacity to change thinking and action. In acquiescing we felt we gave up the opportunity to change how delis were conceived and merchandized, and ultimately shopped by all of us. This failure was felt as a failure in our engagement with our clients, a failure to ourselves as anthropologists, and as a failure for the influence and impact of anthropological thinking; in other words, for the field of anthropology as well.

## Inspirational Cries: The Home Organization Project

Beyond the moral underpinnings, the cry for theory also persists, at least in part, because of its capacity and expectation to inspire both our clients and us. When we are successful, what we, as anthropologists, bring to our clients in business worlds *is* a different kind of thinking, a different theory, which can be enlightening. We can help clients get beyond an impasse or out of a quagmire because we provide a new way of thinking about or framing an issue. This explicit "thinking tool" aspect of anthropologists' contributions, this bringing in of theories or cosmologies, is actually a crucial aspect of the practical work that needs to be accomplished. In consumer research circles at least, it is part of the value that we bring to clients. For us, this has taken the form of introducing notions of linguistic and behavioral marking and indexicals in a study of everyday celebrations for the same snack food company that commissioned the deli work, or the theory of metaphors brought to bear in a home organization project detailed here.

In 2004, we embarked on a project to study how people organized the "stuff" in their homes. The goal was to mine insights for innovation opportunities in organizational products or services. Our theoretical inspiration was Lakoff and Johnson's (1980) classic *Metaphors We Live By*, along with a number of other more contemporary metaphor theorists, no doubt in part because we had, at that time, recently written about cultural metaphors (subsequently published as Denny and Sunderland 2005). In our analysis, we pointed to the ways that people's organizing actions and artifacts were caught and animated by the tension between two dif-

FIGURE 7.1. Container metaphor. Bins on left hold clean, wear-in-home, "comfy" clothes, separated from wear-outside-the-home hanging clothes. Bin in the middle is for worn clothes, but still clean enough to wear before washing. Large bin on the right is a hamper with dirty clothes to be washed before wearing again.

ferent organizational metaphors: on the one hand, a container metaphor in which everything had its place (see Figure 7.1); on the other hand, an emerging "array" metaphor which seemed built on experience with visual arrays and scanability learned in everyday computer usage (Figures 7.2 and 7.3).

FIGURE 7.2. Array metaphor 1. Closets in which mutable visual array is key.

FIGURE 7.3. Array metaphor 2. Mutable visual array; immersion in the array is also key.

We combined this array insight with other fine-grained Lakoff and Johnson–inspired observations of spatial orientation metaphors. We noted the way in which in-use objects were signaled by a flat orientation (as in a book lying flat on a table or files laid out on the floor); ready-to-use was signaled by a vertical orientation (as in a book vertical on shelf, or clothes hanging in a closet or arrayed vertically on shelves in a walk-in closet); not-in-use or not-yet-in-use was signaled by stacks (as in a stack of books by the bedside or the clothes stacked on the bin next to the dresser; see Figures 7.4–7.6).

This framework provided a springboard for ideas for new home organization products and services that were not grounded by outdated container metaphors, but instead were based on arrays. The important corollary insight was that the organizational need was better means of retrieval, not storage. Combined with fine-grained considerations of the spatial metaphors, and the need to easily transform flat to vertical without ending up stacked (or lost), we could provide a clear and focused platform for innovation. It was useful. In 2009, five years later, our

FIGURE 7.4, above. Flat equals "in use."

FIGURE 7.5, right. Vertical is "ready for use."

FIGURE 7.6 Stacked is "packed,"
which often means lost.

client, working in a different innovation space, called us back because she needed the anthropologists. The metaphors, and their impact on corporate thinking, were remembered. Moreover, it keeps repeating. In the last year, two other individuals who had been part of the client team called us when they needed insight for a product development issue. Both now worked at other companies, but each of them remembered the home organization analysis we had provided, akin to the way we had remembered Lakoff and Johnson analyses when we had been presented with the problem of how to think about the organization of stuff.

## Survival Cries: Beauty and the Beast

If theory is part of the work that needs doing in consumer research, academic exposition and the celebration of theory for theory's sake are not. At least in the United States, theory must often be brought in implicitly and casually; theory must be represented and invoked as easily understandable and practical. It is not about engaging in heady intellectual theoretical debates with the client as coparticipant. In U.S. commercial spheres, anthropological theory is an aspect of the clients' practical work that needs doing. But, the currency of theorizing, and its accorded status as noted before, and even its fun, are located in academia (Tracy 1997). Given our socialization, the habitus of academia while in graduate training, explicit theorizing is a currency—and source of fun—that is sometimes missed. To return to the subjective urge for theory, it is also understandable given theory's currency in the academy, and our own socialization into realms of anthropological theorizing in the academy, that we often tend to look there for new theoretical ideas. Given the dimensions of currency—in terms of cultural capital generally and the interrelated notion of temporality—it is perhaps not surprising that anthropologists in practice often rely (explicitly or implicitly) on the academy for new theoretical ideas. There is a feeling that we need to stay abreast, informed, to continue to be helpful to clients as well as to remain ("good") anthropologists.

Nonetheless, the cry for more theory (flowing in from the academy, implicitly or explicitly) is at once a practical, on-the-ground need and a lament that by its very locution constitutes outdated theorizing. The lament and locution presupposes a one-way course, a shoveling in, a bringing in, a tidal flow into an otherwise empty space (just as practitioners themselves migrated, flowed, went, occupied another "space" called applied work). Theory, however, is not something "imported" and "applied"; rather, theorizing is implicated in the work that is done under any circumstances (whether all involved recognize it or not). As many have noted, it can thus be more fruitful to conceptualize industry as a field site where theory is enacted, a site that includes the very real positioning of the researcher as an actor in the proceedings (Robinson 2005; Welker et al. 2011). In other words, theory is emergent and there is no "there" here, only a "we here." The cry for more theory, then, is best understood not as a cry for more importing per se, but rather a plea to theorize the "we here" situation at all. For anthropologists, this means problematizing, querying assumptions, and explicating both the knowledge production and use of which we are a part.

The persistence of the plea for theorizing, I would also argue, is a response to industry practices in which the "we here" is negotiated. For lurking monsters, theorizing is at once a survival strategy and an act of responsibility within the matrix of project work. Drawing on the logics of commerce and industry, theorizing becomes a pragmatic activity, a response to the situational matrix of relations and practices. It becomes a way to negotiate identity, contribution, and influence. In the doing, theorizing also becomes a form of resistance to industry practices (see Cohen 2005; Denny and Sunderland 2008; Morais and Malefyt 2010; and Sunderland and Denny 2007).

In 2009, Jerry Lombardi spelled out the business practice of deskilling for ethnographers in industry (Lombardi 2009). He observed that ethnographic work was increasingly subject to budget-controlled piecework, systemization of process, and extraction of creative mental effort. In the past few years we have experienced the deskilling process, becoming caught in the corporate craw of procurement policy overhaul. Corporations have developed systems of prequalifying research "suppliers" based on the cost of distinct research methods and abstracted from any real research question at hand (e.g., the cost of an in-home interview, a focus group, a diary). In focusing on the difference of our anthropological analysis, theorizing thus becomes a survival tactic, a form of resistance, and a means of practicing skilling.

If deskilling is a rational, capitalist, pragmatic process in support of fiscal efficiencies, deskilling is also consonant with business and industry inclinations towards simplifying theorizing. Still a pragmatic survival skill, theorizing practice in this case is not born of budgets and inexorable fiscal policy concern, but rather of having a say, of being influential. In a rumination on ethnographers' impacts on practices and practice theory, Cefkin (2010) reflected on conundrums experienced by ethnographers in business brought about by industry's theorizing of practice (how it is "reified and rendered" [Cefkin 2010:55]). If practice theory is an effort to illuminate broader social dynamics combined with the situated relations that account for (and count in) subjective experience, business tends to codify and stabilize ("best") practices. One effect is that ethnographers in industry can fall short in implementing the implications of analysis because corporations see social matters such as power and hierarchy to be beyond their purview, "externalities" over which they have no control. Cefkin suggested there is a price paid in not pushing theorized practice forward with as much intellectual and practical gusto as can be mustered. If not pushed, are we ethnographers limiting the ability to negotiate contribution and influence, "being positioned as technicians, problem solvers for addressing immediate issues, rather than holders of vital social and cultural knowledge worthy of broader strategic consideration?" (Cefkin 2010:55). Just because business practices are not reflexive of broader social dynamics does not mean conversations should be limited: "by avoiding naturalistic, reductive treatments of practice and instead recognizing the powered dimension of their existence, might not our work better realize the transformational power to change structures?" (Cefkin 2010:56). Problematizing or querying assumptions (both of which count as theorizing) of the things with which we are engaged thus become survival strategies.

Beyond its merits as a survival strategy, theorizing the "we here" situation (instantiated in proposals, analysis, presentation, meetings, etc.) is a form of responsibility, an obligation that stems from the signifying practices that characterize anthropology as a discipline. In a disquisition on industry's preoccupation with "users" in design research, Cohen (2005) made a persuasive case that "user" is more than a word: "it is a concept which establishes some of the material, social and cultural conditions for our research" (2005:14). Users, much like Flynn's (2009) "my customers," not only become a reified entity that serves to organize creative development and economic investment within the corporation, but they are grounded definitionally by exclusion, by a contrast to nonusers (or "not my customers"). Importantly, as Cohen (2005) emphasized, how products and services function and for whom has implications for a larger public. Mobile phones, to cite his example, designed for "users" definitionally excluded homeless mothers and, in so doing, excluded them in ensuing design. How users, my customers, delis, celebrations, the home, cars, clothes, stores, or organizations are conceptualized has an impact on all of us. If the work that we do influences—which is the position of practitioners—then practitioners bear responsibility for their impact on the publics within which those products or services circulate. In the end, then, theorizing is the work that needs doing if we, as lurking monster–practitioners, are to turn our positions into ones of anthropological beauty, theoretically, pragmatically, and responsibly.

# References

Baba, Marietta

2005 To the End of Theory-Practice 'Apartheid': Encountering the World. *EPIC* 2005:205–217.

2009 Disciplinary-Professional Relations in an Era of Anthropological Engagement. *Human Organization* 68(4):380–391.

Blomberg, Jeanette

2005 The Coming of Age of Hybrids: Notes on Ethnographic Praxis. *EPIC* 2005:67–74.

Cefkin, Melissa

2010 Practice at the Crossroads: When Practice Meets Theory, A Rumination. *EPIC* 2010:46–58.

Cohen, Kris

2005 Who We Talk About When We Talk About Users. *EPIC* 2005:9–30.

Denny, Rita, and Patricia Sunderland

2005 Researching Cultural Metaphors in Action: Metaphors of Computing Technology in Contemporary U.S. Life. *Journal of Business Research* 58:1456–1463.

2008 Engaging Anthropology's Cultural Muscle. *QRCA Views* (Fall):13–17.

Fischer, Michael M. J.

2006 Culture and Cultural Analysis. *Theory, Culture & Society* 23(2–3):360–364.

Flynn, Donna

2009 "My Customers are Different!" Identity, Difference, and the Political Economy of Design. In *Ethnography and the Corporate Encounter: Reflections on Research in and of Corporations,* edited by Melissa Cefkin, pp. 41–57. New York: Berghahn.

Greenwood, Davyyd

2000 Theory-Practice Relations in Anthropology: A Commentary and Further Provocation. *NAPA Bulletin* 18:164–175.

Hamilton, Jennifer, and Aimee Placas

2011 Anthropology Becoming...? *American Anthropologist* 113(2):246–261.

Lakoff, George, and Mark Johnson

1980 *Metaphors We Live By.* Chicago: University of Chicago Press.

Latour, Bruno

1993 *We Have Never Been Modern* [Catherine Porter, trans]. Cambridge: Harvard University Press.

Lombardi, Gerald

2009 The De-skilling of Ethnographic Labor: Signs of an Emerging Predicament. *EPIC* 2009:42–49.

Morais, Robert, and Timothy de Waal Malefyt

2010 How Anthropologists Can Succeed in Business: Mediating Multiple Worlds of Inquiry. *International Journal of Business Anthropology* 1:45–56.

Mullins, Paul
  2011 Practicing Anthropology and the Politics of Engagement. *American Anthropologist* 113(2):235–245.

Plowman, Tim
  2005 Ethnography, Operations and Objective Practice. *EPIC* 2005:53–66.

Robinson, Rick
  2005 Let's Have a Conversation: Theory Session Introductory Remarks. *EPIC* 2005:1–8.

Slater, Don
  2011 Marketing as a Monstrosity: The Impossible Place Between Culture and Economy. In *Inside Marketing*, edited by Detlev Zwick and Julien Cayla, pp. 23–41. Oxford, United Kingdom: Oxford University Press.

Sunderland, Patricia, and Rita Denny
  2007 *Doing Anthropology in Consumer Research*. Walnut Creek, CA: Left Coast Press.

  2011 Consumer Segmentation in Practice: An Ethnographic Account of Slippage. In *Inside Marketing*, edited by Detlev Zwick and Julien Cayla, pp. 137–161. Oxford, United Kingdom: Oxford University Press.

Tracy, Karen
  1997 *Colloquium: Dilemmas of Academic Discourse*. Westport, CT: Praeger.

Wasson, Christina
  2006 Making History at the Frontier. *NAPA Bulletin* 26:1–19.

Welker, Marina, Damani Partridge, and Rebecca Hardin
  2011 Corporate Lives: New Perspectives on the Social Life of the Corporate Form. *Current Anthropology* 52(Supp. 3):S3–S16.

## Notes

1 As is perhaps evident in the terminology of "purified" and "monstrosity," Slater is drawing on Bruno Latour's theorizing of modernist oppositions. For Latour, the existence and purity of modernist conceptual oppositions (e.g., nature versus culture, science versus art) is achieved by the simultaneous proliferation of hybrid entities that must be continually denied, rendered impossible, or denied as monstrous aberrations. The erasure of the hybrids, these monstrous hybrid beings that are not supposed to exist, is part of the work that recreates and maintains the existence—and the purity—of the oppositions. See for example, Latour (1993).

2 See, for instance, the way the *Journal of Business Anthropology* (http://rauli.cbs.dk/index.php/jba/index) makes a distinction in the foregrounding of theory in papers versus case studies versus field reports.

3 The projects cited in this chapter were collaborative endeavors with Rita Denny. Moreover, both chapters in this volume were collaboratively written.

Chapter 8

# The Cry of Practicality

*Rita Denny*

> Pasteur encountered a vague, cloudy, gray substance sitting meekly in the corner of
> his flasks and turned it into the splendid, well-defined, articulate yeast
> twirling magnificently across the ballroom of the Academy.
>
> —*Bruno Latour*

## Dilemmas

In "The Cry for More Theory" (Sunderland, this volume), we tackled the question of why the oppositional dualism between theory and applied work persists. We argued that persistence results from the practitioner's subjective positioning vis-à-vis the logics of anthropology as a discipline (whose imprimatur in the past 60 years comes from its academic profession) and the opposing logics of commerce and industry. Using Slater's (2011) analysis of marketing-as-monstrous-hybrid as a muse, we suggested that anthropological practitioners hold an analogous position as an impossible-object: Practitioners are neither here (industry) nor there (academia) in the purified logics of either realm, but at the same time practitioners are both here (industry) and there (academia) in subjective experience. Importantly, persistence of the dualism is propelled by workplace dynamics: first, anthropological practitioners often feel a moral obligation to theorize in the face of industry practices (as a form of resistance, as an ethical obligation given positions to influence, or to preserve self-identity); second, theorizing is a pragmatic strategy for claiming power and identity within a corporation (in which theorizing becomes a survival skill and strategy).

This chapter turns away from concerns about the persistent opposition between theory and (applied) work to contemplate more fully the experienced tension. Why do practitioners experience theorizing and the work that needs doing as a zero-sum game? As a (seemingly unending) series of skirmishes in which there are winners and losers? We suggest that the experienced tension is not between theorizing and practical needs but rather about the theorizing itself and, more specifically, about whose theory prevails. My focus here is on illuminating and problematizing the work of theorizing *in* the practicality of the work that needs doing. The practitioner's dilemma, I will argue, lies in articulating the terms of

*Advancing Ethnography in Corporate Environments: Challenges and Emerging Opportunities,* edited by Brigitte Jordan, 136–150. ©2013 Left Coast Press Inc. All rights reserved.

negotiation. To illustrate the role of theory (and what we would say is the work of theory), as well as the parameters of practitioner dilemmas, I am opting to start with two very different examples of failure (if for no other reason than failure serves to focus the mind).

## Failures

In the fall of 2009, we conducted a project for a food company on a particular brand offering designed for children.[1] The brand team's goal was to double the size of its business. This would be no small feat given stagnant growth in the previous five years (despite various marketing initiatives in pricing, advertising, and product offerings). The team's strategy, in their terms, was to earn the trust of mothers while simultaneously delivering a product enabling kids' choice and control (in what was offered or how it was consumed). In practical terms, what might the company do to and with a kid-focused meal to make it popular not just with kids, but also with parents? The consumer insight manager assigned to the team felt an ethnographic approach would yield greatest insight about the brand's potential and current consumers; she called us.

To meet the team's objective, we saw our goals to be an investigation of mothers' food priorities, routines, and decision-making around their children's eating and, particularly, to understand the stigma, barriers, and opportunities for children's foods and the company's brand. We conducted group discussions with moms (who met the specifications of the brand's target consumers), spent an afternoon or evening with mothers and their children in their homes, and had mothers create video or audio diaries of food in everyday life. Sixteen diaries provided us with a week of on-the-ground, real-time documentation of moms, children, and food. In creating the diaries, we asked participants to document all kid-related food and beverage activities from morning to night, "each and every meal, snack, whatever, whether at home, restaurant, car, wherever: show us the situation, who is involved, outcome, how you felt about it, anything difficult or easy."

In the analysis, we became fascinated by the socialization of personhood that engagement with food fostered between mothers and children. We observed ubiquitous routines of necessary choice-making in the diaries, with parents asking children to make food decisions, often in a forced, false-choice way. Did they want cereal or waffles for breakfast, peanut butter or grilled cheese for lunch? That choices and the terms of choices were socialized was made readily apparent by a toddler who, in repeated response to his mother's two lunch choices, kept saying that he just wanted "TV." The more she tried to confine his answer to the two food choices, the more he resisted and the more adamant he became that TV was really his preferred choice for lunch. In viewing the diary, one could not help but laugh, as well as feel the pain of both mother and son.

Aside from comedy and emotion, the data in this project were fascinating because the socialization of choice, via food, was about the socialization of other key attitudes and behaviors, entailing American notions of democracy, individualism, and personhood. Our interests in language and culture dated to graduate school.[2] And here we were, witnessing parenting (in its ideals and tensions) through the lens of food and mediated by language practices, in more than 30 hours of diary footage. Perfect.

In an all-day presentation to the client team, we presented our analysis and implications in four sections. We started at the broadest level by speaking to what we saw as the pertinent cultural ideas framing parenting. We then focused on the goals and tensions surrounding food choices, the routines and practices of eating and, finally, on our client's brand challenges and opportunities. We had more than two and a half hours of edited media, largely excerpted from diaries. By the end of the first section, the brand manager on the team had literally turned her back to the screen (and us). Postures did not significantly improve as the day went on.

From a professional perspective, this project failed. While we pulled through (inspiring) findings to business implications, we had lost the audience. The report and edited media was too much an ethnography of parenting through food and not enough, at least in the first section of the report, on the implications for the brand team's business issues. In the end, there was no sharing in a joint, engaged conversation (for reasons that also went beyond our preoccupation with socialization theory, and had to do with internal dynamics within the brand and research team members). But in this case, bringing in the theory and engaging in the theory tripped us up. We needed to be speaking in terms of products, ingredients, and cartoons: rethinking the brand and its products was the work that needed doing. We needed to be vigilant observers of our clients' implicit theorizing (about brand trust or child empowerment). The "wow" of socialization through language practices was our wow, and our conversation, not theirs.

The second example of failure took place in a very different venue. In the fall of 2010, a yet-to-be-tenured scholar gave a talk in a business school colloquium. Like traditional academic colloquia, this monthly meeting is conceived as a forum for speakers to share current work and gain benefit of audience perspectives via constructive comments and suggestions. Unlike traditional academic colloquia, audiences and speakers come from an array of disciplines. The common ground is an interpretive perspective on consumer behavior. The forum includes culturally oriented marketers and social scientists interested in consumption, and is typically a mix of students, faculty, and the occasional practitioner.

On this November morning, the speaker (and scholar) was making her case for experiential (opposed to material) consumption, arguing that knowledge has value as a resource in identity creation: that experiences rather than things were the "hope chest" of today. The audience loved her data; they were deemed "great data." But the ensuing discussion by the audience, and the challenge posed to the scholar, focused on finding the theory or theoretical framework with which to frame these data to get it published (by a particular A-level journal). To replicate Bourdieu would be disappointing, journal-wise. Other theoretical frames were offered as possibilities, all of which would entail a reworking of the paper's framework. If the story, the details, and the ideas energized the audience in the telling, the subsequent discussion extinguished the palpable enthusiasm engendered by the thoughts and observations of this scholar. The only way the data, *the work*, could count as knowledge and see its fruition in a journal publication—which was the work that needed doing—was by surrounding it with relevant theory. She had failed to make her case as a scholar.

On initial examination, these two examples of failure might be taken as further evidence of a theory and work opposition. In our project with the children's food brand, one could view it as a case where we let theory get in the way of the practical work that needed doing. In the colloquium case, the scholar had not privileged "theory" over "data." This reading would be too pat. Rather, we suggest, both examples provide a lens for illuminating the role of theory *in* the work that needs doing, whether that work is a consulting project or academic journal writing.

## The Work that Theory Does: Establishing a Community of Practice

In each of the failures described here, the tension between the work to be done and the cry for theory is best understood as a communication problem. Unless the findings are framed appropriately, they will not be heard, will not count as knowledge, and will not be acted upon. The tenure-seeking scholar had data in need of a (better) theory. "Appropriate theory," in her case, meant theories her colleagues had already put into play via journals, books, and other forms of scholarship. Her offering would constitute a gambit into that larger conversational discourse. Establishing interlocutors, then, is the communicative work that theory or theorizing does. It establishes the participants in a community of practice.

In the academic's case, explicit theorizing was the practical need. In Latour's terms, she needed to identify her own yeast particulate and send it twirling across the ballroom floor of the academy. Theorizing was the expected form of talk in a venue that prioritizes demonstrable competence in the circulation of ideas (see Tracy 1997 for a detailed conversational analysis of academic colloquia). Delivery, I would suggest, whether a talk, a paper, presentation, or PowerPoint document, is a form of narrative; only when it adheres to expectations does it become knowledge.

The practitioner's case is more complicated, as there are competing theories (and epistemologies) and competing forms of narrative in play. As Robinson (2005) has noted and others have rued, "what is going on" is mediated not only by models (theories) that practitioners bring to bear but also by clients' models (and, indeed, research participants' formulations as well). In the children's food project, the client team's goals of "earning trust" and "enabling choices" implicitly theorized the issues: it assumed that trust is a relevant construct or condition for purchase (versus, for example, symbolic resonance), and that choice-making by children is an ideal to pursue and design for. It is fair to say that we failed to engage with at least the first idea; the term "trust" does not appear once in our hundred-page report. Success in applied work depends on client engagement. As the case of the kids' meal brand illustrated (as did delis in Sunderland, this volume), engagement cannot be taken for granted. With the stakes of various managerial agendas in play, engagement is not always easy to pull off. What I hope to show, however, is that engagement is at least in part a negotiation of terms (which speak implicitly or explicitly of models or theories).

In the communicative work that theory does to establish participants as a community, having multiple models in play puts a spotlight on language. What language is used? How is "what is going on" framed? What counts as knowledge? For whom? And, importantly, whose language prevails? The answer to the last question has significant consequences. In a classic article on the implications of linguistic practice, Carol Cohn (1987) talked about the experience of working with defense intellectuals (the people who map the arms race, formulate deterrence models, and model nuclear war). She discovered that acceptance as a member of the community was contingent on speaking in their terms; her ability to influence depended on her ability to talk, to be an interlocutor in the conversation.

As Cohn became an ever more powerful participant, she also discovered an inability to express her own ideas and values. Linguistic practices defined the terms of engagement. Thus, for example, there was no concept of peace ("peace" as a word was not a part of the discourse). As she wrote, "The problem, then, is not only that the language is narrow but also that it is seen by its speakers as complete or whole unto itself—as representing a body of truths that exist independently of any other truth or knowledge" (Cohn 1987:712). And the power of language seduces. As Cohn put it:

> Suffice it to say that the issues about language do not disappear after you have mastered technostrategic discourse. The seductions remain great.... But as the pleasures deepen, so do the dangers. The activity of trying to out-reason defense intellectuals in their own games gets you thinking inside their rules, tacitly accepting all the unspoken assumptions of their paradigms. You become subject to the tyranny of concepts (1987:714).

Cohn's dilemma, I would suggest, is the practitioner's plight more generally. For anthropological practitioners, the practices of language in commercial arenas erupt as dilemmas. There is a price to be paid in a project's outcome when adhering to the discourse of client models. Too much adherence to client terms and implicit theories means a loss of identity and lack of power to evoke change, as was the case in the deli project (Sunderland, this volume). Too little adherence, as in the case of kids' meals, results in incomprehension and, again, no power to effect change. When it works, there is a messy, negotiated, and fine balance. Cohn goes on to conclude that engagement provoked questions that she would have been incapable of asking of herself had she not been "inside." Thus, engagement can provide a vantage point not otherwise obtained; but, at the same time, in the doing, explanatory models are being contested (or not) and communities are being established (or not) by language practices and language choices.

## The Work that Theory Does: Establishing the Future

If theorizing does communicative work, establishing participants in a community, it does so within a set of peopled relations that bespeak of power hierarchies and managerial or corporate agendas. In the case of the kids' meal brand, rejection of the cultural framing for gaining insights (at least in how we presented it) was simultaneously a rejection/dismissal of the research manager (who had hired us). It was a gauntlet thrown, a challenge to the assembled team, as to which explanation of consumer behavior would end up framing the team's future actions. Theory, as Brenneis (2008) noted, is a polysemic term, a term with multiple meanings, that "carries with it a range of assumptions about what constitutes significant and worthwhile research questions, appropriate and productive ways of pursuing those questions, and the implications of our findings" (2008:156). My point, then, is that not only does theorizing (in the form of questions asked or terms of explanation) establish participants as a group in the here and now of doing, but establishes the terms or groundwork of future action. In a linguistic sense, explanations "perform" the future.

Similarly, sociologist Michel Callon (1998, 2007) has drawn on linguistic theory and notions of linguistic performativity (e.g., Austin, Searle) to ground his arguments about performativity of economic theory in which he has argued that the very discourse of how the economy works creates the economic realities it purports to theorize and explain. Anthropologist Doug Holmes (2009) extends this idea to the linguistic practices of central banks in which, Holmes suggests, the banks' pronouncements surrounding future expectations condition or shape subsequent consumer prices. Using wine talk as his muse, Michael Silverstein (2006) elaborated on the sociocultural work that language-in-use does. Discursive practices indexically identify membership and status within a group: "Mastery of a register, a characteristic way of talking about some area of experience, indexes one's membership in the social group that characteristically does so" (Silverstein 2006:491). Simultaneously, discursive practices (or "enregistered language") are located within institutional structures ("networks of institutional authorization") where status, power or identity is actively negotiated through language events, for example, a scholar talking about consumption, or us talking about mothers as consumers of children's meals. It was only when Cohn mastered the register of defense intellectuals (the institutional authority) that she became an accepted and potentially effective voice in the discourse. In Silverstein's (2006) case of wine talk, participants' alignment is mediated by the *representation* of wine. Likewise, I would argue, it is the *representation* of consumers, delis, mothering choices (or whatever) that becomes the fodder for alignment among members of research teams in industry.

Entangled within institutionalized hierarchies, the terms of talking are the in-the-moment means of representing what is going on. Terms reflect the implicit theoretical stances of those involved. Is it "purchase drivers" or "cultural symbols," "motivations" or "resonance"? Is the subject "consumers" or "families" or "people" or "users"? Negotiation of terms is done within existing discursive hierarchies and has an impact on how teams subsequently think. Crucially, language practices, discursive practices, or registers create as much as reflect in the doing. To return to wine talk, "to the extent that intersubjective alignments are achieved in interaction by negotiating relevant aspects of how wine is described in language, wine's dimensions of evaluation over its existential course are, in effect, thus projectively constructed as much as reflectively construed" (Silverstein 2006:484).

The practitioners' space, by definition, is one of influence. In Robinson's words (2005), practitioners' engagement conditions the future. Cohen (2005) noted the responsibility of practitioners for the impact of their projects on larger publics. I would note that the terms of linguistic engagement perform. Which is to say, discursive practices theorize: the terms of talk construct as well as construe to use Silverstein's terms. The work that talk does, then, is landscape the terms of knowledge and understanding about the way the world works or the what-is-going-on-here. In the framing, telling, reporting, and presenting, there is no neutral position. All positions perform the future.

## A Success Story

If examples of failure illuminated the theorizing implicit in the practicality of work, I turn now to success—a story about the representation of art—to emphasize the performative implications of discursive practices. In the summer of 2006, we conducted a project for the Detroit Institute of Arts (DIA). The DIA was undergoing a massive renovation of its galleries at the time and had awarded Perich Advertising + Design, an Ann Arbor–based agency, the account for creating the campaign that would reintroduce the public to the DIA when it reopened in the fall of 2007. Even though the DIA had attitude and usage information on its audience from a number of quantitative sources, Perich argued strongly that this was insufficient for crafting an effective, inspiring creative strategy, and what they really needed was insight provided by Practica Group. We had a history of collaborating with Perich dating to the early 1990s when Perich was the agency of record for the then Ann Arbor–based Borders bookstore. That collaboration resulted in an award-winning and category-altering national campaign, "Are you curious?", which helped Borders Books and Music redefine the meaning of "bookstore" on a national scale.

Perich was awarded the DIA account in early May of 2006, with a mission to "ignite" museum attendance when it reopened, nothing less. By mid-May, they had not yet convinced the DIA that additional research was required, but had called us to craft an approach. Perich's May 19 draft of proposed research to the DIA stated Practica's rationale in the form of a hypothesis:

## Hypothesis:

By developing an understanding of how people think, feel and live with art, we can gain valuable insight into what key messages will have the greatest opportunity to impact consumers and get them to consider a visit to the DIA.

The term "hypothesis" was not ours (though all the other words were), but the content served to highlight what we saw as the relevant avenue to explore, and it was our first gambit in negotiating the terms of art's representation. From the beginning, we were asking the DIA to shift their focus from museums to aesthetic experience more generally and from ART writ large (masterpieces) to art writ small (everyday life). The hypothesis format served to focus subsequent discussions among Perich, the DIA, and us on relevant questions to pose and relevant ways to query. In the final proposal (accepted in early June), we explicitly met the DIA's concern for actionable results via our approach in our wording of the implications, "By awakening, renewing, igniting art in everyday life, we will need to ensure a connection to awakening a desire for museums."

If the DIA took a leap of faith in agreeing to Perich's request for a particular research partner, it was clearly not without consternation. Beyond the multiple phone calls about both objectives and methods, the discussion guide was scrutinized. In an email from Perich to the DIA team that served to frame how the discussion guide should be evaluated, our client at Perich more or less copied and pasted my words (from a prior email to Perich).[3] Our goal was to preempt a discussion with the DIA on which questions, exactly, we would ask during the interviews:

From: cjohnson@perich.com
Sent: Tuesday, July 11, 2006 10:40 a.m.
To: tom.smith@dia.org, mike d, sarah e
Subject: Ethnographic discussion guide

Hey everyone,
Attached is the discussion guide that has been developed for the in-home ethnographic interviews. It is designed to give some structure to the interviews by outlining the topics we want to cover, but please remember that these discussions will be a bit "free-form" as we want the participants to have the freedom to express themselves in their own unique ways.
A few things to note.

(1) The background section at the beginning is where we spend a little time getting the participants at ease and talking about themselves. It's the prep work for what's ahead.

(2) The section on the daily routine helps establish a foundation for where we take the conversation about where art fits into their lives.

(3) We really want to come away with information on the topics listed in bold—what's life like, art, aesthetic lives, etc.—the specific questions under each of those are guidelines to help bring that information out. Don't be too concerned about the language of those specific sub-questions as it's the general direction we're focused on here.

At this point we'd like you to review the discussion guide and note any areas that you feel may not be covered by the main points. If there are we should discuss those with Rita, which we can do Wednesday (she's doing interviews on another project today). If not, please let me know that the guide is OK and I'll let Rita know we're good to go.

Thanks.

From: tom.smith@dia.org
Sent: Thursday, July 13, 2006 12:53 p.m.
To: Chris Johnson
cc.: Mike Dobbs, Sarah E
Subject: RE: Ethnographic discussion guide

I just tried to call you but our phones are currently down. Anyway, thanks for sending this document. We are going to review this today and get back to you ASAP. On another couple of notes:

Is there a way we can have the taped version of Sunday's sessions on Monday morning so we can review them. Even though Mike, Sarah and I are scheduled for later sessions, it would be great to get a feel for how these are going early in the process so we can ask questions/make suggestions before it's too late. Please advise. Let me know if you have any questions.

Thanks

The in-home interview itself was seen as something that could and should be evaluated in terms of success or failure, a metric we pushed against. Once in the field, the DIA team requested a mid-fieldwork debriefing to assuage (or gauge?) their concerns about actionable outcome. In all of these interactions, I would contend that theorizing was the implicit subject. In keeping with Brenneis' notion of theory, we were negotiating with the DIA in what counted as worthwhile research questions as well as what counted as legitimate avenues for exploration.

In November of 2007 a campaign with the tagline "Let yourself go" opened in Detroit. A downtown building was wrapped (Figure 8.1); print (Figure 8.2) and TV

FIGURE 8.1 Building wrap in downtown Detroit, November 2007 (Courtesy of DIA).

spots emphasized the interactive, imaginative, immersive experience that people have with art in their lives while simultaneously referencing DIA masterpieces. Letting yourself go literally and figuratively even extended to jumping through canvases (Figure 8.3). The transformation experienced with art was indicated symbolically by color: in one 30-second spot, a black and white figure approaches a painting, peers attentively into it, and reaches out a hand that, as it comes close to the canvas, takes on its colors (red, blue, and yellow). The figure looks at her arm, the painting, and then, with a leap, jumps through it. On emergence, she has taken on all the colors of the canvas. She has been transformed.

Into 2008, the DIA was getting 10,000 visitors a week. In February 2008, *The Detroit News* headlined, "Clever ads transform DIA into getaway":

> Let's start with a simple question: "What pleases you about your home?" This is the question that somehow wound up as an award-winning advertising campaign for the Detroit Institute of Arts. You may have noticed the quirky commercials for the DIA, because they're striking and simple. They've been running since last fall and somehow cutting through commercial clutter with few words, animated line-drawings and a jazzy cello soundtrack. In two 30-second spots, museum patrons wander around the museum. In one spot, the patron reaches out and—voila—goes from black-and-white to color (Berman 2008).

FIGURE 8.2 Introductory print ad, November 2007 (Courtesy of DIA).

FIGURE 8.3 Screenshots from one of the two TV spots introducing the new DIA, November 2007 (Courtesy of DIA).

The campaign was embedded in the insight that folks looking at a Diego Rivera mural (DIA masterpiece) or a glinting sunset while commuting home were comparable aesthetic experiences, that each offered a respite in getting away from the everyday.[4] Further, it was an equivalence that not only should be respected, but embraced. That a figure could burst through a museum canvas was testament to the shift in DIA thinking and theorizing of art. It acknowledged that art was not about "seeing" or 'learning" but was rather about losing yourself for a moment, a time out from responsibility, productivity, and obligation, a moment of getting away. For the DIA, art was calibrated in terms of museum masterpieces, pedigree, and the Western canon of culture (evident in their initial and ongoing question of "motivating desire for art" in which the implicit subject was *their* art). We offered a different vocabulary, an expanded register in the representation of art, for thinking about and conceptualizing art writ large. To date, the ads are still running (now updated with different wordless conversations; see http://perich.com/work/dia). The DIA did not lessen their commitment to pedagogical, Western-canon views, but enlarged their register in conceptualizing museum art to include "getting away," transformation, and conversation. The terms of new understanding were discursively performed for the future via the campaign.

If the DIA campaign was a great success for the museum, success was contingent on and embedded by interpersonal engagement. On the museum's side, it was a process of extricating itself from "museum mode" and putting itself into "art mode."[5] From our side, it meant listening to the DIA's implicit concerns, the most important of which was to respect the status of ART writ large. Ignoring the DIA register by "dumbing down" art, for example by equating masterpieces with a pop music Top 10 list, was not an option. The terms of their concerns provided a lens into their own theorizing about art and the nature of the problem (high versus low, a thing versus an aesthetic experience), which we explicitly addressed when we outlined a communications strategy that embraced the primacy of individuals' interactive experience with art in everyday life while also embracing the specialness of *this* art (or ART writ large). What made it all possible, though, was the interpersonal commitment of all involved: the implicit agreement was not leaving anyone in the lurch—whether it be Perich, the DIA, or Practica—which permitted a negotiation of new arenas of understanding even when concerns or consternation erupted among each of the players at different points in time.

## Conclusions: The Work that Needs Doing

For anthropologists who practice in industry it would seem, at face value, that the work that needs doing is dictated by industry's terms (see Hepsø and Brun-Cottan, this volume, and Cefkin and Isaacs, this volume, on the temporal dimension of project work). There is a contract to be fulfilled, a promise to be met. What I hope to have shown in this essay is that theory, for practitioners, is always lurking. Engaging with theory (in the we/here) is a crucial aspect of the work that needs doing if for no other reason that clients are bringing in their own. Corporate counterparts have theories too, theories that they propose in interaction, though they are not labeled as such. The work that needs to get done then, the engagement, revolves around a mutual accommodation of participants' implicit or explicit theorizing. Further, in establishing alignment among those involved (a necessary entailment of engagement) theorizing—in the modes of representation, assumptions made or queried, questions asked or the means of answering—is always present. And finally, discursive choices matter, practically for the outcome of a particular project, but more fundamentally because discursive talk, inextricably tied to networks of actors and institutional authority, not only reflects, but performs.

Given the ubiquity of the corporate form (Welker et al. 2011) in all spheres of life, I would suggest that anthropologists must find ways to be effective interlocutors. Toward this end, Clarke (2010) has noted that students are increasingly combining anthropology with professional training in law, business, or health. Beyond the perhaps pragmatic strategy of employment opportunities, this form of professional multilingualism allows access to, and membership in, other communities (for Clarke, "regimes of practice"). I would suggest that wherever anthropologists sit, engagement is a reality and engagement entails a position to influence. As practitioners (of the lurking monster type; see Sunderland, this volume), the moral obligation to the field of anthropology is no less onerous and no less felt; it just takes place on a complicated, contingent landscape in which footing must be found (compare with Bestemen 2010; Guyer 2011; Spencer 2010). If we negotiate a language that performs, there is hope.

## References

Berman, Laura
    2008 Clever Ads Transform DIA into Getaway. Detroit News, February 12. Available at http://www.detnews.com/apps/pbcs.dll/article?AID=/20080212/OPINION03/802120364. Accessed July 2009.

Bestemen, Carol
    2010 In and Out of the Academy: Policy and the Case for a Strategic Anthropology. *Human Organization* 69(4):407–416.

Brenneis, Donald
    2008 Telling Theories. *Ethos* 36(1):155–169.

Callon, Michel, (ed.)
    1998 *Laws of the Markets*. Oxford: Blackwell.

Callon, Michel
    2007 What Does It Mean to Say That Economics is Performative? In *Do Economists Make Markets?*, edited by Donald Mackenzie, Fabian Muniesa, and Lucia Siu, pp. 301–357. Princeton: Princeton University Press.

Clarke, Kamari
    2010 Toward a Critically Engaged Ethnographic Practice. *Current Anthropology* 51(Supp. 2):S301–S312.

Cohen, Kris
    2005 Who We Talk About When We Talk About Users. *EPIC* 2005:9–30.

Cohn, Carol
    1987 Sex and Death in the Rational World of Defense Intellectuals. *Signs* 12(4):687–718.

Guyer, Jane
    2011 Blueprints, Judgment, and Perseverance in a Corporate Context. *Current Anthropology* 52(S3):S17–S27.

Holmes, Douglas
    2009 Economy of Words. *Cultural Anthropology* 24(3):381–419.

Latour, Bruno
    1999 *Pandora's Hope*. Cambridge, MA: Harvard University Press.

Robinson, Rick
2005 Let's Have a Conversation: Theory Session Introductory Remarks. *EPIC* 2005:1–8.

Schieffelin, Bambi
1990 *The Give and Take of Everyday Life: Language Socialization of Kaluli Children.* New York: Cambridge University Press.

Silverstein, Michael
2006 Old Wine, New Ethnographic Lexicography. *Annual Review of Anthropology* 25:481–496.

Slater, Don
2011 Marketing as a Monstrosity: The Impossible Place Between Culture and Economy. In *Inside Marketing*, edited by Detlev Zwick and Julien Cayla, pp. 23–41. Oxford, United Kingdom: Oxford University Press.

Spencer, Jonathon
2010 The Perils of Engagement: A Space for Anthropology in the Age of Security? *Current Anthropology* 51(Supp. 2):S289–S299.

Tracy, Karen
1997 *Colloquium: Dilemmas of Academic Discourse.* Westport, CT: Praeger.

Welker, Marina, Damani Partridge, and Rebecca Hardin
2011 Corporate Lives: New Perspectives on the Social Life of the Corporate Form. *Current Anthropology* 52(Supp. 3):S3–S16.

# Notes

1    The projects cited in this chapter, with exception of the DIA project, were collaborative endeavors with Patricia Sunderland. Moreover, both chapters in this volume were collaboratively written.

2    Patti had been steeped in a language socialization perspective; Bambi Schieffelin had been an advisor. Professor of anthropology at NYU, Bambi Schieffelin's work on the cultural socialization of children with and through language routines and practices was critical in the formation of the language socialization perspective (Schieffelin 1990).

3    Names, other than my own, have been changed.

4    Robert Moise was an integral member of the Practica Group research team. We are indebted to him for his insights.

5    Personal communication in an email to Practica Group from the DIA in 2008 articulating the shift in their own thinking.

Chapter 9

# Doing Corporate Ethnography as an Insider (Employee)

*Vidar Hepsø*

## Introduction

In the last 20 years or so, ethnography has made major inroads in corporations, other large organizations in government, and the not-for-profit sector, organizations that used to rely almost exclusively on quantitative data for strategic decision making. That situation has changed slowly but dramatically, and today practically all global companies hire anthropologists or other ethnographically trained and experienced experts to help them understand, from the inside out and from the bottom up, how their organizations work and how they function within the larger context of customer relationships and supply chains. Ethnography has thus gained a new, strategic legitimacy, which has also led to the reemergence of employees hired for other reasons now claiming their ethnographic skills.

In surveying the landscape of ethnographic employment in industry, it is clear that at the present time, ethnographers work in two primary situations: either hired as full employees to provide a presence and steady input at the hiring company, or as consultants who focus on particular issues that require special attention. I have worked for a multinational oil company for the last 20 years, doing what might be called "petroleum anthropology." In this chapter, I will paint a picture of what it is like to work as an insider where one has available the resources of the company but at the same time must confront issues that are peculiar to the insider position. Many of these same insider issues are also encountered by ethnographers working as temporary consultants; as a matter of fact there is a great deal of overlap, which is also discussed by Francoise Brun-Cotton (this volume). My intent is to give readers an idea of what to expect when hired as an ethnographic employee, and at the same time to give business people or employers an impression of what they can anticipate if they hire an ethnographer as an employee rather than as a consultant.

What company ethnographers actually do varies tremendously, but there are some key characteristics of insider work that they all share to a greater or lesser degree. I will attempt to sketch out some of these characteristics by describing my involvement in a project carried out among offshore oil workers and crane operators on the coast of Norway. This chapter is organized along the lifecycle

*Advancing Ethnography in Corporate Environments: Challenges and Emerging Opportunities*, edited by Brigitte Jordan, 151–162. ©2013 Left Coast Press Inc. All rights reserved.

of an insider ethnography project, starting with a description of the situation, to gaining access, to doing the work of an insider, to wrap-up and lessons learned. I will aim to present the insider issues both from an ethnographer's perspective and a business person/employer's perspective. This project, in many ways typical for my work as an insider, had as its overriding aim the improvement of the quality of working life for offshore crane operators.

## The Project

First, some background: all cargo for offshore oil installations in the North Sea is transported to the continental shelf by supply boats. The vessels are loaded with containers at several supply bases on the west coast of Norway. After loading, these supply vessels call at installations every day or at regular sailing intervals.

When a supply ship arrives at an installation, a crane operator leads the lifting process and communicates with the other participants to make sure that operations are carried out safely. The activity starts when seamen (crew members on the supply vessel) prepare the cargo for transfer to the offshore installation. The crane operator on the installation lowers a cable with a hook to which supply-ship seamen fasten the cargo. The cargo is then lifted onboard the installation platform, where banks men unload it. Crane operations are inherently high-risk activities due to often-extreme weather conditions and high seas. The coordination between crane operators, banks men, and seamen is of paramount importance for safe operations.

FIGURE 9.1. Offshore crane operations in the North Sea. A supply vessel arrives at the installation and crane operations can begin (photo by Øyvind Hagen, Statoil).

FIGURE 9.2. Operator doing his work in offshore crane cabin (photo by Marit Hommedal, Statoil)

An ethnographer working to describe how crane workers collaborate must command a thorough set of ethnographic skills to understand their safety culture.

The employer who hires an internal ethnographer most likely wants to see ethnographic skills applied to company-specific objectives. In this case, the overall goal of the project was to improve the quality of working life for offshore crane operators, with safety of course being an important consideration (Hepsø 2009;

Hepsø and Botnevik 2002). As a company ethnographer, I was asked to take part in an effort to improve both the skills and the status of crane operations crew. It happened that at this time there was a movement throughout the oil industry toward flatter, team-based organizations. These new work designs give much more responsibility to the individual employee. They also set tougher demands on people's skills and lead to more autonomous interaction between technical disciplines and across functional borders. Traditionally, very few crane operators move up in the hierarchy of the company to become middle managers or are promoted to senior positions on the installations. As a consequence, few managers know the skills demanded of crane operators. The effect this had for crane and lifting professionals was that their work was stereotyped as "simple," and therefore unimportant. As an insider, I gained access to the community and helped to describe the key elements of their practice through ethnographic fieldwork. This input was valuable for the company and relevant for organizational development processes that could improve the safety practices of the company. What follows are some of the issues that arose in the course of this project.

## Negotiating Access

A student of corporate ethnography might correctly assume that it is easier to negotiate access when you are an insider in an organization. And it is true that while gaining access is often a major challenge for outsiders (e.g., Jordan with Lambert 2009), for insiders it is generally less problematic. For example, a company badge and access to company email and information technology (IT) systems will ease your work and ability to move around on your own in the company, something that is increasingly important as more and more of the information you need is buried in digital archives and accessible only through company proprietary computer systems. For the employer to have an insider that knows where to go to find backstage arenas and uncover hidden information is a great asset. This process is always more troublesome for outsiders. It is also true that because I am a company employee, colleagues are generally willing to speak to me and share information. The insider therefore needs less time and resources to develop the necessary background understanding of a challenge. This is especially important for employers who tend to need informed input quickly (see also Cefkin, this volume).

I was invited to participate in the project on offshore crane operations because of previous work I had done and because of my personal and professional networks in the organization. Important decision-makers either knew me directly or heard of me via old colleagues who trusted me and advocated my participation. It was thus relatively easy for me to mobilize support, not only for gaining access, but also later on for endorsement and encouragement in the course of fieldwork. I've come to believe that for the inside ethnographer most engagements happen in this way, via invitation or request based on a foundation of personal relationships and networks, maintained in overlapping groups inside the organization. Over time, the ethnographer gains the necessary contacts and absorbs local knowledge about the ways of management and other powerful stakeholders. You learn as an insider to understand the internal structures, sensing formal and informal attitudes and expectations when doing your work. A great deal of the insider's local knowledge revolves around which company words and phrases should be used when, and what strategies should be taken when embarking on a new project (see also Denny and Sunderland in this volume). This also means that the insider knows the corporate agenda and can communicate with the employer far better than an outside consultant. Outsiders can never develop this deep and long-term local knowledge of the company setting since their involvement typically is too short. That an internal ethnographer can gain access more quickly and more effectively than an external consultant is often a motivating factor in hiring an ethnographer in the first place.

## Insider by Degree

It may not be evident to the casual observer that being an insider is a question of degree. Even when you are an employee, no matter how and where you begin a project, your team members will speculate on your identity and presumed allegiances. They will ask: Does he (or she) represent HR (Human Resources)? The Research Department? Or maybe Corporate IT? You will have to work with and negotiate these initial perceptions to be able to work efficiently with the group that carries out the work in which you are becoming a participant. The "negotiating access" and "insider by degree" issues are related. There is a difference between gaining access formally, within the organizational structure that gives you your ID card and officially assigns you to a project, and access to the community of practitioners where you will be doing your ethnography. So even as a card-carrying insider I had to negotiate access to and become accepted by the group of crane operators. Thus, the insider also exists as a quasi-outsider because ethnography in some sense will always have a certain outsider flavor. For the employer, an insider by degree means that the internal ethnographer can easily switch location and objects of study within the organization. Now, let's take a closer look at the "insider by degree" issue as it pertained to the crane operators project.

Crane operators form a group of people that have similar interests and objectives. When they pursue these interests and objectives in their work they use common practices, and a shared vocabulary, and work with the same tools. Through this shared practice and activity they come to develop similar beliefs and value systems. Such a group has come to be called a community of practitioners (Jordan 1989) or a community of practice (CoP; Lave and Wenger 1991). There is an important issue here for employers. It is easier to use internal ethnographers to grasp the essence of these CoPs in the organization.

Often, Legitimate Peripheral Participation (LPP) can ease an "insider by degree" issue. LPP is a practical mode of engagement in which a learner—in this case the inside ethnographer—participates in the actual practices of experts (e.g., crane operators) to a limited degree and with limited responsibility for the product that the experts develop. Most companies use "on the job training" to involve newbies in the activities of the organization, so an internal ethnographer can also easily fit into this category and use that as an entry point. The internal ethnographer's role is therefore formally sanctioned by the organization's learning routines. The legitimacy here does not have to be associated with formal, official sanctions, but the concept of LPP means that the ethnographer is accepted as a peripheral member of the CoP. In other words, everybody, including the ethnographer, sees the newbie as a legitimate member of the community while in the position of participating learner and contributor. In this way, the insider develops a unique understanding of the CoP's practices that could inform development work in the organization.

Most people become accepted members of their groups by capitalizing on apprenticeship-type situations where experts of varying degree provide role models and support for newcomers. Newbies then become "legitimate peripheral participants" in the activities of the established members of the group. Newbie participation was also a way for me to deal with the "insider by degree" issue. I was certainly peripheral in many ways. I am not an expert in crane and lifting operations, and nobody would have taken me for a crane engineer or a manager in that community. I did not know the everyday language and work practices of the crane community. I wanted to learn about the situated practices of the crane operators more or less as an apprentice, which I perceived as vital to comprehend how knowledge and identities develop in this group and to understand the dynamics of the community more generally. In the course of fieldwork I moved from distant observation to more direct participation in discussions over work practices that the community initiated. In this case I was allowed by the community to participate, but in a peripheral kind of role where everybody knew about and took into account my status as a novice, knowing that for me a full insider position would never be an option. The issue that you will only be an insider within certain communities in the company cannot be escaped. The nature and extent of the degree obviously depends on many factors, including the nature of the project, the degree of familiarity, and the kind of relevant background the newbie brings to the work. The advantage for the employer here may be that an employee ethnographer might be seen as less troublesome than an outside consultant who might more easily be perceived as an instrument of management. Also, the outsider often cannot take advantage of "on the job" organizational learning mechanisms since such offerings are reserved for employees only.

## Meaningful Participation and Contributions to the Group's Work

My participation as a peripheral participant was legitimate in the sense that I was there to learn as an apprentice, but participation in a CoP also means meaningful participation and contribution to the work that is undertaken. Participation in a community leads to role expectations about making contributions to the activities and development of the group. As one of the operators said, "We will teach you how we work if you can help us to improve our practice." When I gained deeper access to the community of crane operators and their practices, I began to be able to contribute to solutions to their problems in a more meaningful way. This contribution was founded on a combination of increased understanding of the CoP's work culture and the capabilities I brought into the community. For one thing, I increasingly took on the role of a middleman or translator between the various stakeholders in the project. This is not an unusual role for an internal ethnographer, as Sherry (1999) also notes. For the employer, the internal ethnographer's other capabilities beyond the ethnographic skills for which they are hired may also become important. For anyone wishing to embark on a career in this domain, it may be useful to develop additional skills. Let me present three examples that would be relevant for both students in this area and for employers fearing that internal ethnographers might be too specialized in their competence and skills.

In the project on crane operations I had to show how ethnographic descriptions and analysis of work practice could be translated into routine, practical work procedures without losing the tacit understanding of the nature of the work. For example, the key communication practices of crane operators had to be translated into practical use in training sessions in a crane simulator (Figure 9.3). I helped develop the scenarios and the detailed training sessions that the crane operators then used in crane simulation training. The crane operators would participate in onshore simulation training every second year to practice for hazardous situations

FIGURE 9.3. Crane cabin in onshore simulator used for crane simulation and skills training (photo by Jørn Adde, Statoil).

that could not be reproduced in their normal work environment. Both the brief-ings before simulation exercises and the debriefings afterwards relied heavily on ethnographic input.

I also set up a groupware database in Lotus Notes (a basic bulletin board kind of application) that the distributed community could use when discussing and articulating their practices. Since Lotus Notes was the company standard for email and project collaboration at the time, and I had the requisite computer expertise, it was possible for me to set up an environment that this distributed group could use. As a company insider I had the necessary access rights to make this software application available on the company's servers. Because of this service, the crane operators experienced me both as an ethnographer and a friendly collaborator, helping them with the editing of their descriptions of work practices. Many of them actually thought I was "the IT guy" that enabled their distributed col-laboration. This tool also enabled me to gather information about how the crane operators discussed and presented their practices without being in their physical presence (see also Riopelle and Gluesing, this volume, on gathering data without being physically present).

A final example of useful peripheral skills is group facilitation. A project group/field group was set up and given the mandate to discuss and define the key elements of a crane operational practice. This group consisted of crane opera-tors, banks men, and engineers responsible for crane maintenance. In a number of workshop sessions, the crane operators from the field defined core elements of their "best practice" based on their long offshore experience. The field group consisted of 10 to 15 people depending on the issues to be discussed in a particular session. I facilitated part of these meetings, presented vignettes, or asked informed questions based on my field experience to keep the conversation going. It is easy to see that an internal ethnographer could fill a facilitation role. The external ethnog-rapher might also be able to do this, but without the trust generated by the insider's deep and thorough understanding of the company, it might have a different flavor. These contributions to the work of the community eased my access, highlighted my input, and enabled me to take a useful role in the project.

## Allegiance and Identity

Another important issue for an inside ethnographer revolves around sometimes conflicting world views: on one side, a disciplinary anthropological identity that comes from many years of training; on the other, the company's work culture with its own expectations and goals. How does the inside ethnographer live with overlapping or opposing allegiances and identities? What if our insider status becomes so strongly connected to the organization, its culture, and its agendas that it threatens to come into conflict with our professional identity and practices as ethnographers? This may become a major issue not only for a novice but also on occasions for experienced researchers. For the employer, this boils down to the question: can the internal ethnographer be trusted? Can the employer be sure that the internal ethnographer will take a company perspective? Let me clarify this with an example from the case being presented.

In the oil company, the term "best practices" is used routinely to describe how work should be undertaken. Formulations of best practices should be the end result of the discussions in the field group. Best practices describe primary work, or the activities that directly address the specific agendas and goals of the work situation, and often are tied into a larger formal structure via an espoused division of labor. However, "best practice" does not address all the improvisation and articulation work necessary to handle contingencies in primary work tasks (Hepsø 1997; Suchman 1985). As a trained ethnographer, I know this to be the case. But the crane community constantly misused the term "best practices," and I could not tell the crane operators that this language was all wrong (and counterintuitive to ethnographers). Still, using the term is a common way to describe such issues in the company and is an ingrained part of company role expectations. As such, best practice thinking was part of how insiders thought and talked about development work in the organization. And the employer of a trained ethnographer wouldn't even recognize this identity issue at all. He or she would simply not understand it.

This belief that a representation—such as best practices—developed in one context can be reified and moved to a new context is problematic for an ethnographer. Best practice thinking clashes with some of the fundamental axioms of anthropology and, therefore, with our identity (Hepsø 1997, 2000, 2009). Still, the discussions associated with the development of these best practice representations triggered sense-making in the community and aroused processes that were more than purely instrumental. "Thin descriptions," like best practices, actually became a vantage point for "thick descriptions" of work practice and action that invoked human sense-making, communication, and construction of meaning in the community.

I thought of best practices and the company standards as native categories and mixed them with my ethnographic concepts. (See also Denny, this volume, for a similar mixture of concepts and categories.) To live with an identity as an ethnographer and maintain allegiance as a company employee can be difficult. For the employer discussing the hiring of an internal ethnographer, the following should be observed. Not only was I obliged to act on behalf of the company, but I was also expected to comply with my company's ethical and business standards. This issue exists for outsiders too, but it is tougher for insiders. An inside ethnographer serves business interests first and has, foremost, a business role as employee that cannot be escaped. You cannot betray the loyalty to your company and your employer.

## Company Allegiance and Teamwork

The obligation to act on behalf of, and to comply with, the ethical and business standards of the company contributes to team spirit and cohesion. It blurs the borders between you and the other participants in the organization. This is also pretty obvious for the employer, but less obvious for the fresh student of ethnography. The employer would expect that company allegiance and role expectations should override your ethnographic identity and practice. In anthropology, this coincides with discussions on "going native" or becoming a part of the phenomenon you study, a discussion the employer would never understand or find interesting. The employer will argue that working together with smart people towards fulfilling shared objectives with a good cause (like improved quality of working life for the crane and lifting community) increases the feeling of a shared mindset and team spirit across domains. He or she has a point here.

Still, it is important to know that as an insider, your informants are colleagues, some even good friends. Role distinctions may become unclear or actually break down altogether. As Diana Forsythe argues (1999:7–8), informant, funder, colleague, employer, grant reviewer, and job referee sometimes turn out to be the same individuals. These people will have considerable power over you since you are part of the organizational structure yourself, but they also read ethnographic texts, find them interesting, and will contest them. This is also why your employer will be showing an interest in your work but not automatically take what you write for granted. The lesson is that teamwork with nonethnographers blurs the distinction between our ethnography work and that of others in the team. This does not mean that an inside ethnographer's perspective becomes identical to that of the other team members. The employer also needs the internal ethnographer's core competence, but in a position where the ethnographer is able to communicate and function in the heterogeneous group (Sherry 1999).

An outside consultant can do this work in the team as well, but it is more difficult for the employer and team members to discard your input when you are an inside colleague. On the other hand, role expectations and group pressure are stronger for me as an inside ethnographer in the team than similar pressures on an outside consultant.

## Conclusion

I participated in development work in the crane community for more than two years (Hepsø 2009; Hepsø and Botnevik 2002), helping the crane operators and banks men articulate their practice, develop action plans to improve the quality of their working life, and more generally improve their competence. In presenting this project I hope I have shown what an inside ethnographer can do. I have tried to address issues both from a prospective employee and an employer perspective. An insider position opens up the possibility to be a much fuller participant in events in the field, a situation that is unlikely to happen for many outside ethnographers under more traditional circumstances where being a visitor or guest may be the only achievable position.

The end result of the teamwork project in which I participated was a significant reduction in crane accidents, compulsory training for all offshore crane operators in simulators, the development of a Norwegian education/apprenticeship program for crane operators, and a Norwegian technical standard for crane operations. Inside ethnography provided important input and made me feel proud both as an inside ethnographer and as a company employee. We managed to make a difference for the group, improving the quality of their working lives.

An internal ethnographer can also be a gatekeeper and manager for novice ethnographers. The insider can open up an organization for students, acting as their internal supervisor and helping them do their thesis work within the organization. This has been possible for me since I am also an adjunct professor at the Norwegian University of Science and Technology (NTNU). Both social science and engineering students did thesis work in the aftermath of the project I have described in this chapter, helping to come up with new technical solutions for lifting equipment and undertaking more detailed studies of the quality of working life in crane operations. Through my work I have influenced the careers of many social science and engineering graduates. In several circumstances, my students have become company employees.

The inside ethnographer can also be a gateway for others by providing access for additional ethnographers to work in the organization. The insider can hire external ethnographers to do work that he or she is not able to do her/himself. Or other stakeholders in the organization might hire external ethnographers to do some project-specific task, and the inside ethnographer guides the planning and execution of their work. The job is then to help the outsider gain access, give hints to directions their work can take, and make sure that the interests of the company are handled. In these cases I may even be their project manager.

Can inside ethnographic practice in companies as presented here also be relevant for outside ethnographers or consultants? I believe the answer is yes, since for both the student and the employer the insider perspective represents alternatives that can enlighten the discussion about outside ethnography practice. Many of the topics I have discussed here are continued in the next chapter by Francoise Brun-Cottan, who is concerned with the complementary role of the external consultant ethnographer.

## Acknowledgments

Thanks to Gitti Jordan for making my thoughts more clear throughout the writing process. Thanks also to Robert Irwin, who did an extensive editing job on my imperfect English and thereby improved the quality of my chapter.

# References

Forsythe, Diana

1999 Ethics and Politics of Studying Up in Technoscience. *Anthropology of Work Review* 20(1):6–11.

Hepsø, Vidar

1997 The Social Construction and Visualization of a Norwegian Offshore Installation. Proceedings of the Fifth European Conference on Computer Supported Cooperative Work, Lancaster, United Kingdom, September 7–11, 1997. Kluwer Academic Publishers. Available at http://www.ecscw.org/1997/08.pdf. Accessed June 2, 2012.

2000 Klovn, hoffnarr, guru og insiderantropolog? Noen tanker omkring et antropologisk insiderethos i industrien (Clown, jester, guru and insider anthropologist. Some thoughts on an anthropological insider ethos in industry). *Norsk Antropologisk Tidsskrift* 11:67–80. Universitetsforlaget.

2009 Leading Research in Technoscience; insider social science in socio-technological change, Saarbrücken:VDM Verlag Dr. Müller.

Hepsø, Vidar, and Rune Botnevik

2002 Competence Development in a Community of Practice. Proceedings of the Participatory Design Conference Malmö, New York, June 23-25, pp. 63-73. New York: ACM Press.

Jordan, Brigitte

1989 Cosmopolitical Obstetrics: Some Insights from the Training of Traditional Midwives. Social Science and Medicine 28:9:2:925-944.

Jordan, Brigitte, with Monique Lambert

2009 Working in Corporate Jungles: Reflections on Ethnographic Praxis in Industry. Chapter 4 in: Ethnography and the Corporate Encounter: Reflections on Research In and Of Corporations. Melissa Cefkin, ed. New York: Berghahn Books.

Lave, Joan, and Etienne Wenger

1991 *Situated Learning: Legitimate Peripheral Participation.* New York: Cambridge University Press.

Sherry, John

1999 Ethnography and Internet Time: Ethics, Politics and Poetics. *Anthropology of Work Review* 20(1):15–21.

Suchman, Lucy

1995 Making Work Visible. *Communications of the ACM* 38(9):56–63.

Chapter 10

# Doing Corporate Ethnography as an Outsider (Consultant)

*Francoise Brun-Cottan*

> History is not merely what happened. It is what happened
> in the context of what might have happened.
>
> —*Hugh Trevor-Roper*

## Introduction

This chapter follows Vidar Hepsø's account of experiences informed by doing ethnographic work for more than 20 years as an "insider" employee at a large corporation. The examples he gives are vivid, the issues trenchant. The very length of his tenure speaks to the value with which he and his work have been held.

For myriad reasons, including rapid technological innovation and new services as well as changing financial considerations, such tenancy is becoming increasingly rare no matter an employee's contribution, or their discipline for that matter. Increasingly companies are bringing in external consultants for shorter time spans to look at new products and ways of working.

For me, working most recently as a freelance consultant, the distinction between doing ethnography as an "insider" or "outsider" has more to do with the ability to accept or reject assignments, the possibility of distancing oneself from the assigning agency and from the final report, and knowing what effect, if any, one's work has had, than with the techniques and methods used in the study.

As you will see, my own experiences, both as an inside ethnographer and as an external consultant, don't really conform to what one might think of as the straightforward vanilla versions of either role. My career experiences place me in a liminal position in both instances. On the one hand, this makes my pronouncements about "outsider" experiences a bit less clear-cut. On the other hand, clear-cuttedness has never been the banner cry of ethnography and shows little sign of becoming more so moving forward. On yet another hand—ethnography being a hydra-handed collection of methods, approaches, and ethical considerations— looking at the borders of "insider" and "outsider" as interconnecting semipermeable membranes facilitates seeing how the work of ethnography plays out in and across real-world examples.

*Advancing Ethnography in Corporate Environments: Challenges and Emerging Opportunities,* edited by Brigitte Jordan, 163–174. ©2013 Left Coast Press Inc. All rights reserved.

I believe this sort of quasi-bipolar looking is in keeping with tensions established early in anthropology's disciplinary ancestry, as set out by Bronislaw Malinowski, who famously said: "The goal of the ethnographer is to grasp the native's point of view, his relation to life, to realize his vision of his world" (Malinowski 1966:25).

Yet, a little later (talking about the Kula ring, a ritual economic exchange system) he admonishes us with:

> Not even the most intelligent native has any clear idea of the Kula as a big, organized social construction, still less of its sociological function and implications . . . . The integration of all the details observed, the achievement of a sociological synthesis of all the various, relevant symptoms, is the task of the Ethnographer . . . . the Ethnographer has to *construct* the picture of the big institution, very much as the physicist constructs his theory from the experimental data, which always have been within reach of everybody, but needed a consistent interpretation (Malinowski 1966:83).

So, our instruction as ethnographers is to focus on the micro and the macro in which it is embedded. Our goal is to realize the natives' (users', workers', informants', participants') values and vision even though those may not (and in global, distributed organizations most assuredly will not) include an understanding of the totality of which he, she, or they are a part.[1] I would note here that maintaining a center between the two poles is akin to balancing a teeter-totter, sometimes leaning toward looking from the individual outward, sometimes from the system inward.

I must confess and acknowledge at this point that in more than 20 years of working in and for institutions I have never produced an "Ethnography," (e.g., a book-length report of a sustained study of natives), corporate or otherwise. I have championed, used, and helped expand a toolkit of ethnographic methods and techniques. (Brun-Cottan and Wall 1995). These tools include some combinations of the now usual suspects: interviewing, observation, participant observation, shadowing, audio and video recording, transcribing, logging, rapid prototyping, and, when very lucky, participatory designing. I use the term "ethnographer" rather than that mouthful of features for convenience. But outside of my own dissertation, I have never had the opportunity or been asked to meld the two ends of Malinowski's teeter-totter. I have never had to try and present thick descriptions of individuals' lives and ontologies and integrate those with understandings of the larger organizational and societal systems in which they are embedded. I use ethnographic techniques and methods to produce ethnographically informed insights for specific institutional interests, not to relate holistic accounts of study participants' worlds. Claiming something is an ethnography carries the weight of, and must answer to, understandings gleaned through 200 years of disciplinary exploration, experimentation, argumentation, and analysis. This is not to devalue in any way the works of ethnographers in industry, but we should be mindful of the difference.

## Straddling the Insider-Outsider Position

It would simplify discussion if the ethnographer steadfastly maintained the position of insider or outsider throughout an engagement. However, in some cases, a person may occupy both roles within the scope of one project. Consider the example of Julian Orr's work at Xerox PARC (Palo Alto Research Center). Orr previously had worked as a service technician on various communications devices before, during, and after he completed his bachelor's degree. He had been conducting ethnographic work in Afghanistan before the political situation made it clear that he was not going to be able to continue his research for a higher degree. He joined Xerox Corporation at PARC as a technician. Not having had prior experience with a particular copier—intended to be turned into a laser printer—he attended school for the technicians who would become the focus of his field observations. He was given the opportunity to finish his interrupted ethnographic research, but in a completely different domain than his previous work in Afghanistan. He approached the study of field repair service technicians as the basis of original research for a thesis but he also maintained a corporate insider's perspective, looking out for what could be of interest and use to his corporate sponsor. Before attending the school, we can say that he was an outsider vis-à-vis the groups he was to come to study.

What he discovered once he turned his attention to technicians servicing copiers in the field was enlightening in terms of revealing the ways that technicians learned and built a knowledge base through the sharing of stories. This insight came to form the kernel of an internal tool intended to facilitate such sharing within Xerox.

However, becoming an insider member of the group he was studying had the effect of rendering certain of the copier service technicians' actions and practices transparently obvious and not worth mentioning. After reading his descriptions of some of these practices, research colleagues—insiders to the company but still external to the technicians' group—called for clarification of what had become so obvious to Orr. This is what he notes about the ways in which becoming an insider (to both Xerox and the technicians' trade) was complicated:

> My practical experience was both a boon and a curse. It was beneficial in that it made my presence in the field less obtrusive, since I needed fewer explanations. It was helpful in winning the trust of the technicians. However, it was a problem in analysis since my notes omitted things that were obvious in the field but are less so at a distance. I also found I had a tendency to regard certain phenomena as unremarkable which are not really so to outsiders. The assistance of colleagues was invaluable in calling my attention to some interesting material. . . . (Orr 1996:7).

Orr moved back and forth between insider and outsider roles and viewpoints for the duration of the project. He operated as a novice learning to fix a particular copier innovation, as a competent technician observing his own and his colleagues' work practices, as a researcher describing the technician communication structure, and as an employee reporting work practice understandings for their relevance to corporate interests. Each of these relations entailed understanding and addressing different sets of recipients and interests.

## The Viewer's Point of View

Labeling an ethnographer an insider or an outsider may well depend on the ethnographer's relationship to the person who is doing the labeling.

For more than a decade, and before turning to freelance ethnographic consulting, I was employed as a research ethnographer, also at Xerox Corporation. Throughout those years, most of the work of the multidisciplinary work practice teams of which I was a member entailed going out and looking at groups outside of the corporation. Generally, but not always, these groups were Xerox clients.[2] I am going to claim that while I was a Xerox employee, from the point of view of the field participants I was studying, I was an external analyst/consultant.

The ethnographic research work we did at that time was commissioned by, and its funding was drawn from, various departments within Xerox. Sometimes funding came from Research, sometimes it was from Engineering, sometimes from a Design Center. We would present our observations and findings within the corporation, often presenting to groups beyond the original requesters. In that sense we were insiders, reporting within the mothership. For those reports, we knew the basic parameters of what had been assigned, what language/s to use, what political icebergs to avoid, and for how long our presentations would be endured. These are advantages the insider can enjoy more easily than an outsider consultant. Even so, different concerns among different internal organizations sometimes posed a presentational, if not existential, challenge in addressing potential conflicts of interests (Brun-Cottan 2009). We had been sent out to observe and understand what entities (schools, colleges, global equipment manufacturers) outside the corporation were struggling with; how they were doing their work; how they were fantasizing about doing their work; what tools they were using; what services they were, or might need to be, using (Brun-Cottan 2011). Often, others in Xerox selected and secured the field sites. On one hand, this could facilitate matters for us in terms of securing permissions to observe, to interview, to videotape, and to gain access to field sites; on the other hand, it could also be constraining in terms of which sites were chosen and how much freedom we were permitted in terms of sharing information about our interests in, as well as our observations about, the field participants.

# Working as an Outsider

For the past 10 years, I have been practicing ethnography as a freelance external consultant. The range of project types and subject matter has been quite diverse. What follows are descriptions of projects illustrating why I feel the terms "insider" and "outsider" are rarely as clearly experienced as the words describe.

## A Straightforward Outsider

In the project example that follows, I was contracted to describe how ethnographic methods could provide special insights for one of the University of Rochester's main libraries, which was faced with transitioning from a paper-based world to a digital one. I had two advocates on the staff. One was an ethnographically savvy computer engineer with whom I had worked previously. The other was an anthropologist newly hired by the library.

My work entailed presenting to various library staff and university administrators convincing arguments why doing ethnographic work was appropriate (for example, anthropologists have a long history of studying tool use) and showing achievements in previous engagements, and discussing the library's current project goals and considering ways to achieve them.

Working with the library's anthropologist and doing some interviews with professors in different departments—noting the very different sorts of materials and ways of working that would have to be accommodated—an initial project schedule with tasks and timelines was drawn up. I left with the understanding I would come back at the midway point to assess how things were going and to help formulate what would be included in the final report. The project—focused on looking at ways to capture and present "gray information"—was meant to integrate with the efforts of libraries from different universities as well as to serve to convince the University of Rochester that these sorts of ethnographically oriented studies should be carried out within its own library as an ongoing enterprise.

When I returned, it was clear that all the librarians and staff who had signed on to participate in the project had done so with gusto. There was a wealth of interesting observations about ways things were done. There was surprise at how willing teachers were to give time and thought to questions asked. There was a lot of excitement. Missing was a clear, actionable path to the sea through the bramble of rich data and possibilities that would produce a presentable final report. Here is one of the places where the external "authoritative" consultant (authoritative about gleaning and presenting ethnographic insights, not the work of being librarians) may have an advantage over internal group members. From the outside, it is easier to swing the axe and clear lesser—if still enticing—debris from the path. In this case, I suggested that the project staff's task was to choose the four most important findings they had discovered, to clearly state their implications, and to describe and emphasize the rich opportunities they presented. It's oh so much easier to be brutal if your own special little discoveries aren't being tossed out!

Rejecting proposals, especially from enthusiastic recruits, is a delicate matter. In the same sort of circumstance, the insider ethnographer is faced with rejecting proposals from coworkers with whom she or he would have to continue working. The external ethnographer is not usually constrained in the same way.

Happily, this project was seen as a success, and the practice of integrating ethnographic inquiry with computational technology development has become a bedrock within that university's library system. But it is not always this much fun.

## Outsider Once Removed

Most typically, as an external consultant, I have been brought into a study by a person or consulting firm that has been hired to conduct the research. As such, I am an extra step removed from the commissioning institution. This has turned out to have special drawbacks. Too often it has meant that I do not set the parameters of the study and that though I partake in drawing up the final reports, I may not actually present them. In such cases, feedback about the study reception is also secondhand. Though I have worked happily with colleagues on projects config-ured this way, I think one risks losing significant understandings at either the front end, or the back end, or both, of the engagement.

## The In Vitro Project

One example of being an outsider indirectly contracted to conduct a study involved a multinational project piloted by an ethnography firm that had been directly engaged by a company in the medical sector. The primary goal was to identify various medical and nonmedical factors influencing women's decisions to initiate or continue in vitro fertilization (IVF) treatments. These treatments are painful, expensive, and (in the last decade) still have only about a 20 percent suc-cess rate. For this project, researchers in various U.S. cities and in other countries used diaries, video, face-to-face and phone interviews, and document analysis to identify similarities and differences across nationalities and describe how expecta-tions and procedures were managed and treatment paid for.

The study participants who the researchers interviewed may or may not have been using the commissioning medical company's product. I was one of the field researchers. We learned late in the day, after most of the fieldwork had been conducted and analysis of patterns across respondents were being shared, that the company had already developed a product they wanted to introduce into the IVF treatment protocol. Perhaps we weren't told this was the case so that we could not inadvertently be asking participants questions in a way that could influence their responses.

The general consensus among the members of the research team was that the product would not make an iota of difference to the women we had studied. Rather, to the researchers, it seemed the product would complicate interaction with other components used in treatment and not manufactured by this particular company. But this left both researchers and the consulting firm in a difficult position. To tell the client "You made a big mistake, why didn't you ask for this study before making the product?" is not the sort of finding wanted in a report that various departments in the client company would see. Nor is it a helpful finding if you are the ethnography firm wishing to continue in a longer-term relationship with the company.

Fortunately, we had all dug pretty deeply into problems the women—and their partners—were having in terms of understanding and complying with various aspects of the treatments. We understood about the emotional upheavals caused by the hormonal earthquakes the treatment produced. We also understood that personal and familial stresses surrounding infertility as well as the cost of treatment could cause as much, if not more, trouble than concerns caused by the actual medical protocols. We had noted along the way various things that might help allay women's fears. We were able to frame these as opportunities for the company to develop. As it happens, they were bona fide opportunities.

Though I contributed to the final report, I and most of the other field research team members did not present it. But not presenting the final report means not seeing how it is being received, the questions being asked or not asked, or the off-report clarifications and suggestions over lunch or drinks that build understandings about expectations and relationships. The insider ethnographer is far better placed to see reactions to, as well as ramifications of, the work that was conducted and the findings that were presented.

There is a difference between an external freelancer directly commissioned by the funding corporation (as in the library example) and one working for an ethnography consulting firm which itself is hoping to make a commission or turn it into a client relationship. Of course, as a freelance consultant, you hope your work is so good and so valued that it is repeatedly requested. But direct contact with the institution funding the study permits greater understanding of what the assignment really is about. It can even mean the terms of the engagements evolve as the relationship progresses (Darrouzet et al. 2009). Working as a third-party contractor can leave you blind—or at least pretty myopic—at both ends of the engagement.

Another problem that may arise is that the internal ethnographer may be asked to perform a study that, for a variety of ethical or practical reasons, they are unwilling to do. For them, refusal may mean dismissal. That is to say, refusing a work assignment may mean losing a lasting institutional job, if not a stable career. The external ethnographer more easily can refuse an assignment and move on to another project, perhaps in a completely different subject domain, without endangering a career. Fellow anthropologist Alice Morton, who often consults in HIV/

AIDS prevention for USAID as well as international nongovernmental organizations (NGOs), relates the time in the 1980s when "I was invited by a Pakistani agriculturalist to work for British-American Tobacco in Pakistan, helping them figure out the kinds of messages they could put in campaigns to get women to smoke. I turned down the offer with righteous indignation" (Alice Morton, personal communication, May 2012). At least she knew the object of the exercise. And it didn't mean a change of institutional employment.

## The "Not Black Ops" Project

I originally wanted to push on this issue of differences in pressures a bit more. To do so for this chapter, I was going to describe a project conducted in the last decade that could serve as a basis for considering ways in which the external consultant's obligations to reporting findings might differ from those of insider ethnographers. I contacted that project's Principal Investigator (a friend and former colleague from PARC). I wrote to see if there were any images I could use that did not have people or places that were identifiable. I was informed that such images existed but that neither I nor anyone else involved in the fieldwork could use them. Moreover, I could not even refer to the project, nor describe it, nor state that it ever happened. What? Apparently, I had signed a nondisclosure agreement (NDA) agreeing to that stipulation. I did not remember signing any such thing. Well, I had signed an NDA with the Principal Investigator who in turn had signed an NDA to that effect with the commissioning entity. That could be. Not worth "hitting the mattresses" to fight.

A lesson to be learned here is that one can be so happy to find "cool" work with outstanding fellow researchers that one does not consider they might not have totally grasped the implications of the assignment. I easily, if carelessly, could have signed such an NDA without looking at the one the Principal Investigator had signed. Still, I was surprised. The project was not a top-secret, covert, military "Black Ops" operation out of "Mission Impossible."

So let me refer to it as the "Not Black Ops" project. It is not even necessary to know what commercial sector/silo it inhabited. (And no, it had nothing to do with tobacco either as a substance, product, or company.) The assignment, which we researchers accepted, was to identify ways of ameliorating a product in order for it to gain greater usership while reducing its well-known downsides. We spent many hours at various field sites doing interviews, observing, and audio- and videotaping members of the public using the product. Several things became clear to us. Increasing usership absolutely entailed an increase in the product's downsides, both in number and severity. It just did, and we couldn't make it otherwise. Moreover, we found out things that might decrease the downsides, but these same findings could also be exploited profitably by the funding agency to actually increase the negative effects. Mind you, the product/activity was totally legal.

Enough of vagueness. What do we do in a situation where we feel—indeed, where we are quite certain—that what we learn would not be used in/for the public welfare, much less that of our actual study participants? In this case, we did not have to produce a macro analysis involving all the layers of societal infrastructures—Malinowski's "big organized social construction"—to understand that significant segments of the public were going to suffer devastating impacts. This opinion has subsequently been confirmed by research reports and sadly has been borne out by history. Not insignificantly, it turns out the "Not Black Ops" institution knew this would be an outcome as well.

To resolve this ethical dilemma, we presented an accurate assessment of several, but not all, the pertinent behaviors that we saw. So we delivered new findings, but not "all" of the new findings: accuracy, but not adequacy in terms of analysis. And we did not expound on ramifications of some of our findings. Facts, and in some cases only the facts, were reported. If, as Cefkin (this volume) posits, institutions engage ethnographers with the expectations of gaining understandings of opportunities and how to best realize those, then we purposefully failed to meet those expectations. You may think we were naive and possibly even remiss in not initially digging more deeply into the general activity being studied. You might be right. However, I would counter that the institution commissioning the study has a responsibility to be straightforward about its state of knowledge and "real" objectives.

We paid a price. We did not pursue Part II of the project's projected expanded engagement. Yes, we could be accused of a certain naivety for accepting Part I. Accepting Part II would have been duplicitous. I am not permitted to say more.

From my experiences, I judge that some of the important differentiators between internal and external ethnographers lie in the varying means they have to gauge the effectiveness of their work. As an external ethnographer, at least I did not have to face the conflicts of subverting findings from my employers while maintaining an ongoing relationship with them, or of short-changing my fellow coworkers of information.

Hepsø (this volume) proposes that the inside ethnographer serves business interests first and has, foremost, a business role as employee. The internal ethnographer—especially a valued, long-term employee such as Hepsø, or myself while I did research at Xerox—will have a strong attachment to the institution he or she is serving, to colleagues within the institution, and to a reputation built on the relationships cultivated there. It is harder not to deliver "the goods." As Jordan pointed out in conversation, "the insider walks the halls, runs into people who ask—in the ordinary course of things—how things went, what was the upshot of the work" (Brigitte Jordan, personal communication, June 2012). It would be hard to be unforthcoming to fellow employees and friends. And refusal to divulge information that you have been paid to produce is not generally a stairway to grander positions. So, it is harder to not share, and hard to lose an institutional career.

Insiders also face greater immediate pressure if they are in disagreement with study participants, whether they be fellow ethnographers or members of the groups they were studying. In the end, if the situation is such that there is no acceptable solution to the ethical conflict, the internal ethnographer might have to seek employment elsewhere. There is hardly any joy to be found in that situation.

However, the external ethnographer is not completely exempt from such stresses. Pressures to divulge project information can be intense for the external ethnographer, especially if he or she is working solo. These pressures also can increase if the ethnographer is part of a team and there is disagreement about what findings to reveal. Possible future relationships with team members can be jeopardized. But in terms of relationships with the funding employer, external ethnographers have greater wiggle room than the insiders. They can refuse to participate in final presentations. As part of a team working in mutual agreement, as was the case in the "Not Black Ops" project, the team members' relationships were not threatened. The external ethnographers may lose future engagements with the employer, but once they cut loose they have greater freedom to move to a different engagement, a different environment, and with fewer ongoing entanglements to weigh them down than does the insider ethnographer.

External ethnographers do not have the Insiders' opportunities to follow the impact of their work. Was it valuable, was it valued? Was it powerful enough to make ethnography integral to a company's work practice, to its ways of understanding its work, or product, or opportunities.

As a final note, as Hepsø also emphasizes: if you are an outsider, a helpful insider can make all the difference (Jordan with Lambert 2009). Having a helpful insider—it needn't even be a fellow ethnographer—might have made all in the difference in the way that Denny's team (this volume) framed their findings about children's food choices and control, and a difference in their reception. And if you are an insider, as was the case for the staff anthropologist in the library example, an outsider can provide new perspectives.

## Conclusion

In the previous chapter Vidar Hepsø gives one story incorporating detailed accounts of issues and activities based on his experience as an insider over the course of a single project. An outside ethnographer, almost by definition, has multiple experiences and outcomes with multiple projects. (An outsider who works for the long term with only one employer is basically an insider without benefits.) I have offered several abbreviated stories intended in one way or another to present the main points I have learned over the course of multiple projects.

Julian Orr's (1996) work stands at one end of a nearly ideal working relationship with study participants while he was employed as an internal ethnographer for a corporation. Initially, for the repair service technicians, his relationship was as an external ethnographer. By training with them and with deep immersion, he became a knowledgeable member of their community of practice. Yet, even he benefited from queries made by research colleagues. His understandings of the technicians' work and practices had become so ingrained, so unremarkable, that he missed seeing how some of their practices were nevertheless opaque to outsiders who were not practitioners.

My experience with the library project stands at the other end of what turned out to be an equally ideal relationship, but as an external consultant directly hired by the commissioning institution. I never became even a semicompetent practicing librarian, yet I was able to inform and coordinate the efforts of the library staff and professors in such a way that they could continue to develop ways to migrate from old analog practices to new digital ones. In this effort, I was aided by an internal staff anthropologist familiar with ethnographic techniques who could champion their use in the future.

In my work as an outsider, distance from the institution originating and funding the research has presented some of the most severe challenges to understanding the nature of the assignments and to attending to ethical issues surrounding what has been discovered through the work and how to represent it.

The IVF example shows that the nature of the assignment can change in fundamental ways and yet one can still provide insightful, actionable findings. One of the drawbacks of the greater distance from the project's initiator is that the external researcher may not be able to gauge reception or instigate follow-through.

With the "Not Black Ops" project, the mission did not change, but understandings gleaned in the course of the fieldwork made it apparent that some observations would be used to the detriment of members of the public. Even without spending months with our participants or becoming versed in most aspects of the social constructions in which they were embedded, we could foresee the harm that would befall them and spread to others.

In that case, the dilemma for the ethnographers was that satisfying their contractual obligations and fully informing their employer of their findings would make them complicit in the ensuing negative impacts. Do we fulfill those obligations to the fullest (and get recommendations and offers of further employment), or do we protect fellow humans (and lose recommendations and further work)?

Rather than focus on differences between the two positions of internal and external ethnographers, I have chosen to elaborate the back and forth commonalities they share, depending on the features of their work projects. I also note that the researcher's inclusion in one position or the other can very much depend on who is looking.

For me, it seems apparent that we can slip and slide between being an insider or an outsider and face many of the same challenges in either role. We can visit extremes and become "natives"; we can have enough of a grasp of larger issues beyond the scope of a given project and be faced with multiple conflicting interests. Whether insider or outsider, we share a desire to reveal useful insights, to be valued, and to create inroads for greater appreciation of what the methodology can bring to both institutions using it and to the people who are subjected to its analysis. How that unfolds is part of the skill of balancing on the teeter-totter that our projects present and our profession enjoins.

## References

Brun-Cottan, Francoise

2009 The Anthropologist as Ontological Choreographer. In *Ethnography and the Corporate Encounter: Reflections on Research In and Of Corporations*, edited by Melissa Cefkin, pp 158–81. New York: Berghahn Books.

2011 Work Practices to Understand the Implications of Nascent Technology. In *Making Work Visible: Ethnographically Grounded Case Studies of Work Practice*, edited by Margaret Szymanski and Jack Whalen, pp. 74–86. Cambridge, United Kingdom: Cambridge University Press.

Brun-Cottan, Francoise, and Patricia Wall

1995 Using Video to Re-Present the User. In *Making Work Visible, Communications of the ACM* 38(5):61–71.

Darrouzet, Christopher, Helga Wild, and Susan Wilkinson

2009 Participatory Ethnography at Work: Practicing in the Puzzle Palaces of a Large, Complex Healthcare Organization. In *Ethnography and the Corporate Encounter: Reflections on Research In and Of Corporations*, edited by Melissa Cefkin, pp. 61–94. New York: Berghahn Books.

Garfinkel, Harold

2008 Good Organizational Reasons for Bad Clinical Records. In *Studies in Ethnomethodology*, edited by Harold Garfinkel, pp.186–207. Malden, MA: Blackwell Publishing, Ltd.

Jordan, Brigitte, with Monique Lambert

2009 Working in Corporate Jungles: Reflections on Ethnographic Praxis in Industry. In *Ethnography and the Corporate Encounter: Reflections on Research In and Of Corporations*, edited by Melissa Cefkin, pp. 95–133. New York: Berghahn Books.

Malinowksi, Bronislaw

1966 *Argonauts of the Western Pacific*. London: Routledge and Kegan Paul Ltd. Available at http://archive.org/stream/argonautsofwesteoomali#page/n5/mode/2up. Accessed May 2012.

Orr, Julian

1996 *Talking About Machines: An Ethnography of a Modern Job*. Ithaca: Cornell University Press.

Szymanski, Margaret and Whalen, Jack (eds.)

2011 *Making Work Visible: Ethnographically Grounded Case Studies of Work Practice*. Cambridge, United Kingdom: Cambridge University Press.

## Notes

1   It is a particularly trenchant aspiration that has bedeviled ethnography since its inception and presents the sort of quandary that sociologist Harold Garfinkel spent a career, with some relish, elucidating. Realizations wrought from his observations helped spawn the disciplines of Conversation and Interaction Analysis, which have become powerful tools in the ethnographic arsenal (Garfinkel 2008).

2   For detailed descriptions of some of these engagements, see Szymanski and Whalen (2011).

Chapter 11

# Accelerated Pattern Recognition, Ethnography, and the Era of Big Data

*Chad R. Maxwell*

## Introduction

> Without analysis, data are worse than useless.
> —*Margaret Mead*

This chapter and the following one by Brigitte Jordan take up the issue of pattern recognition and its relationship to evolution, ethnography, and the field of anthropology at large. In a world that seems to be changing faster than ever with the onset of advanced digitization and technological influence, we believe these issues are essential for understanding where we as a species have been and where we are going. The impact of digital technology and the massive amounts of data it creates are charting a new course for ethnographic practitioners. How do these environmental, analytical, and technological changes connect to our evolutionary and ethnographic past, present, and future?

This pair of chapters tackles a spectrum of issues that are tied together through the central concept of pattern recognition. I begin by exploring technology-enabled pattern recognition and how that is shaping culture in implicit and explicit ways today. I argue that in a world of increasing data, our species has to augment our biological pattern recognition skills through accelerated pattern recognition analytics.

In the next chapter, Jordan builds on these ideas and demonstrates that we as a species have a long history of configuring ourselves and our environments through tools and technologies. She details how the theory of paternality posits that all living beings need to recognize patterns effectively and with ease to survive and adapt.

This chapter explores my reflections on the relationship between ethnography, technology, analytics, and understanding people's lives.

*Advancing Ethnography in Corporate Environments: Challenges and Emerging Opportunities,* edited by Brigitte Jordan, 175–192.

## The Idea of Ethnographic Analytics

For the sake of this chapter, we will call the fusion of ethnographic practices with the craft of analytics, as well as the application of ethnographic methods to understanding the cultural implications of analytics, algorithms, and massive data, "ethnographic analytics."

This idea of ethnographic analytics was born out of a career epiphany. After graduate training in anthropology with H. Russell Bernard at the University of Florida in 2004, I started a career in web design user research. User research is the study of how a person uses a product, service, or human-computer interface in an effort to improve it. The practice focuses on user needs states, ease of use (usability), and how user understanding can lead to better design. It is a large field that uses a variety of research techniques (surveys, ethnography, in-person usability testing, focus groups, and other approaches).

Soon, however, in my digital-design/user research career, I came toe-to-toe with web analytics. Put simply, analytics is the craft of gaining user understanding from passive data collection (data automatically collected through technology systems without solicitation) to make data-driven judgments and decisions about design and usability. (For web analytics, these metrics often concern point-of-origin metrics, search engine rankings, cookie-tracking, click patterns, time spent on pages, etc.).

I started to find conflict and competition between user research and analytics. Both attempt to explain user behavior in an effort to improve a product. Which is right? Which has better validity? Which approach better helps us understand people, their motivations, their needs, and their behaviors? Practitioners of analytics emphasize the fact that they have a much larger and more robust data set that can generate true behavioral insights, whereas the user researchers tout that they can explain more deeply the variables underlying people's behavior through the richness of ethnographic insight.

I question where we as a culture are going in a world forever changed by the digital landscape. I also question the massive amounts of data the digital age has brought forth, and how our development is being shaped as a consequence. The world encompasses more data than ever before. In many industries, these massive amounts of data are critical for understanding long-term trends, making real-time decisions, or evoking a more precise answer. The data are macro, micro, a "moment in time," longitudinal, past, and present all at the same time. These data sets are large and ever-growing; they are often terabytes and exabytes large and cannot be handled by standard software and computers. This type of data is called Big Data.

The algorithms that drive analytics are the engines that process all these data. Although actual people create the systems and algorithms that power analytics, once in place, those systems become largely automated to drive efficiency, scale, and profit in processing the data. Thus, Big Data technology is enabling a massive amount of passive data collection and passive data analysis to produce big understanding, insight, and/or profit. The promise and opportunity of Big Data and analytics are huge. Where does ethnography fit into this burgeoning analytics-driven world?

To attack these questions, I explore pattern recognition, analytics, and the ethnographic practice in four sections. The first focuses on how technology is driving unprecedented data collection and how the nature of data itself is changing, which affects pattern recognition. I connect this to Jordan's discussion on sociodigitation (Latham and Sassen 2005) and hyperconnectivity. Next, I look at how humans use technology, analytics, and algorithms as an adaptation to accelerate pattern finding in our digitally changing environment. The third section examines some possible implications and considerations for the impacts of accelerated pattern recognition on our culture: how is extrasomatic pattern recognition changing us? I look specifically at the concepts of evolution and the invisible digital ecosystem. The fourth section explores this technologically driven data collection and pattern finding as it relates to the ethnographer and the future of ethnography: what are the opportunities for anthropologists looking at pattern recognition in a digital age? How can we demystify the algorithms, systems, and digital ecosystems interacting in the cloud and elsewhere? I conclude by reflecting on our environment, ourselves, and our practice as we continue down the path of hyperconnectivity and digital pattern recognition.

## Data Growth and Change

Understanding pattern recognition in analytics must begin with tracing the tremendous growth and changes in types of data. Since the very start of our species, environmental conditions and tool development have led to a stronger understanding and interpretation of the world around us. In recent times, the proliferation of technology has expanded data types, speed, granularity, interpretation, and quantity.

When I worked at Razorfish as a user researcher and consumer insights professional, there was a vision that "All things that can be digital will be digital." The corollary is that if all things that can be digital will be digital, then all things will be trackable, measureable, and subject to pattern recognition and interpretation. Latham and Sassen (2005) explore this concept and extend it beyond the digitization of things such as books, art, and banking, to the digitization of culture itself, which Latham calls "sociodigitization." Sociodigitization is the process by which human activities are digitally encoded, read, and stored.

It is important to note that, in addition to the quantity of data, the nature and type of data has changed as well. This is important because, considering how human behavior has changed and my story of the competition between user research and analytics, it has caused some of the changes in pattern recognition strategies and in the practice of ethnography. Data have changed in four primary ways: (1) granularity, (2) passivity, (3) hybridization, and (4) connectedness.

First and foremost, data sets are more granular than ever before because of technology. In a world of digitization, tracking behavior at the most minute level is easier to do than ever. For example, when you visit a website, that site's technologists know where you came from, where you went when you left, which other pages you browsed, where your mouse hovered on a page, the time you spent on any given page, and every action (scrolling, highlighting, copying) that you took on that page. The goal is to collect as much data at the lowest level of contrast possible and then interpret it (mine it) later. This level of granular data tracking is also used in financial/banking industries, in video surveillance, and in many other situations where a digital interaction or observation occurs.

Much data are collected by technology without the knowledge of or direct solicitation from the person: this is sometimes called passive data. Data such as cable TV viewing information, power consumption habits, Facebook activities, and shopping patterns tracked by loyalty cards are all examples of passive data. Passive data differs from primary data in that primary data require a question, observation, or a human conduit through which to create the information exchange.

With the digitization of our lives and devices, and the proliferation of technology in general, we have moved from mostly active data collection (surveys, interviews, elicitation techniques, and other recall tasks) to more passive data collection (back-end technologies, tagging systems that record our web browsing and online media interaction automatically, monitoring technologies such as closed-circuit video, and the like).

An example of passive data collection involves remote insurance rate calculation. A recent device called Snapshot, released last year by Progressive Insurance Company, transmits passive data about driving style (braking, acceleration, speed, distance, driving locations, and other variables) back to the company, where actuaries calculate the driver's insurance premium to develop a customized month-by-month billing (rather than the typical six-month premium) that is based on the insured's driving behavior as recorded by the device.[1]

In addition to data granularity and passivity, data are becoming increasingly hybridized. Instead of being exclusively qualitative or quantitative, digitization and analytical power have made it possible to move between data types more easily. For example, ethnographers can take a stack of millions of photos and use face recognition software to code, sort, and analyze their visual data. Technology-driven pattern recognition and data collection technologies are blurring the lines between qualitative and quantitative data and data analysis. Perhaps more important, however, digital technologies are blurring the lines between what are data and what are not.

Social media and social listening technologies are an excellent example of how these hybridized data are formed and automatically analyzed. Social listening tools are designed to harvest all digital mentions of a key word or phrase across the Internet and process them into "meaningful" human understanding. Think of social listening as automated text analysis, both grounded and structured, for all content generated by users (blogs, comments, status updates, forums, communities, etc.). Businesses can use social mining tools to understand what social media users think or feel about their products or services.

Chicago bars are harnessing the power of visual pattern recognition analytics with a mobile app called SceneTap (Rowinski 2011). This new app for smartphones connects users to bar scene data created by in-bar cameras with facial detection analytics. Without identifying specific bar patrons, it posts information such as the average age of a crowd and the ratio of men to women, helping barhoppers decide where to go. Think of both of these examples as "film" being read by machines to code and quantify visual information. The data are both qualitative and quantitative at the same time, and come to scientists, analysts, and users in real time. This is an example of digital hybridization of data.

Finally, technology is changing the nature of data in a fourth way: connectedness. Rather than data collections being separate and unique, technology is driving the unification of data collection to create single-source sets. This means that the

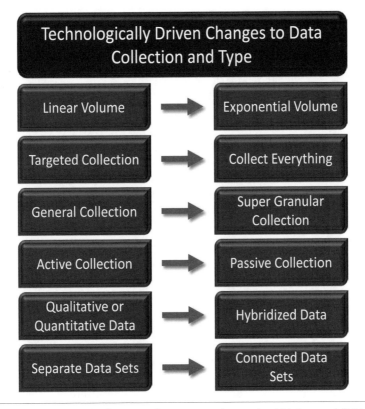

FIGURE 11.1. Summary illustration demonstrating the ways in which increased digitization and technology have transformed the type, quantity, collection approach, and connectivity of data.

data sets become larger not just in volume, but also in terms of the number of variables they can potentially cover. The databases interact and "form relationships" with one another in their own digital ecosystem.

A great example of this is grocery store loyalty club card data. This data set details past purchases in terms of product type as well as the frequency of purchase. Loyalty cards also record number of store visits, time between visits, and coupons used. All this information gained through just using a loyalty card (positioned as a cost savings incentive, rather than a passive data collection tool) is also linked to an email address. With an email address in hand, marketers can potentially append loyalty card data to web browsing, social media, and even TV viewing data to find relationships between what people watch on TV or do online and their purchase behaviors. Thus, multiple data sets are linked together with a single email address. The key to gaining the larger data picture in terms of behaviors is finding matching data to connect disparate data sets and get those sets talking to one another.

The relationship between technology and data has resulted in the amplification of passive data collection's reach and the type of data tracked and measured, as well as the very nature of the data itself. The changes have been cumulative and accelerative, leaving many people overwhelmed. The proliferation of technology that gave rise to massive amounts of data also gave rise to a pervasive data predicament. However, just as humans have adapted in the past to interpret their environment and the world around them, we are adapting today through the use of analytics and algorithms to make sense of this digital environment.

## Analytics: An Adaptive Pattern Recognition Strategy

With unprecedented data volumes, researchers and people in general quickly faced a growing challenge: how to process it all. People who are used to dealing with data sets in the hundreds or thousands found themselves dealing with data in the millions and billions. Matrix sizes expanded and data coding, cleaning, management, and processing challenges were rampant. With all the granular, passive, hybridized, and connected data at our fingertips, the traditional senses were not enough to process it all.

Jordan (this volume) discusses pattern recognition throughout our history. She discusses patternality, which is essentially the ways in which people order things in the world, the way they make sense (and, by consequence, meaning) through the construction of or discovery of patterns. Analytics is a way of applying order to our changing environment; it is a tool and adaptation strategy to this explosion of data and new environmental conditions.

The simplest definition of analytics is the craft of gaining insights from passive data collection to make data-driven judgments and decisions. As mentioned, this is known as Big Data in my field of marketing and many other industries such as healthcare, public-policy, sports, telecommunications, etc. Analytics concerns itself with the  processing and analysis of Big Data for increased user understanding, sales, forecasting, and other insights, optimizations and predictions. The decisions that analytics can drive may concern customer experience management, online performance and optimization, spread of disease, DNA pattern recognition, sales and return on investment, performance enhancement, or processes improvement such as supply chain logistics and power supply management. The application opportunities stemming from the analysis of Big Data are virtually infinite.

Data-driven decision making, modeling, and prediction are all key components in analytics. Think of analytics as the tools for digesting Big Data. The growth and importance of analytics is already apparent in the number of job positions open in this advancing field where new job titles such as database architect, analytics scientist, Big Data engineer, Big Data developer, solution architect, and analytics technologist are becoming established.

As do most things statistical, analytics hones in on relationships and understanding them. Due to the complex nature of analytics and the multiple active data systems often rolled into data processing, when we hear about analytics we often hear about algorithms as human-generated prescriptive rules to create data calculations and judgments.

We see these algorithmic rules at play all the time. When we are shopping online at Amazon, a preference algorithm drives suggestions for purchases that you may like based on the computation of your purchase and browsing history compared with the purchase behavior of other people who are like you. The website LinkedIn has algorithms that suggest people to you who you may know and want to include in your network, based on other people with whom you are already "friends." Insurance companies are calculating risk and premiums based on a series of algorithms (actuarial sciences) that determine who should and should not be insured, and at what rate. Algorithms automatically make data decisions, produce more manageable bits of information, and often output a conclusion.

The rise of analytics as a product of massive data growth, the application and proliferation of embedded algorithms, and practitioners working through Big Data all act to extend human pattern recognition. The data judgments and decisions that analytics computes in some ways act as a sixth sense extending humans' natural ability to decode the world around us. To circle back around to patternality, analytics and algorithms reorganize the world in an effort to apply order and structure to it.

This reorganization is apparent in augmented reality applications on our mobile devices. You can hold your smartphone up to a street and the phone's camera will "read" the street. On the image of the street, it superimposes data from a number of different data systems to show the user restaurant types, ratings, and reviews; homes that are for sale; and other information. My smartphone camera and the data feeds funneling into it are augmenting our natural senses by bringing forward information culled together by data systems and algorithms. Another more cyborg-like example comes from augmented reality contact lenses (Parviz 2009). These lenses, which are still experimental, are claimed to project images on retinas so that a wearer's biological vision is supplemented in real time by data and analytical feeds. And in a dramatic display, IBM's computer Watson recently beat a human opponent on Jeopardy by understanding questions (human language) through a series of algorithms to pull together the winning answers and take the championship.

Analytics and the algorithms that drive them are supplementing our understanding of the world around us in new ways. They are helping us to process information about our actions, feelings, and communities and, in some cases, are making our decisions. Biometrics, biochip implants, neuroscience, continued digitization, integrated data systems, and other technology, data, and human fusions will continue to take algorithmic decision making and informing even further. Analytics, by preprocessing large amounts of data, extends our pattern-making senses and enhances our decision-making abilities.

## Cultural Implications and Cautions

Although analytics and algorithms have helped us manage the data volume challenge, provide more order to the world, and develop some "processing" solutions in our new sociodigitized environment, their increasingly unquestioned acceptance, application, and cultural pervasiveness warrants consideration. danah boyd and Kate Crawford outlined some of the issues with Big Data in their paper "Six Provocations for Big Data." They detail the exaggerated claims around Big Data accuracy, how Big Data is changing the definition of knowledge, and explore how the limited access to Big Data can create unintended divisions between the "data haves" and the "data have nots" (boyd and Crawford 2011). I expand upon these points in the following, and share some additional considerations.

Analytics and the algorithms are a human system. And like all human systems, they are products of worldviews, values, and interpretation that may affect the system and our decision-making skills. What are the algorithms and data rules deciding for us that would be better decided by ourselves and vice versa? How will we know when a systematic decision-making algorithm is chronically wrong and introducing widespread misinformation?

Analytics often happens in a black box, offering up a response without context or clear transparency around the algorithmic rules that computed a judgment, answer, or decision. Analytics software and hardware are being sold as a single-source, easy solution to make sense of today's digital complexity. The promise of these solutions is that seemingly anyone can be an analytics guru. There is real danger in this do-it-yourself approach to analytics, however. As with all scientific instruments and approaches, whether it be statistics, a microscope, or even a thermometer, without proper knowledge of the tool, expertise in the approach, and knowledge of the rules that govern the process, the results will be questionable. The paradox between ease-of-use and dependable results may have prompted

Nicola Hughes's comment at the 2012 SXSW Interactive conference, "Big Data allows us to be wrong with infinite precision."

In the world of databases, analytics, and algorithms, the computations are even more difficult to decode and perceive than in earlier statistics programs. The algorithmic instructions that guide the program's decisions are not transparent or accessible. They are incredibly complicated, and only a few select people may know their operations. This leads to issues of who owns the data and, consequently, issues of privacy and power. Often the algorithms themselves are proprietary information that is not shared in an open-source way. It is ironic that this processing power and pattern recognition analytics is all around us—devices, cameras, in the cloud, on our computers—but nowhere to be seen at the same time. Algorithms and Big Data are rather mythical in this way.

Further challenges arise when the black box of algorithms increases in size. Algorithms are built upon algorithms and are inextricably connected, sometimes operating autonomously in their own digital ecosystem with their own rules. This takes "cowboy statistics" to a whole new level. At the same time, I do not mean to dispel the power of analytics or to say that we are quickly becoming a sci-fi movie that looks like a cross between "The Matrix" and HAL from "2001: A Space Odyssey."

The thinking and knowledge systems that govern analytics and our accelerated pattern recognition are becoming mechanized, commoditized, assumed, and culturally embedded. In this regard, algorithms are bringing order to the world, but what kind of order is it? And what do the results really tell us about the world, culture, and us? Perhaps ahead of his time, Chris Anderson in his piece "The End of Theory: The Data Deluge Makes the Scientific Method Obsolete" suggests how Big Data challenges the most basic principle of science itself—the scientific method. Whereas historically scientists have built explanatory models to connect disparate data sets with some amount of reliability and validity, currently, "faced with massive data, this approach to science—hypothesize, model, test—is becoming obsolete" (Anderson 2008:109). If analytics is a pattern recognition extension that adds meaning to the way we live and behave, then it should integrate with, and augment, our understanding of the world around us. It should also invent new order and meaning where and when appropriate. All algorithms can have significant cultural, environmental, and structural implications, but unbounded algorithms may pose a particular risk. A recent financial phenomenon provides a cautionary tale about algorithms.

The single greatest one-day point decline in the stock market (7 percent) was a product of mysterious algorithms and computers being in control. Evan Newmark of the *Wall Street Journal* stated, "It's a safe bet that after the trader's initial error, high-frequency trading computers remorselessly running their algorithms took over." Going a step further, he continued, "Today's (May 6, 2010) market was neither orderly nor efficient nor trustworthy. It was just a bunch of computers making ugly, messy love with each other. And your money hung in the balance" (Newmark 2010). This is but one example of powerful algorithms exerting influence in an unquestioned and unmonitored way that had significant impact on the cultural infrastructure and institutions that drive our society. The massive implications and future cautionary measures of this event should extend to other societal institutions such as transportation, energy, government, and healthcare.

The potential consequences of assisted pattern recognition and automated algorithms are not all negative, however. Analytics and algorithms are being used in profound ways to drive human understanding and improvement. For example, the United Nations' Global Pulse project leverages vast amounts of technology and data to advance human well-being. One of the studies the Global Pulse Project recently published (2011) studied social media cues as a real-time predictor of unemployment. Based on the prediction, policymakers can potentially anticipate design solutions for unemployment (United Nations Global Pulse Project 2011). Another example of a benefit from Big Data processing comes from Deb Roy and his team at the Massachusetts Institute of Technology Media Lab and founder of Bluefin Labs. In a recent TED talk, Roy discussed how he captured the birth of words for his newborn son using social, video, and "space time worm" analytics (Roy 2011). Roy recorded every utterance, movement, sound, and image in his home for three years, collecting 90,000 hours of video and 140,000 hours of audio of natural, longitudinal data. He and his team imported the data streams into an analytics program that converts space, time, and sound into a single output that demonstrated the influence of social interaction on language development and the movement from utterances to language development over time in unprecedented ways.

Roy's analytics not only changed language understanding but how the interactions between space, time, and language are represented. When we think about language development, linguistic anthropology, and social structures, this project is a powerful example of technologically enhanced ethnography coupled with "analytic steroids" to produce a deeper understanding of the human condition.

The key point is that as we move forward in the space of augmented understanding we need to think critically about the inputs and outputs. We need to question analytics-assisted pattern recognition so that it doesn't completely supplant human judgment, logic, and intuition. If data processing in this form imposes a new way for humans to organize the world, then we must question the rules, powers, and judgments that govern it, the inherent values and biases the human-created algorithms contain, and the users who implement and craft the analytics that make the decisions.

## Opportunities for the Ethnographer in Analytics

In a world of optimized, efficient, automated, and mechanized observation, tracking, measurement, analysis, and decision-making, what is the role of the ethnographer? How can we as social scientists and participant observers bring new and unique value? In what untapped space can ethnographers contribute and add explanatory power in the era of analytics? The competitive pressures from analytics and passive data are strong. If the ethnographer is traditionally the instrument of observation, data collection, and analysis, and if that role is being outsourced to Big Data and algorithmic pattern recognition, do ethnographic practitioners become dated? Just as print journalism, music, and TV have been transformed by digitization, so, too, will ethnography and anthropology be changed.

In my field of marketing and digital design, the "ethnographic push out" is a real challenge for two reasons: efficiency and value. Analytics is often cheaper and quicker than ethnography, although we could get into validity, reliability, and value-added arguments here. For example, analytics often has troubles with tagging systems, click fraud, cookie clearing, multiple users on the same device, and lack of cross-device measurement and understanding. So many of the same research design challenges are as present in analytics, such as data quality, sampling, and instrumentation, as they are in ethnographic approaches.

In either case, in fast, digital business environments, cheaper and faster frequently trumps quality and understanding. The other reason analytics can be seen as more competitive is the real-time value it offers. Anderson argues that correlation is enough and causation is no longer as relevant as it once was in a world that is moving so quickly. He asks, "Who knows why people do what they do? The point is they do it, and we can track and measure it with unprecedented fidelity. With enough data, the numbers speak for themselves" (Anderson 2008:108). Analytics can monitor, learn, and deduce in real time while simultaneously implementing an optimized, efficient solution. Ethnography is inherently a more longitudinal and iterative craft than a real-time solutions approach.

Another example is in cross-screen TV watching: watching on your mobile device, computer, gaming system, tablet, or traditional TV. Some programs tend to be watched more often on mobile devices, whereas other programs are watched primarily on traditional TV sets in the home. As an advertiser or content publisher, I can tell who, at the household level, is watching what programs, where, when, and on which platform. This means I can more effectively connect customers to advertisers in meaningful, real-time ad placements. This analytical approach has real return-on-investment implications for advertisers, marketers, and media professionals in terms of advertisement placement, sales, and revenue generation.

Traditional market research and ethnographic work might have taken weeks to explain why some people watch some programs at certain times on certain devices while other people do not (see Gluesing and Riopelle, this volume, for discussions on why and how traditional ethnography methods take time). As technology and sociodigitization continue to grow, so too will the back-end analytics and algorithms, increasing competitive pressure on ethnographers and the value we bring to the table.

In sum, we face the following two problems: (1) analytics and algorithms are offering up accelerated pattern recognition but are unchecked and are influencing our world in unknown ways; and (2) analytics and algorithms *seem* to be pushing the ethnographer and ethnography out of the insight equation.

On the other hand, these problems present several opportunities for ethnographers in analytics and in shaping the next chapter of our craft. Instead of framing the situation as a problem of how analytics works against ethnography or how ethnography works against analytics, we should continue to demonstrate how the two can work together to form a more comprehensive picture and to make the understanding brought forth from each approach stronger. Fusing together practices such as analytics, ethnography, and Big Data has become widely visible at conferences, where the issues are discussed from a variety of standpoints (Data-Edge Conference, SXSW, Ethnographic in Praxis Conference, SAS Analytics, IBM Information on Demand, IEEE International Conference on Data Mining, etc.). Ethnographers bring considerable skills to the table to contextualize and make greater meaning of analytics, while analytics and algorithms are presenting a new field site and complementary data sets for ethnographers. In the following, I outline some of these opportunity areas for more study.

First and foremost, there is an enormous opportunity for ethnographers to help demystify algorithms, to make them less nebulous. If analytics truly is a new scientific paradigm fueled by the digital age, we should try to understand and deconstruct it. We need to apply ethnographic approaches in pursuit of grasping how it shapes the human condition and how we assign order to the world.

Much as anthropologists have questioned and studied systems of knowledge, power, language, and influence in the past, so too is there an opportunity to dig into the implicit rules that govern analytics and algorithms. What cultural rules or biases do human-generated algorithms carry? How are they subtly shaping the world around us? What are their impacts on privacy and individuality? What assumptions are being built into coding, decision-making, and data processing that are critical to consider? What cultural implications do these algorithms carry? Databases, algorithms, and analytics can become our new field sites, while engineers, code developers, systems creators, and other professionals in the field become our new informants, participants, and collaborators. For example, Genevieve Bell in her presentation at the Web Summit 2.0 Conference described Big Data as a person, hence anthropomorphizing the very idea of Big Data and who it may be (Bell 2011). Big Data in this setting becomes a tool as well as an agent, a character with personalities. Rick Smolan is a photographer who acts as a visual anthropologist exploring the quantified self. In his work "The Human Face of Big Data," Smolan is capturing how Big Data will affect virtually everything we know through a "human" lens. An increasing amount of work is being carried out in this area of ethnographic analytics, and it is an important frontier.

A second opportunity for ethnographers is to help analytics practitioners contextualize their work using human and cultural frameworks. Analytics is often focused on reporting, prediction, and modeling, but the human implications and meanings are lost on the audience. Anderson et al. (2009) illustrate this humanization of analytic data. In their work, researchers showed participants data visualization demonstrating the intensity of the participant's computing device use. Participants were asked to interpret what they saw in their own visualization—referred to as "ethnomining." This approach combined the robustness of Big Data with the interpretative human narrative. By coupling algorithms and analytics with cultural and human understanding we can better understand the systems in place. Along this same line of thought, Slobin and Cherkasky (2010) asked whether, in a world of analytics, ethnography can still add value and whether the deep understanding of "why" that ethnography provides is even important anymore. He concluded that a focus on experiential/interpretative understanding coupled with data modeling is a stronger way to get a true "360 view of the customer." So a collaborative approach between the ethnographer and the analytics practitioner is a rewarding model.

FIGURE 11.2. Potential opportunities for ethnographers in the growing field of analytics, Big Data, and algorithms.

When I coach my research teams, I encourage ethnographic researchers to become the "quilters of fact." More and more, I find that the strongest opportunity for ethnographers lies in creating connective tissue between micro and macro data sets and to stitch them together through a form of shared cultural understanding. In this situation the ethnographer also reconciles the tension between disparate data sources and sews them together with cultural theory, storytelling, and deep, meaningful understanding.

In this model, the focus is less on the analytics and the algorithms and more on the strategic thinking the analyst or social scientist brings to the table. This is an important distinction: ethnographers can become data agnostic and stewards of multiple hybridized data sets (as described here) to compete more effectively in the era of analytics. The opportunity here for ethnographers is to close the gap between analytics and people-centric understanding framed in social theory and close the gap between meaning and extraneous data noise.

We are doing more and more of this type of ethnographic analytics work in marketing, where we are fusing analytic power and automation with larger cultural models. For example, at Razorfish, I worked with Teresa Caro on a study that looked at the lifetime value of airline customers and how they interacted with different marketing communications channels (Maxwell and Caro 2011). In that study, we had many different data inputs that told us how customers were engaging with the brand that came from back end analytics and algorithms. I could tell how many tickets you bought and whether you visited the website, opened email newsletters, checked in to a flight via Twitter, and so on.

We examined almost every single point of contact with the brand, so that it was possible to see which one (or which groupings) most affected the monetary value of the customer to the airline. From that analysis, we found that there were several strong customer segments that revealed what factors most influenced lifetime value, but we had very little data regarding why and how people were engaging with the brand in different ways, and how their brand interactions related to their larger cultural context. By placing the analytical modeling within a larger cultural construct, we created a vehicle through which to tell the story and gain broader, more manageable understanding of the use of communication touchpoints. Furthermore, with an ethnographic analytics approach, we were able to explain how, when, and why people move from one lifetime value segment group to another. Their motivations became clear through the ethnographic approach (Maxwell and Caro 2011). The results from the study also inspired marketing innovation from the fused ethnographic analytics that drove a Big Data story as well as a human interest story for the client (Zoninsein 2011). Ethnographers can help companies keep track of the "human" in all the algorithms and analytics. I would say that the airline lifetime value study was a step in the right direction of hybridized research design, but more work can be done.

If analytics and algorithms are the new scientific paradigm and a growing patternality, then they need to be studied as such. For example, just as biological anthropologists have studied evolutionary advantage and observed primates for centuries in terms of behaviors, survival, communication, and language, it is critical that we consider analytics and algorithms as just such an adaptation that needs to be studied in a similar way. In a world of so much information and exponential data growth, we are adapting though technology enhancements such as augmented reality, data systems, biofeedback monitors, tracking, and biotechnology to change our world and ourselves. There is a substantial opportunity for anthropologists and ethnographers to review how these adaptations are coming into play in our daily lives and how they are shaping larger cultural trends. What are the impli-cations for language, biology, knowledge systems, power, identity, community, family, and other cultural attributes? Ethnographers are well positioned and trained to help make sense of the automated, accelerated, and algorithmic cultural ecosystem. Cyborg anthropology is a burgeoning field that is taking on more and more of these challenging, pioneering arenas (see http://cyborganthropology.com/ for more information).

Analytics is in a place to make ethnographic understanding stronger. Video coding is a laborious and tedious process. Ethnographers sift through hundreds of hours of video footage to find clips that best illustrate their findings. Now, through analytical reduction and face recognition programs, we can look at only the clips that are relevant. Analytics can help the ethnographer carry the burden of data aggregation, coding, and synthesis. A close relationship between the analytics practitioner, the technologist, and the ethnographer can preserve the integrity of the ethnographic approach without analytics completely supplanting the ethnographic method. Substitution is not the solution, but leveraging the benefits of both might be.

## Looking Ahead

This chapter has traced the acceleration of data collection and the empowerment of analytical pattern recognition. I reflected on how the very nature of data is changing to become more hybridized in quality. In short, the technology-made component of our environment has increased immeasurably in volume, scope, and complexity. New information and communication technologies have generated global connectivity; they have spawned social networking sites and virtual worlds. Sociodigitation and technology are making the volume of data expand, and solutions are needed to make sense of this "new world."

To cope in this changing environment, pattern recognition through analytics has supplemented our natural human senses as a way in which we digest, distill, and make sense of the new sociodigitized world around us. Advanced technologies are expanding humans' ability to detect patterns—new kinds of patterns that were formerly hidden.

I have brought forth some of the challenges of pattern recognition in analytics and some considerations to keep in mind when working with Big Data. For example, I maintain that the black box nature of analytics, lack of access, and confounding governing structures are all problematic.

Finally, I have discussed how the role of the ethnographer is changing in this analytics age, how analytics might shape ethnography, how ethnography may shape analytics, and, perhaps most important, how ethnography can thrive in these transformative times with an ethnographic analytics approach. Ethnographic analytics may make analytics and algorithms more human and extend the relevance of ethnography. The relationship can be symbiotic. This approach is ripe with opportunities for both new topics of investigation and methodological innovation.

In a time of automated measurement, decision-making, and observation, it is more important than ever to question these systems within our cultural context and understand the influence they have over our lives. It is also more important than ever to understand the role of ethnography and the ethnographer in a passive, massive data-collecting technology machine. In addition to focusing on "why and how" we have the opportunity to quilt data streams and package analytics in a more digestible way.

I am convinced that analytics and algorithms, and their seamless, automatic incorporation, are the next phase of our cultural evolution. Ethnographers can embrace this idea and understand this as a biocultural adaptation. Meaning-making, which always had been grounded in physical, corporeal realities, is now struggling with a virtual electronic environment where the old ways of detecting patterns and making sense are not necessarily applicable. The methodologies and technologies for pattern recognition that had evolved, and earlier ways of ordering the world, no longer work as they once did. Digitization has outstripped human sense(s).

I am also convinced that for the ethnographic enterprise to remain competitive in the marketplace and present a value-added approach in the world of Big Data and analytics, ethnographers must sit side by side with analytics practitioners. As my own career path continues to merge with this area, I attempt to find new ways to push a fused, integrated ethnographic analytics approach forward. Perhaps we can view Big Data as our next field site and coders as the next "tribe." We need to work in collaboration with analytics, and leverage the strengths of both approaches.

Our job as anthropologists, and humanity's concern at this point, is to find ways of dealing with this invisible, algorithmic world. To understand our present society and the implications algorithms bring to it, we must enter the digital field site and algorithm ecosystem to understand the rites, rituals, and rules that encompass that space. Society now needs an ethnographic approach to how the world has changed, and what this global digital existence is like for society. The methods and approaches to undertake those investigations will come from a fusion of data inputs (databases, active, primary, and passive data) and ethnographic understanding of spaces involving computer science, systems thinking, and further development around concepts such as digital patternality and sociodigitation.

# References

Anderson, Chris
> 2008 The End of Theory: The Data Deluge Makes the Scientific Method Obsolete. *Wired Magazine*, June 6, 2008, pp. 108–109. Available at http://www.wired.com/science/discoveries/magazine/16-07/pb_theory. Accessed August 6, 2012.

Anderson, K., D. Nafus, T. Rattenbury, and R. Aipperspach
> 2009 Numbers Have Qualities Too: Experiences with Ethno-Mining. *EPIC Proceedings* 2009:123–140.

Bell, Genevieve
> 2011 Big Data as a Person. Paper presented at Web Summit 2.0 Conference, October 17–19, San Francisco, CA. Available at http://www.youtube.com/watch?v=Nvn_l_Vh3hw. Accessed August 9, 2012.

boyd, danah, and Kate Crawford
> 2011 Six Provocations for Big Data. Paper presented at "A Decade in Internet Time: Symposium on the Dynamics of the Internet and Society," September 21, 2011. Available at SSRN: http://ssrn.com/abstract=1926431 or http://dx.doi.org/10.2139/ssrn.1926431. Accessed August, 12, 2012.

Latham, Robert, and Saskia Sassen
> Digital Formations: Constructing an Object of Study. In *Digital Formations: IT and New Architectures in the Global Realm*, edited by R. Latham and S. Sassen, pp. 1–33. Princeton, N.J.: Princeton University Press.

Maxwell, Chad R., and Teresa Caro
> 2011 Virgin America: Creating an Itinerary that Identifies and Leverages Customer Influence. Available at http://liminal.razorfish.com/?page_id=19. Accessed July 20, 2012.

Newmark, Evan
> 2010 "Mean Street: Crash—The Machines Are in Control Now. *Wall Street Journal*, May 6, 2010. Available at http://blogs.wsj.com/deals/2010/05/06/mean-street-crash-the-machines-are-in-control-now/. Accessed July 20, 2012.

Parviz, Babak A.
> 2009 Augmented Reality in a Contact Lens. *IEEE Spectrum*, September 2009. Available at http://spectrum.ieee.org/biomedical/bionics/augmented-reality-in-a-contact-lens/0. Accessed July 20, 2012.

Rowinski, Dan
> 2011 Coming to a Bar Near You: Facial Recognition & Real-Time Data. *The New York Times*, June 10, 2011. Available at http://www.nytimes.com/external/readwriteweb/2011/06/10/10read writeweb-coming-to-a-bar-near-you-facial-recognition-50989.html. Accessed July 22, 2012.

Roy, Deb
> 2011 The Birth of a Word. TED Talks, March 2011. Available at http://www.ted.com/talks/lang/en/deb_roy_the_birth_of_a_word.html. Accessed July 20, 2012.

Slobin, Adrian, and Todd Cherkasky
> 2010 Ethnography in the Age of Analytics. *Ethnographic Praxis in Industry Conference Proceedings* 2010:188–198.

Smolan, Rick
> 2012 The Human Face of Big Data. Available at http://launch.thehumanfaceofbigdata.com/ and http://vimeo.com/37869516. Accessed August 24, 2012.

United Nations Global Pulse

2012 Using Social Media and Online Conversations to Add Depth to Unemployment Statistics. Available at http://www.unglobalpulse.org/projects/can-social-media-mining-add-depth-unemployment-statistics. Accessed August 1, 2012.

Zoninsein, Manuela S.

2011 For Virgin America Marketer, Taking New Media to New Heights Makes Flying Fun. *Ad Age Digital*, April 7, 2011. Available at http://adage.com/article/special-report-digital-conference/virgin-america-marketer-media-makes-flying-fun/226878/. Accessed July 20, 2012.

# Note

1   http://www.progressive.com/auto/snapshot-common-questions.aspx, accessed July 23, 2012.

Chapter 12

# Pattern Recognition in Human Evolution and Why It Matters for Ethnography, Anthropology, and Society

*Brigitte Jordan*

> You can take the human out of the Stone Age but
> you can't take the Stone Age out of the human.
> —*Anonymous*

## Introduction

This final chapter is concerned with a world that has been irrevocably changed by the arrival of the Internet and the massive amounts of data its affordances have generated. It speaks to issues that are of fundamental concern for all of us who are thinking about where we are coming from and where we are going, given that we find ourselves in a present that experiences unprecedented changes in the material and symbolic environments in which we live, facing an uncertain future, and, significantly, coming from a more or less unexamined past that goes back several million years. What do these versions of the world have to do with each other? Why are we "we" and "here," and not "something other" or "somewhere else"?

We are concerned then with a number of wide-ranging issues, from the basic existential questions that confront society today to specific questions about the role of anthropology and ethnography in a world of ever-increasing complexity. This chapter attempts to build a case for the significance of evolution for ethnography as a methodology, for anthropology as a discipline, and, in the end, for the future of our society.

I begin our conversation with two central concepts: first, the idea (or image, if you like) of a helix with spiraling, evolving strands that allows us to conceptualize human evolution not so much as a series of discrete steps or thresholds, but as slowly emerging possibilities and opportunities; and second, a theory of patternality that says that all living beings depend on recognizing patterns in their environment to survive. I use these concepts as a foundation for exploring the question of potential parallels with the situation we are facing today. I will suggest that looking at the kinds of processes that have occurred throughout history and especially prehistory may give us some clues about our current situation, where again we are

*Advancing Ethnography in Corporate Environments: Challenges and Emerging Opportunities,* edited by Brigitte Jordan, 193–213. ©2013 Left Coast Press Inc. All rights reserved.

confronted with an utterly incomprehensible environment that may also require substantial pattern reorganization.

This chapter has two major sections: Part I positions us in "The World That Was." It paints a picture of transformation after transformation in the evolution of our species that individually and jointly changed us into the creatures we are today. Part II asks: "That Was Then. And Now?" Seeing our existence as a long line of slow transformations, I propose that we are again facing a changing world for which we might (or will have to) undergo major changes, thereby grounding the conversations begun by Maxwell, Riopelle, and others in this volume.

## The Helix

Thinking in terms of a twisting, turning, spiraling helix that takes energy from the environment, both physical and human-made, allows a view that focuses on growth and development through processes of mutual influence, of coevolution, of imbrication, of a path taken when others could have been taken: a view that says it is the combination of many different influences that in the past drove the direction of evolution and most likely will continue to do so as far as our future is concerned. Of the many strands of the human helix, I have chosen to focus on the physical, cognitive, and social strands and their intricate linkings and interdependencies, where a tentative move in one opens up possibilities in the others, some of which may or may not be taken depending on a variety of often unknown ecological, climatic, or other changes in the environment in which our precursors lived. By invoking the image of the helix throughout this chapter, I invite us to focus specifically on the exceedingly slow coevolution rather than on the popular "stages" and "thresholds" that tend to get constructed around famous archeological finds (such as Lucy). I see rather a delicate, multifaceted helix with a variety of strands that eventually gets us to what and who we are, a development that at any point could have taken a different direction (and did so in other hominins).

I suggest that these strands and their paths became somewhat discernible some millions of years ago with anatomical changes such as slowly developing upright posture and bipedal locomotion, changes that fundamentally affected our ability to recognize patterns and with that not only led to further anatomical adjustments but also to cognitive and social changes that produced new pattern configurations. Slowly and persistently, over millennia, these became neurologically fixed and thereby available for more exploration and use.

## Patternality and Pattern Recognition

The second concept that will be central to our conversation is patternality, the ability to discern (and ultimately make) new patterns in the environment. Patternality is common to all life forms. It represents a deep instinct, a drive, a need to impose order on the world so as to make it usable and survivable. I suggest that this concept provides a powerful way of looking at the central questions we are investigating here.

Patternality with its affordances shapes how we and all creatures make sense and meaning of the environment within which we exist and the world within which we live. At the biological level, it drives survivability. At the cognitive and social levels, it drives learning and meaning-making for humans and many other social species.

There are two views of patternality. The first assumes that patterns (recognizably regular arrangements of "things") are out there in the world and can be detected through an organism's sensory capabilities. Thus, our ears detect certain frequencies in the space around us and not others. Pattern detection is present-oriented and descriptive, matching sensory capacities to particular configurations of things in the environment.

The second view emphasizes the process through which particular patternalities come into existence and is thus inherently temporally and evolutionarily oriented. On the social level, it asks questions about the construction of conviviality; on the cognitive level, it is concerned with making symbols and establishing categories and coherent "mental models" that serve as templates for making sense of the world. The difference between these views is between processes of recognizing existing orders and actively imposing them. In the literature, authors frequently do not distinguish between these views. I, similarly, invoke both aspects.

Patternality is built slowly by conspecifics (individuals belonging to the same species or group) experiencing similar conditions. In humans it leads to a common, consistent, and coherent web of meanings that is constantly ratified in use. Thus, for social species, a major part of the ability to detect patterns that have meaning is consensually constructed and changeable in the crucible of an undependable physical and social environment.

To look ahead a bit, the key thread I am following throughout the course of evolution in this chapter has to do with changes in the environment, both given and human-made, that provide the energy for continuous amplification of patternalities, producing ever new ways of ordering and making sense of the world. There is little hard evidence for this story, so I sometimes employ what Maria Bezaitis and ken anderson (2011) have called "informed fictions", a device for opening up new thinking spaces in order to fill in the white spaces in our evolutionary history.[1]

## Part I: Pattern Recognition in Human Evolution

### Arbitrary Beginnings

Let us step into the picture millions of years ago when our ancestors started to manipulate objects in their environment, things like sticks and stones, to maybe scratch or scrape or dig, thereby beginning a process which in the long run changed the environment in ways no other species has done. We will go back about five or six million years to start tracking the ways in which our prehuman ancestors have seen and constructed the patternalities of their worlds. Archeologists, paleobiologists, paleoecologists, and other specialists in reading the past tell us that somewhere in the hominin line there was a class of furry, quadrupedal animals that made a living scurrying around in the underbrush. They might have looked something like this (see Figure 12.1 below).

Eventually, these creatures found it advantageous to go upright and bipedal. Why is anybody's guess. Maybe it was because they sniffed and found things to claw from tree trunks, or they noticed that rising up allowed them to get at low-hanging fruit. Maybe it was because of the incursion of competitors. We don't know. The best guess is that there was some change in their environment that invited, maybe even propelled, them to change their behavior.

For the creatures who happened to get up on their hind legs, what was different for them? How did their perceptions change? Their ears now drew input from an expanded audiospace; their eyes saw things previously invisible, out of sight; their snouty nose, no longer to the ground, sensed new odors. The front paws that had always been exploratory became even more so. Their footpads began to differentiate between what they sensed from the ground and the tactile feedback they got from a little higher up. Increasingly, hearing, seeing, and sensing what was above ground opened new opportunities when they searched for food, for shelter, for mates. Above all, it increased the likelihood that they would not be eaten.

The quadrupedal posture had limited them to a rather confined field of vision. The patterns they had recognized through their senses had been very, very local,

FIGURE 12.1. A contemporary furry, four-legged, mostly ground-dwelling animal (photo by the author).

quite literally down to earth. With upright posture, their world opened up. They now saw landscape. Distance. Perspective. A new patterning of the world emerged that allowed them to understand that some of the small things out there could actually be large things. Slowly, as they explored the possibilities, their understanding of what is an obstacle, what is dangerous, and what were the opportunities in this new spatiovisual field changed, and with that, their behavior. Little by little their bodies and brains adjusted. Their memory of what leads to success and failure reconfigured and rewired itself, building templates for recognizing new patterns and in the long run establishing a new patternality that encompassed a novel view of the world.

## Getting Up from the Ground

Between 6 and 3 million years ago (mya) there may have been several groups that were on the way to walking upright.[2] Our best example is *Ardipithecus ramidus*, a group of creatures that lived about 4.4 mya and left us an almost complete female skeleton that scientists affectionately nicknamed "Ardi." (Images of Ardi are proprietary. Any Internet search engine can find a representation of her skeleton and a reconstruction of what she might have looked like.[3])

Ardi definitely walked upright on two legs, and with that forever destroyed the myth of our ancestors swinging in trees like chimps. (She doesn't have the proper shoulder structure for that. Her anatomy had already changed.) While the ancestors of apes went up into the trees, ours acquired the ability to walk on the ground. The two lines developed different physiological, cognitive, and social modifications as their helices spiraled into somewhat different directions. Ardi and her kind had perfectly formed hands for fine manipulation, and feet that, though somewhat odd with a splayed-out big toe, were fully capable of supporting walking on two legs. But about their cognitive development we know almost nothing. Their brains were no bigger than chimps'.

We can only speculate about what happened during the millennia when these creatures explored the possibilities opened up by their upright posture and increasingly efficient bipedality. Informed fiction tells us that they found themselves adapting to every kind of change, whether that came from transformations in their environment—the climate changing, new predators coming in—or from the ongoing alterations in their anatomical and neurological makeup. They managed the transition by exploring their new lifescapes, learning (often the hard way) what aspects of their patternality didn't work anymore and, most important, experiencing what types of new patterns could be constructed with the resources the new environment provided. This surely was a long drawn-out process. Other groups of creatures engaged in it as well. Many followed similar paths, but at some point their helix took an ever so slight turn that led to extinction. I imagine that our line faced the same potential fate many times. But here we are, and we are *Homo sapiens*, not chimps hanging out in the trees or the creatures whose massive skulls (and skulls only!) survive in our lectures as *Paranthropus*.

## Hands

But let us return to Ardi and her group. Not only had their sensory capabilities changed with upright posture, but the achievement of hands must have produced a fundamental reordering of the "things" in their world (like what is reachable and carryable). New behavior patterns emerged as things in their environment became accessible and available to them in a way that was radically different from what had been possible with the sensorimotor capabilities of the quadrupedal way of life.

The hands now could do much of what the mouth had done before and as the old mouth traditions slowly gave way to hand traditions, they could do it better. With that, their prognathous snout and those massive canines became less useful and then less prominent. Smell became less important; vision, more so. Hand-eye coordination established itself, especially for fine manipulation (Stout 2008). Over time, exploring and becoming familiar with these new resources, new *categories* of patterns emerged. There were now touchables and untouchables, graspables, transportables, maybe even giftables that expanded not only in quantity but also in practical meaning.[4]

With hands, as had been the case with upright posture, a tremendous potential opened up. Again there was a world out there that was full of uncertainties and unknown dangers, but it was also a world of vast opportunities, at the same time scary and promising. It was an inflection point for the human helix that opened new paths for our line while closing up others it might have taken.

The ancestors of chimps and gorillas, for reasons too complex to speculate about here (fun as it would be), made different choices, choices that laid out a route to stiff hands and stiff backs which are good support for hanging around in trees, rather than to the nimble hands and flexible backs that led to the complex beings we are today. The two lines diverged in other ways as well. As the hands of creatures like Ardi became adept at grasping and picking up things in their environment, our precursors realized that they could transport stuff from one place to another. Here too, the ape helix moved into a slightly different direction so that today they may manage to carry a nut or a rock a few meters to a more convenient site, but that's about all. They are neither good at walking any distance nor at carrying. For our predecessors, on the other hand, the ability to carry stuff again opened up their world for exploration and adaptation, mentally as well as socially.

## Rocks, Tools, and Community

We know that our ancestors carried raw materials and stone tools (and surely all other kinds of things that were important to them) by 2.6 mya. I believe the importance of stone tools has been vastly overemphasized because they are the only hard evidence of purposeful human activity that has survived. Their presence actually says little about what must have been an extraordinarily slow accumulation of experiments and experiences with natural (and naturally perishable) materials. The stick they might have poked into a rock crevice to scare out a lizard, decayed. The rock grasped to bash a nut survives as only a rock, not a tool.

It is reasonable to assume that ever since they went upright and developed hands that could grasp, our ancestors must have picked up things from nature and explored their affordances. Some turned out to be useful, became popular, and congealed into recognizable patterns and traditions, as always closing down some options, but also opening up new possibilities. Others simply disappeared.

During these eons, the helix slowly was energized by experimentation with multiple kinds of materials and substrata, organic as well as hard, generating an ecology of what we might think of as potential tools, pseudotools, tools-in-waiting, or simply tools in early stages of development. They must have played around with rocks of the kind I picked up in the Andean Altiplano, where the landscape is practically littered with such things. What is often identified as the earliest evidence for tool use (a bone with cut marks from about 2.6 mya) may well have been produced not with a recognizable tool but with such a rock (see Figure 12.2).

Tinkering and experimenting with what was possible with such objects fostered further pattern detection in the natural environment. It also stimulated pattern *making* in the modifications that their tryout tools underwent in the course of time. I suggest that it was this drawn-out process that eventually produced the traditions archaeologists now identify in surviving hard artifacts.

FIGURE 12.2. Naturally occurring "proto-tools" from the Andean Altiplano (photo by the author).

These strands of experimentation spiraled with the multiple neurophysiological and anatomical changes that made them possible and were thereby altered themselves. We can assume that all of these activities were embedded within a rich prototool ecology, an assortment of materials and techniques that were used certainly for beneficial practical results but possibly also for esthetic reasons.

Our informed fiction here is shaped by the fact that when stone tools do become identifiable, they appear not as single artifacts but as patterned collections, well-established traditions, and recognizable regional assemblages. By 2.6 mya, stone tools and resources were transported from place to place in the paleolandscape, maybe as much as 20 kilometers (Toth and Schick 2009:292). This implies a long period (maybe as much as 1.8 million years) during which skeletal, biomechanical, cognitive, and social strands cospiraled and developed, finally spitting out what became visible as stone tools. Thus it was in a perishable world that our ancestors must have first established the experimental artifacts, the behavior patterns, the skills, and the social relationships (and with that the patternalities) that were foundational for what we now recognize as "tools."

Our predecessors left stuff in heaps and piles numbering hundreds and sometimes thousands of pieces of raw material: flakes, cores, partially finished tools, and lithic residue in places that look like worksites. These accumulations indicate social activity and use over substantial periods of time. We can imagine that toolmaking practices were learned by observation and imitation, in small groups and workshop-like gatherings in what we would now call Communities of Practitioners, or COPs.[5] This suggests that collaborative work practices and the required social structuring must have been developed and perfected, supporting a now invisible exchange system, a "First Economy" if you will, long before they became evident in lithic traditions.

Could we imagine then that there were gatherings at known sites where we might have seen a group twisting vines to make rock carriers? Or prehistoric snugglis, for that matter? Had they established a fashion of bead and feather necklaces? And what kind of social life did those artifacts have? Could they be given as gifts? Did they acquire symbolic meanings beyond their use value? Ritual meanings? Were they indicators of prestige? Of accomplishment? Were they traded? We do not know, but it seems safe to assume that there was, long before the production of stone tools, a flourishing protoeconomy of objects that carried not only use value but also social symbolic meanings.

## A Human-made Environment

As their world became dotted with traces of human activity, human-produced patterns added a new layer to the increasingly deep and consequential reach of our ancestors' ability for pattern recognition. Sensory input now differentiated between the things in the world that were out there because they were made by them or others of their kind, and other things that were part of nature. They recognized the remnants of a camp, the debris from a production site, the cast-off coconut shell, as indications of presence and activity of their own kind: a new category of pattern that significantly increased awareness of conspecifics and opened possibilities for social interaction and collaboration. Their world was now doubly populated: by things independent of human existence, and others that had never before existed.

Looking into the future (our present), the start of the transformation of the natural into a human-made environment generated an autocatalytic process by which the human component grew, eventually exponentially, not only as the modification of the physical environment was driven by increasingly nonsustainable practices, but also by new ways of gifting, distributing and trading, and ordering "things" both physical and of the mind.[6]

In time, social life in emerging communities generated an environment rich in interaction, observation, and imitation where the inherent plasticity of neural circuits eventually allowed for sensory inputs to be replaced by inputs from physical entities and representations (Coolidge and Overmann 2012; Skoyles 2012; Stout 2008). Symbol remapping provided neural circuits with the capacity to support culture and ongoing cultural innovation, and with that, new patternalities based on symbolizing, intersubjectivity, language, domestication, hierarchies, automation and, eventually, the Internet.

## Part II: That Was Then: And Now?

### Setting the Stage

For the rest of this chapter, I propose to examine the possibility that we are indeed witnessing another inflection point, another point at which the helix is nudged ever so slightly but ever so significantly into a new path. I intend to examine some of the most visible indicators of a changing patternality and then explore what that might mean for society, for us as individuals, and particularly for investigative methods and topics of concern in ethnography and anthropology.

Let me begin by painting the digital environment. I will briefly pull up some of the phenomena that I see as instrumental in powering the transformation, such as sociodigitization, the data deluge known as Big Data, an increasingly powerful underground economy, the linking of online and offline information, and analytics as it attempts to make sense of the digital environment. I connect to Maxwell's accelerated pattern recognition as I explore augmented realities and an augmented self. Throughout, my eye will be on what ethnography and anthropology can do to help guide the helix into a more rather than less beneficial course.

### *Sociodigitization and the Second Economy*

We have had digitization (transformation of text and other logocentric representations into digital form) for years now. What is truly new is the extension of digitization to all aspects of social and cultural life, an extension (or invasion)[7] that has become possible only with new digital technologies and the emergence of the global Internet. Sociodigitization involves drawing social and cultural phenomena up into the cloud, in digital codes, images, and text, thereby transforming the social, geophysical domain of human activities into something that is no longer "grounded," no longer detectable with our senses (Latham and Sassen 2005). It is what provides much of the energy for the spiraling of the helix now and, I believe, will provide the parameters for a new digitally based patternality.

Sociodigitization liquefies not only nondigital bodies, artifacts, and properties—like the money in your pocket or the house you are trying to sell—but also immaterial properties such as the music you are composing or the business proposal you are writing, even the book you are reading, giving them a kind of hypermobility which makes them instantly available and globally actionable.

In just the last few years, sociodigitization has become expansively self-perpetuating (autocatalytic), which we recognize as a feature of the evolutionary process that began with the "humanizing" and technologizing of the environment. This process has already dislocated pattern recognition abilities that were trained on physical realities accessible through our senses.

As a consequence, communication and exchange systems (including markets in physical assets like real estate and virtual assets like expertise) will never be the same again.[8] Much economic activity is now carried out over cyber linkages that run all parts of global financial and communication transactions in what Brian Arthur, a pioneer in the field of complexity economics, calls a "Second Economy" (Arthur 2011). He points out that almost all movement of goods and services now occurs over a global network of servers and sensors that operate autonomously, meaning that human beings are no longer directly involved in running them. They track and make decisions that affect sales and inventory, financial transactions, commercial real estate operations, designs of physical and virtual entities, air traffic and shipping control, and just about every other global operation that can be digitized, growing slowly, invisibly, and with no end in sight. They archive automatically, sense and execute remotely, run in parallel, reconfigure themselves on the fly, and increasingly have properties of self-organization and self-healing. They could be seen as embodying something like a neural layer for the physical economy (Arthur 2011).

### The Data Deluge and Data Mining

Another defining feature of the new sociodigital landscape is the data deluge, usually now referred to as Big Data. Facebook alone uploads 300,000 photos a day and globally data grows at a rate of five trillion bits a second (Overbye 2012).[9] Maxwell (this volume) said, "What can be digitized will be digitized." I would now amplify that by saying "What can be archived will be archived": automatically, continuously, and relentlessly. The result is mega data streams that are channeled into gigantic holding depositories in the cloud. They are fed not only by the "click data" that automatically note every keystroke, but also by data coming from remote sensor technologies and other digital devices that record practically everything that moves in the digital universe. With the explosive expansion of social networking sites, machine-generated data have been augmented by human-generated, personal data, making a rich mix of information that is begging to be analyzed. In spite of widespread questioning of the meaning of these data, their "mining" has become standard procedure in industry, government, and partisan politics.

## Linking Online (Digital) and Offline (Physical) Information

An absolutely critical feature of the present-day digital environment for establishing new pattern categories is the linking of online and offline personal information (Jordan 2009). It has deep existential implications since it disturbs and potentially recasts our notions of what it is to be a human being. But it also has given rise to wide-ranging controversies about privacy, as we will see later in this chapter.

The structure of human society is built on social relations where individuals have access to carefully regulated kinds of information about each other, depending on their role and position in society. Our social interactions have been built around who we know, closely or distantly, from family to friends and strangers. The delicate negotiations about what we allow others to know about us or what we believe we have a right to know about them are part of building any kind of relationship for us. These understandings and the ability to give or deny access are fundamental to our sense of self and the borders between self and society. One highly significant way in which these borders are being breached is through the connecting of online with offline information that is now possible.

Consider this: we have been offloading large amounts of personal information to the web now for some time, in blogs, pictures, personal websites, and social networking sites, assuming in some unacknowledged way that this information has a level of accessibility that is negotiable and rather similar to the access control we have over our file cabinets and storage sheds. With online/offline merging of personal data, awareness of who has access to this information and what they can do with it is growing (amazingly slowly) in the public consciousness. When access control slips, the "augmented individual," whose physical (offline) reality is supplemented by (or merged with) information about him or her from the cloud, is beginning to tug at deeply held convictions about privacy and the self.

## Analytics and Algorithms

The driving force in attempts to develop tools that could detect meaningful patterns in Big Data agglomerations is what has become known as "analytics" (which originally simply meant "the analysis of meaningful patterns"). It now refers to a collection of algorithms that are applied to massive digital depositories in attempts to coax meaning out of them. Big Data, data mining, and analytics at this point are lightning rods for both the promise of digital technologies and the uncertainty surrounding their implications for the future.[10]

In analytic operations, algorithms (statistical computations with clearly defined steps) are central, having attained new significance in searches for meaning in digital depositories. They are involved in sense-making (pattern detection) as well as in meaning-making (pattern building) through existing recognition algorithms and by actively constructing algorithms that will lead to a desired outcome. Typical data mining requires multiple, conjoined sets of algorithms and multiple iterations during which the correct series of steps is determined.

Algorithms are a crucial feature of the digital transformation. But it is important to remember that they are not neutral; they have a language and a politics. They incorporate a certain worldview.[11] In analytics, we are dealing with a concatenation of different algorithms whose relationships and assumptions interact and quickly become untraceable. Ethnographers need to understand what kinds of algorithms affect their research and what interests, technical knowledge, and resources drive their construction.

Significantly, we often do not know what assumptions algorithms are built on, nor do we know much about the communities of specialists that produce them. This calls for insider studies similar to the laboratory studies of the 1990s, with apprenticeship in the academic and corporate research labs where algorithms are produced. A central question is in what ways new algorithms could be developed that are based on and interact with ethnographic data about what matters for the future. Riopelle and Gluesing (this volume) have begun to move in this direction.

## Ethnography: Making Sense and Making Meaning

As we explore this new digital landscape, opportunities for contributing to solving its problems offer themselves at every turn. Specifically, I believe ethnographers need to be tracking and documenting the many small changes that cumulatively lead to pattern reorganization while at the same time exploring the existential mega problems that are emerging in the digital society. In this, we need to keep in mind what Francoise Brun-Cottan (this volume) has called the Malinowskian teeter-totter: the need to pay attention to the micro *and* the macro at the same time, as the contributing authors in this book have done. We need to do both fine-grained, on-the-ground ethnographic documentation of what people do and say, and integrative system analysis of what those behaviors could add up to in a historical global systems perspective. We need to understand the helix and the strands, the paternality and the patterns; and we have available for this the whole arsenal of ethnographic methods, including technology-aided tools.

## Observations at the Inflection Point

If we are in fact at an evolutionary inflection point, where would we find the subtle changes that indicate a shifting patternality? In everyday life, of course! We see daily routines transformed, such as lunch (Denny), city parking (Isaacs), or just plain "categories for arranging stuff" (Sunderland, Rijsberman; all this volume). Or, check out the baby that tries to "open" a magazine picture with the finger motions that work on her iPad but don't work on paper (Graff 2011). Is there a new pattern category emerging for her that distinguishes between things that are "openable" and those that are not? Or observe that stress and overload are taking on a different flavor. What we see now is not so much particular events that threaten to overwhelm people, but a very large, ever-expanding task environment that, instead of requiring a brief spurt of energy, generates a constant floating attention, a highly stressed scanning of the environment that expects trouble on multiple fronts.[12] Or you notice the mass of photographs sent out over the web that evaded shoebox purgatory and wonder what else has become newly mobile or is still locked up in personal lives, physical communities, and histories. Walking through a Las Vegas casino you notice zombie-like behavior induced by the hypnotic effect of fast-action digital screen presentations. You start to think about the role of sequentiality in what humans do and, reaching back into evolution, you wonder if there are basic ways in which the brain processes information that get disturbed when familiar things go by too fast. You also begin to notice that people treat each other differently; hanging out on social networking sites, they now know different things about each other. People are building new expectations about face-to-face interaction and across digital media, as Martin Ortlieb (2011) has observed.

There is also a greater willingness to be playful, to be different, to stick out, that you see in people's clothing and activities that are now tolerated, even appreciated, for their scent of freedom, difference, tolerance, and release. Take, for example, the recent urban phenomenon Parkour (Figure 12.3 next page). In an impressive combination of discipline with noncompetitiveness, young adult practitioners train in loosely integrated groups to master very difficult physical skills. In this highly supportive environment, philosophy is as important as body, equipment, and technology.

For building one's intuition about where society is heading, self-observation is a powerful tool. It may involve tracking things that make you slightly uncomfortable or unreasonably happy, and explicitly noticing what responses and anticipations of behavior don't arise automatically anymore for you. A while ago I was about to explain to a stranger what I look like so she would recognize me in a crowded restaurant, when she said, "Oh no, I know you. I've looked at your website." A major advantage of auto-ethnography, of course, is that you know the context and that often you can go back and see in what ways things have changed.

I would love to see classrooms of students required to go out and produce blip diaries of this sort: on the fly, quick jottings on paper, a brief comment on a picture just snapped on their phone, video clips and snippets from public media.

FIGURE 12.3. A practitioner of Parkour practicing in a periurban setting (photo by Matthew Downey).

Of course my hypothetical classroom (or group of young business leaders) would then get together and jointly analyze their various observations. They would see patterns newly emerging and others fading. They would build a coherent image of a system undergoing change, checked against insights from a cadre of peer observers.[13] It does not take much imagination to see that such insights would be of value to all kinds of interests, academic as well as corporate and commercial.

We have lots of aggregate data, be they from public opinion surveys or data mining, about what people *say* they do, but observation tells you what they are actually doing, and as you show them the great picture you just took, they also tell you the whys and hows, the history and the meaning. What people say is often not what they do, so this is why observation of actual behavior is so important. At the same time, of course, we want to know how people think and talk about that because that is what feeds into the discourse of marketing and public consciousness.

## Mega Issues

Working from the bottom up invariably surfaces systemic issues. Some of them are highly charged and in the public eye. Others live subsurface.[14] (They tend to emerge with "what-if" questions.) It is when we are faced with major societal issues that the systemic aspects of anthropological research become relevant. Mega questions require a deep understanding of the ways in which sociodigitization generates problems while at the same time embodying their solution. This suggests that what is important for understanding how the system works is to carry out research on multiple levels, with multiple methodologies and multiple kinds of researcher embeddedness, in the technology sector, in industry, and in governmental policy settings. Relying on in-depth ethnographic interviewing and observational shadowing, in person and remotely, and employing all of the technologies available to us, we need to re-articulate, as Sherry Ortner suggests, the practices of social actors on the ground with the big structures and systems that both constrain those practices and yet are ultimately susceptible to being transformed by them (Ortner 2006:2).

## Privacy

Privacy, certainly, has now become a societal mega issue. If you listen to how people talk about privacy, you quickly realize that there are actually two topics: the first revolves around what constitutes the self and how much of that is confined to the physical body. It asks how much of your activities and knowledge you can offload without affecting your identity. The second question revolves around rights to commercialize the personal information people have uploaded to the web.

Regarding the first, we do not know to what extent people now actually consider their online representations to be a part of their identity. If everything you have on the web disappeared, who would you be? Or, *what* would you be without your memory, your history, your connections? We have long espoused the notion that the self is private and have regulated access by others socially and legally. But what if those regulations and assurances have become ineffective? What if the information we have deposited on the web becomes available to others (as Nardi et al. asked as early as 2004)? As a matter of fact, this is happening today. It is now possible for anybody with the right resources to strip away the cloak (or protection) of anonymity.

For example, researchers at Carnegie Mellon University (CMU) have shown it is possible to identify social security numbers (SSNs) (plus much other sensitive information) using minimal data from the web, such as a person's photo along with a place and date of birth. They do this with face recognition software that connects the unidentified photograph to public online data. (They use other algorithms to determine birth information, and then employ algorithms modeled on patterns detected in the Social Security Administration's public Death Master File to predict SSNs [Acquisti and Gross 2009; Acquisti et al. 2009, 2011]).

These kinds of experiments are carried out in multiple scientific and industry labs. At this point they don't scale, but there is every expectation that they will. Online information, still regarded as private and restricted in the old pattern, is in the process of transforming into public information that is accessible by unknown others.[15] It may well be that our idea of what makes a person is slowly changing to include not only physical but also digital enhancements, and the idea to give others access or control may become deeply threatening.[16]

The question then arises: what rights do consumers have to keep the information (the parts of their self?) they have deposited on Facebook, Twitter and other social networking sites from commercialization, and what rights do the big Internet companies have to use this information for profit?

## A Changing Discourse

The existential privacy question turned acerbic when it became clear that the vast amounts of personal information that are archived in social networking sites can now be mined for commercial purposes. In the ensuing discourse (or battle), the big Internet companies insist that they provide a service that improves the searchability of information for subscribers and enables better design and placement of advertisements with more of the types of ads that customers are likely to want. Their language is one of service to the customer and the industry.

Consumers complain that the companies don't tell what data they collect and what they do with them. Companies, consumers say, hide behind privacy policy written in legalese and use duplicitous language where information that has been "removed" may not mean that it has been deleted. And if you unsubscribe, the company keeps the information it has collected. As a matter of fact, it is for all intents and purposes impossible for a subscriber to find out what information is being held, much less get it deleted.[17] Consumers seem to have a point.

This conflict is visible not only in legal skirmishes but also in more general arguments that employ the language of service provision, democratization of surveillance, and Do-It-Yourself analytics, suggesting the shared benefits of the new technologies. The phrase "publicly available" has come to mean "usable by anybody." For example, the CMU group and others emphasize that the data they use (from social networking sites, voter registration lists, and such) are available to anyone, and the software (e.g., PittPatt) can be bought in any computer store. But nowhere in their presentations do they emphasize that running these programs requires massive computing resources.[18] There is no way that "the general public" can do the data mining that can be done by using the massive resources Internet companies and scientific establishments have accumulated. This—if I may borrow a phrase from Bourdieu and Passeron (1977:42) here—provides "a market for material and especially symbolic products of which the means of production are virtually monopolized by the dominant classes." It is pretty clear that there is a major gap between users and providers. Can ethnography make a difference here?

Any ethnographer will see research questions and issues in this terrain for which basic ethnographic documentation could provide clarifying information, such as: to what extent do consumers consider their web presence a part of their identity? What do they consider "personal information," and how does that overlap with providers' definitions? Are consumers more concerned about disclosure of personal information or about its commercial and political use?[19] What do they actually object to? Are they concerned about violation of the self or about sharing the wealth? Do they actually read privacy policies and if so, how does that affect their behavior? What do people believe about the protection of their uploads and how does that correspond to the de facto situation? What kinds of service do people want from Internet sites and service providers, and how does that correspond to what they get? Answers to such questions should provide guidelines to lawmakers and regulators as well as industrial designers.

There are untold numbers of splendid, indeed awe-inspiring research issues waiting for us in the new digital landscape. I see a vibrant, exciting, new ethnography emerging that helps document and guide its development.

## Conclusion: From Then to Now and into the Future

We have followed the path of the human helix from early beginnings, millions of years ago, and have seen how miniscule, opportunistic, arbitrary changes in one combination of strands have opened up opportunities that provided energy for the others. And we have seen that the fundamental process that drives the evolution of the helix is pattern recognition, the increasingly sophisticated ability of living creatures to arrange things in the world in such a way that their potential becomes apparent and can be exploited for further useful adaptations.

Repeatedly, the creatures who eventually became our ancestors were confronted by situations of immense uncertainty, with momentous transformations in their lifescapes. For example, when they got up to walk on two legs rather than four, an unknown world opened up to them to which they responded, as our species has done again and again, through massive realignments in their sensory capabilities, their anatomy, their cognition, and their social relationships. I have been suggesting that the transformation of our environment brought on by the digital turn has taken us to such a point again; that we are witnessing an alternate, augmented patternality being constructed, a new way of life for the species where new pattern recognition capabilities are now in the process of being shaped, albeit by fits and starts. The existential question is how to develop this new patternality in such a way that it keeps the species' options open for a positive future.

Our job as anthropologists and ethnographers, and humanity's concern at this point, is to find ways of dealing with this invisible world. Continuing a long ethnographic tradition, making visible what is invisible, should help drive the field from mechanical data mining closer to what Maxwell calls ethnographic analytics, that is to say the committed collection and analysis of meaningful data in a sociodigitized world.

## Acknowledgments

I am grateful for helpful discussions with Dennis Biggerstaff, Mary Lynn Buss, William Clancey, Ron Simons, Mark Vanderbeeken, and Michele Visciola. Kimsey Jordan Ruettimann deserves thanks for wielding her machete to cut the chapter to manageable size. My friends at the monthly Silicon Valley ethnobreakfast meeting kept me from sloppy thinking on more than one occasion. I gratefully acknowledge Brian Arthur, Robert Irwin, and Chad Maxwell as my best critics as well as most inspiring support. Part I of this chapter (on evolution) is based on work supported by the National Science Foundation under Grant No. 0837898.

# References

Acquisti, Alessandro, and Ralph Gross
   2009 Predicting Social Security Numbers from Public Data. *Proceedings of the National Academy of Science*, 107(27)10975–10980.

Acquisti, Alessandro, Ralph Gross, and Fred Stutzman
   2009 Face Recognition Study FAQ. Available at http://www.heinz.cmu.edu/~acquisti/face-recognition-study-FAQ/. Accessed June 1, 2012.

   2011 Faces of Facebook: Privacy in the Age of Augmented Reality. Video of BlackHat presentation. Available at http://www.youtube.com/watch?v=fZQ7Th9L5ss. Accessed June 1, 2012.

anderson, ken, Dawn Nafus, and Tye Rattenbury
   2009 Numbers have Qualities Too: Experiences with Ethno-Mining as in *Proceedings of EPIC* 2009:123–140.

Arthur, Brian W.
   2009 *The Nature of Technology: What It Is and How It Evolves.* New York: Free Press.

   2011 The Second Economy. *McKinsey Quarterly*, October. Available at http://www.mckinseyquarterly.com/The_second_economy_2853. Accessed June 1, 2012.

Bezaitis, Maria, and ken anderson
   2011 Flux: Creating the Conditions for Change. *Proceedings of EPIC* 2011:12–17.

Bourdieu, Pierre, and Jean-Claude Passeron
   1977 *Reproduction in Education, Society and Culture.* London: Sage.

Churchill, Elizabeth, and Elizabeth S. Goodman
   2008 (In)visible Partners: People, Algorithms and Business Models in Online Dating. *Proceedings of EPIC* 2008:86–100.

Coolidge, Frederick L., and Karenleigh A. Overmann
   2012 Numerosity, Abstraction, and the Emergence of Symbolic Thinking. *Current Anthropology* 53:2:204–225.

Graff, Amy
   2011 "Baby thinks magazine is broken iPad." *The Mommy Files, SFGate.com*, October 15, 2011. Available at http://blog.sfgate.com/sfmoms/2011/10/15/baby-thinks-magazine-is-broken-ipad/, accessed June 12, 2012.

Ho, Karen
   2009 *Liquidated: An Ethnography of Wall Street.* Durham, North Carolina: Duke University Press.

Jordan, Brigitte
   2009 Blurring Boundaries: The "Real" and the "Virtual" in Hybrid Spaces. Introduction to Special Section on Knowledge Flow in Online and Offline Spaces. *Human Organization* 68(2)181–193.

Ladner, Sam
2008 Watching the Web: An Ontological and Epistemological Critique of Web-Traffic Measurement. In *Handbook of Log File Analysis*, edited by J. Jansen, A. Spink, and I. Taksa, pp. 64–78. Hershey, Pennsylvania: Idea Group Information Science Reference (IGI Global).

Latham, Robert, and Saskia Sassen
2005 Digital Formations: Constructing an Object of Study. In. *Digital Formations: IT and New Architectures in the Global Realm*, edited by Robert Latham and Saskia Sassen, pp.1–33. Princeton: Princeton University Press.

Maass, Peter
2012 How a Lone Grad Student Scooped the Government and What It Means for Your Online Privacy. *ProPublica*, June 28, 2012. Available online at http://www.propublica.org/article/how-a-grad-student-scooped-the-ftc-and-what-it-means-for-your-online-privac. Accessed July 12, 2012.

Nardi, Bonnie, Diane Schiano, and Michelle Gumbrecht
2004 Blogging as Social Activity, or, Would You Let 900 Million People Read Your Diary? Proceedings of the 2004 ACM conference on Computer Supported Cooperative Work (CSCW), pp. 222-231, Chicago, November 6-10, 2004. Published by ACM, New York.

Ortlieb, Martin
2011 Unclear Social Etiquette Online: How Users Experiment (and Struggle) with Interacting Across Many Channels and Devices in an Ever-evolving and Fast-changing Landscape of Communication Tools. *Proceedings of EPIC* 2011:311–321.

Ortner, Sherry
2006 *Anthropology and Social Theory: Culture, Power, and the Acting Subject.* Durham, North Carolina: Duke University Press.

Overbye, Dennis
2012 Mystery of Big Data's Parallel Universe Brings Fear, and a Thrill. *New York Times*, June 4, 2012. Available at http://www.nytimes.com/2012/06/05/science/big-datas-parallel-universe-brings-fears-and-a-thrill.html?_r=1, accessed June 12, 2012.

Skoyles, John R.
2012 Neurosignifier-Neurosignified, Symbols, and Anthropological Possibility. *Current Anthropology* 53(3):356–357.

Stout, Dietrich
2008 Tools and Brain Size. *General Anthropology* 15(2):1–5.

Tett, Gillian
2009 *Fools Gold: How Unrestrained Greed Corrupted a Dream, Shattered Global Markets and Unleashed a Catastrophe.* London: Little, Brown.

Toth, Nicholas, and Kathy Schick
2009 The Oldowan: The Tool Making of Early Hominins and Chimpanzees Compared. *Annual Reviews of Anthropology* 38:289–305.

Wedel, Janine
2009 *Shadow Elite: How the World's New Power Brokers Undermine Democracy, Government, and the Free Market.* New York: Basic Books.

# Notes

1   I provide some key resources for the voluminous scientific literature on which my claim to *informed* fiction is based in the references.

2    Important dates for finds mentioned in this chapter are: Ardi (*Ardipithecus ramidus*), 4.4 million years ago (mya); Lucy (*Australopithecus afarensis*), 3.2 mya; bone with cut marks (first evidence of proto human behavior), 2.6 mya.

3    Most instructive is a 2009 special edition of *Science*, which is readily available (with free registration) at http://www.sciencemag.org/site/feature/misc/webfeat/ardipithecus/, accessed June 12, 2012. The report of the 47 scientists who worked up the findings was published in 2009, though Ardi was discovered in 1992.

4    It has been suggested that the emergence of new competencies in pattern recognition may have drawn on the inherent malleability of neurological structures together with very ancient "feral" cognitive capabilities such as numerosity. Numerosity, the ability to appreciate quantity, is also present in preverbal infants and nonhuman animals and the inherent malleability of neurological structures (see Coolidge and Overmann 2012 and comments therein).

5    Ongoing discussions in paleoneurology suggest that sustained behavioral repetition and habituation are associated with complex integration of neural substrates (Coolidge and Overmann 2012; Skoyles 2012; Stout 2008). It is possible, then, that it was precisely these rhythmic, repetitive, social activities suggested by the remains of these workshops that might have supported the kind of improved pattern recognition ability required for increasingly sophisticated, patterned tool use.

6    This self-referential, exponential "up-ratcheting" has been identified by Brian Arthur as a characteristic of technologies in general (Arthur 2009).

7    You will see me sitting on the fence about evaluative aspects of these phenomena. I deeply believe that there are potentially both immensely positive and immensely negative outcomes of this turn.

8    Things that formerly were fixed can now appear any place in the world, albeit in a different form. For example, a luxury house for sale on a remote tropical island now appears as an ad on the front page of the *New York Times*, and your own face now stars in an ad courtesy of Facebook.

9    Note that these numbers don't mean anything anymore. There is no real-world experiential equivalent that would give them meaning. They are metaphors and should be investigated as such.

10   Of the several types of early studies with a social science approach, let me mention the insightful experiments of anderson et al. (2009) and the early work of Churchill and Goodman (2008), which anticipated many of the issues that are lively now. For questioning the meaning of algorithm-based research, see Ladner (2008).

11   Cory Doctorow, author of *Makers*, said algorithms are "statistically expressed opinions." For embedded assumptions, see Ladner (2008).

12   Linda Stone, a former Microsoft and Google Vice-President and dedicated self-observer, talks about attention, stress, email apnea, and physiological changes in our now continuously connected world. She argues that our connectivity is changing the way our brains function (http://lindastone.net/; accessed June 12, 2012).

13   http://trendwatching.com, a website for businesses, uses a process that incorporates some of these ideas. They use 700 spotters across the world to collect concrete instances of behaviors, products, and installations that speak to emerging business trends (such as "transumers" or "pop-up stores").

14   See James Ferguson's forthcoming book on the new politics of distribution; also Karen Ho (2009), Gillian Tett (2009), and Janine Wedel (2009). Many of the digital mega issues are tied to economics and financial markets, where ethnographically informed analysis has barely begun.

15   The extreme formulation of that possibility would be something like: If everything that can be digitized is digitized, and everything that is digitized is archived, and everything that can be archived is connected, there IS no privacy.

16   Is there a parallel case in the wide acceptance of physical augmentations such as artificial body parts, surgical reconstructions, organ transplants, extreme cosmetic surgeries, and the like?

17    It took Max Schrems, a 24-year-old law student from Vienna, to force Facebook to hand over the 1,200 pages of data they had recorded on him. As suspected, his dossier contained items he had deleted, including photos he had detagged himself, email addresses and location information he had never provided, plus the names of everybody he had ever "poked" or chatted with. To get the information he finally had to file a complaint in Ireland, where privacy laws are much stronger and tend to be enforced. The Federal Trade Commission in the United States is hamstrung with insufficient funding and personnel (Maass 2012).

18    In the SSN project, the researchers had access to high-performance computing resources, including the Pople system with 768 processors and 1.5 terabytes of memory. They worked with a core dataset of about eight gigabytes and used 100 processors for up to eight hours for each of seven runs, not to speak of human resources like four highly trained graduate students. See http://www.psc.edu/science/2009/privacy/, accessed June 12, 2012.

19    Should we see parallels here to indigenous people objecting to having their blood and DNA used for commercial (and scientific) purposes?

# Index

Numbers followed by *f* indicate figures.
Numbers followed by t indicate tables.

# About the Contributors

**Melissa Cefkin** is a member of IBM Research–Almaden. She is a business and design anthropologist specializing in workplace ethnography, services research, product and service design, and organizational learning. Cefkin was previously the Director of User Experience and member of the Advanced Research group at Sapient Corporation and a Senior Research Scientist at the Institute for Research on Learning (IRL). She is the editor of *Ethnography and the Corporate Encounter: Reflections on Research in and of Corporations* (Berghahn Books, 2009) and has served as the cochair and board member of the Ethnographic Praxis in Industry Conference (EPIC). A Fulbright award grantee, she has a Ph.D. in anthropology from Rice University.

**Rita Denny** is an anthropologist and a founding member of Practica Group, LLC, where she applies an anthropological framework to consumer behavior, calling on linguistic, semiotic, and symbolic traditions in interpreting consumer attitudes, perceptions, and behavior. Rita's preoccupation with "the talk" of clients and consumers has led to textual or semiotic analyses of advertising, packaging, retail display, and magazine editorial. It also accounts for near obsessive attention to ways clients and consumers talk—alone or together—about products, advertising, and consumption. With Patricia Sunderland, she is the author of *Doing Anthropology in Consumer Research* (Left Coast Press, 2007). Denny and Sunderland are also coeditors of the forthcoming *Sourcebook of Anthropology in Business* (Left Coast Press, 2013).

**Patricia Ensworth** is President of Harborlight Management Services, a consultancy specializing in project/program management, business analysis, and quality assurance. She is the author of *The Accidental Project Manager: Surviving the Transition from Techie to Manager* (Wiley, 2001), and her articles appear in both technical and general interest publications. In her career as a business anthropologist, she has worked for employers and clients in financial services, telecommunications, healthcare, government agencies, and nonprofit organizations. She is a faculty member at the American Management Association and the City University of New York. Additional information is available at www.harborlightmanagement.com.

**Francoise Brun-Cottan** received her Ph.D. from the University of California, Los Angeles, in cultural anthropology and conversation analysis. She retired from Xerox PARC's satellite base in Rochester, New York, as a senior research scientist.

Since 2002, she has been an independent consultant living in Los Angeles, working for libraries, corporations, and government agencies. She can be reached at fbcinla2@yahoo.com.

**Julia Gluesing** is President of Cultural Connections, Inc. and is an anthropologist with more than 25 years of experience as a consultant, researcher, and trainer in global business focusing on global organizations, global teams, and cross-cultural communication. From 2003 to 2011, Gluesing was a Research Professor in Industrial and Systems Engineering at Wayne State University, where she served as codirector of the Global Executive Track in the Ph.D. program. She has published professionally in journals and books, most notably as an editor and contributing author of *Mobile Work Mobile Lives: Cultural Accounts of Lived Experiences* (Blackwell, 2008), *Virtual Teams that Work: Creating Conditions for Virtual Team Effectiveness* (Jossey-Bass, 2003), *Handbook of Managing Global Complexity* (Blackwell, 2003), and *Crossing Cultures: Lessons from Master Teachers* (Routledge, 2004).

**Vidar Hepsø** has a Ph.D. in social anthropology from the Norwegian University of Science and Technology (NTNU). He has worked as an internal ethnographer and project manager in the Norwegian oil and gas industry for more than 20 years. Through his work he has studied crane operators, process and production engineers, and subsurface and reservoir specialists. His main interests and publications are within emerging collaborative practices enabled by new information and communication technology. He has also written several publications on methodological issues associated with insider research. In addition to his job in the oil company, Hepsø is Adjunct Professor in the Department of Petroleum Engineering and Applied Geophysics at NTNU.

**Ellen Isaacs** is a user experience designer and an ethnographer at the Palo Alto Research Center (formerly Xerox PARC). She received her Ph.D. in cognitive psychology from Stanford University and has since worked at a variety of Silicon Valley companies—from startups to large research labs—designing and evaluating technology to improve people's lives. Her role sits between ethnography and engineering, translating ethnographic observations about human practice into opportunities for technology innovation, and working with engineers to iteratively design, develop, and test novel technology that meets people's needs. Her papers and designs can be found at www.izix.com.

**Brigitte Jordan,** after a career change from university teaching and international research in ethno-obstetrics and medical technology, has worked for 25 years as a corporate anthropologist based in Silicon Valley. She has held positions as a Principal Scientist at Xerox PARC (now the Palo Alto Research Center) and as a Senior Research Scientist at IRL (the Institute for Research on Learning). The recipient of numerous professional acknowledgements, including the Margaret Mead Award of the American Anthropological Association and the Xerox Award for Excellence in Science and Technology, she has published widely during both of her careers. Her interests continue to revolve around research methodologies adapted to the new lifescapes emerging in a global digital world. Many of her publications are available on her website at www.lifescapes.org.

**Chad R. Maxwell** is an applied anthropologist with a passion for understanding the intersections of culture and technology. His primary research interests include design anthropology as well as consumer research for marketing, media, and advertising. Maxwell's professional experience has primarily been with digital marketing and advertising consultancies, where he works as an integrated measurement researcher and people-centered consultant. His clients include Fortune 100 companies in the financial, technology, publishing, entertainment, and consumer packaged goods (CPG) industries. While at Razorfish, Chad coauthored "Liminal: Customer Engagement in Transition," an investigation that fused ethnography, CRM, analytics, and social media strategy approaches. Chad studied Spanish and cultural anthropology at Illinois Wesleyan University, and earned his M.A. in anthropology from the University of Florida.

**Marijke Rijsberman** is currently a design ethnographer with Motorola Mobility/Google, focusing primarily on the experience of mobile imaging and media. As an independent consultant, she studied the role of a vast range of products in the everyday lives of individual Americans, from cosmetics to social networking, from genomics to financial tools, and from search apps to health insurance. Rijsberman holds a Ph.D. in comparative literature from Yale University, which gave her excellent training in the analysis of patterns and meanings.

**Ken Riopelle** is an educator, entrepreneur, management consultant, and retired research professor at Wayne State University. His professional career spans over 40 years in both the auto industry and academia. His primary research interests include accelerating the diffusion of innovations in globally networked organizations, which was funded by a National Science Foundation (NSF) grant from 2005 to 2010, the study of Collaborative Innovation Networks (COINs), and the science of team science using coauthor and cocitation analysis as a method to visualize, measure, and understand scientific collaboration.

**Patricia Sunderland**, based in New York, is a founding partner of Practica Group, LLC, a consumer research and strategic consulting firm. Along with Practica partner Rita Denny, Patricia is author of the 2007 book *Doing Anthropology in Consumer Research* and coeditor of the 2013 *Sourcebook of Anthropology in Business*. As a specialist in ethnographic consumer research, Sunderland's work has run the gamut from brand positioning and new product innovations to the metaphoric examination of entire categories and cultural terrains. Nuances of language and visual representations are key sources of intrigue and inspiration in her work; international projects help keep life interesting.

## green press
### INITIATIVE

Left Coast Press, Inc. is committed to preserving ancient forests and natural resources. We elected to print this title on 30% post consumer recycled paper, processed chlorine free. As a result, for this printing, we have saved:

2 Trees (40' tall and 6-8" diameter)
1 Million BTUs of Total Energy
159 Pounds of Greenhouse Gases
863 Gallons of Wastewater
58 Pounds of Solid Waste

Left Coast Press, Inc. made this paper choice because our printer, Thomson-Shore, Inc., is a member of Green Press Initiative, a nonprofit program dedicated to supporting authors, publishers, and suppliers in their efforts to reduce their use of fiber obtained from endangered forests.

For more information, visit www.greenpressinitiative.org

Environmental impact estimates were made using the Environmental Defense Paper Calculator. For more information visit: www.papercalculator.org.